Perspectives on Development in the Middle East and North Africa (MENA) Region

Series Editor

Almas Heshmati, Jönköping University, Jönköping, Sweden

This Scopus indexed book series publishes monographs and edited volumes devoted to studies on the political, economic and social developments of the Middle East and North Africa (MENA). Volumes cover in-depth analyses of individual countries, regions, cases and comparative studies, and they include both a specific and a general focus on the latest advances of the various aspects of development. It provides a platform for researchers globally to carry out rigorous economic, social and political analyses, to promote, share, and discuss current quantitative and analytical work on issues, findings and perspectives in various areas of economics and development of the MENA region. Perspectives on Development in the Middle East and North Africa (MENA) Region allows for a deeper appreciation of the various past, present, and future issues around MENA's development with high quality, peer reviewed contributions. The topics may include, but not limited to: economics and business, natural resources, governance, politics, security and international relations, gender, culture, religion and society, economics and social development, reconstruction, and Jewish, Islamic, Arab, Iranian, Israeli, Kurdish and Turkish studies. Volumes published in the series will be important reading offering an original approach along theoretical lines supported empirically for researchers and students, as well as consultants and policy makers, interested in the development of the MENA region.

Ribaz C. Biro

Political Challenges of Economic Development in Rentier States

The Case of Kurdistan Region 2003-2020

Springer

Ribaz C. Biro
Economic Research Center
Soran University
Erbil, Kurdistan Region, Iraq

ISSN 2520-1239 ISSN 2520-1247 (electronic)
Perspectives on Development in the Middle East and North Africa (MENA) Region
ISBN 978-981-96-0565-1 ISBN 978-981-96-0563-7 (eBook)
https://doi.org/10.1007/978-981-96-0563-7

This Springer imprint is published by the registered company Springer Nature Singapore Pte Ltd.
The registered company address is: 152 Beach Road, #21-01/04 Gateway East, Singapore 189721, Singapore

To Ruxsar, my beloved spouse, who has unwaveringly supported me in achieving my aspirations.
I express an overwhelming sense of gratitude to my cherished parents, to whom I owe an eternal debt of gratitude for their exceptional nurturing.
In addition, I wholeheartedly dedicate this book to all those who have provided me with unwavering support throughout this arduous journey.

Acknowledgments

I would like to acknowledge gratitude to the following:

Professor Almas Heshmati for his continuous support, careful advice, patience, the sharing of his expertise extended to me in the entire process of my Ph.D. studies, and his valuable guidance and follow-up during the research, reflected in the quality of this book.

The Soran University, Faculty of Law, Political Sciences, and Management, Department of Political Sciences and International Relations, and Ph.D. committee, for providing me with all the necessary support and facilities for the research.

I would like to extend my heartfelt gratitude to the esteemed presidency of Soran University, particularly the University President for their invaluable support in assisting me in overcoming numerous challenges encountered during my research.

Finally, I am deeply grateful for all the support of my family, especially my wife Ruxsar, who has provided me with the necessary cozy environment and am indebted to her for the sleepless nights before deadlines and many weekend and evening research work endurance.

About This Book

The manuscript explores the political barriers to Kurdistan-Iraq's economic development from 2003 to 2020. It uses a systematic mixed research approach and a large database to assess how political instabilities impact different aspects of economic development in rentier states, economic liberty, institutional quality, and economic development. Thus, the study is especially focused on the Kurdistan Region of Iraq (KRI) as an illustration of a rentier state case. Drawing from the available literature, there exists a direct and positive relationship between the countries possessing better-quality institutions and the GDP growth rate. This is due to rentier mentality, a high level of corruption, favoritism, and external and internal conflicts that hinder the development of this region's economy. Thus, the analysis calls for immediate changes inside the KRG and asserts that new approaches must be adopted toward techniques, the private sector's growth, diversification of the economy, and reduction of the oil dependency for sustainable and strong economic development.

Contents

Abbreviations

BOI	Board of Investment
CBI	Central Bank of Iraq
CEDAW	The Convention on the Elimination of All Forms of Discrimination against Women
CPA	Coalition Provisional Authority
CPI	Consumer Price Index
EFW	Economic Freedom of World
EIU	Economic Intelligence Unit
FDI	Foreign Direct Investment
GCC	Gulf Cooperation Council
GDP	Gross Domestic Products
IMF	International Monetary Fund
IOC	International Oil Companies
IQ	Institutional Quality
IS	Islamic States
KDP	The Kurdistan Democratic Party
KRG	Kurdistan Regional Government
KRI	Kurdistan Region of Iraq
MNC	Multinational Corporations
NGO	Non-Governmental Organizations
OPEC	The Organization of the Petroleum Exporting Countries
PSC	Production Sharing Contracts
PUK	The Patriotic Union of Kurdistan
SDGs	Sustainable Development Goals
SMEs	Small and Medium-Sized Enterprises
UNHCR	United Nations High Commissioner for Refugees
UNSC	United Nations Security Council
VIF	Variance Inflation Factor
WDI	World Development Indicators
WGI	World Governance Indicators

List of Figures

List of Tables

Chapter 1
Introduction

1.1 Context

The economy of Iraqi Kurdistan is closely connected with politics and exerts a strong impact on its development trajectories. In this context, where simple problems practically do not exist, various intricate problems resulting from the interlinkage of political and economic factors define the further evolution of the given region and its sustainability. The sources of complexity can be summed up as the following: the broken nexus between the government and business; remaining political insecurity; deeply rooted corruption; internal tensions; and weak institutional endowments. The web of relationships complicates efforts to seek new sources of income, reducing the non-oil economy to a minimum. Abdullah and Gray (2022) highlighted that most attempts at establishing economic diversity are always met with major resistance by strong political forces, whose forces are usually in divergence with the trend that seeks to diversify the economy.[1] The clash of self-interest, that is, the major political parties' interests in pushing their agendas practically at the expense of development, is a major hindrance to the advancement of development.

Moreover, it should be noted that the social structure of Iraqi Kurdistan is to some extent traditional, while at the same time, it has many more signs of modernity, which creates extra layers of difficulty for the implementation of transformative changes. The high interdependence of these factors hampers the possibility of making vital changes. This contributes to the other challenges encountered when implementing the privatization of the control and leadership of public sector companies. The process of privatization, which is a very sensitive process, causes

[1] This book is an expansion of the journal article: Ribaz Chato Biro and Almas Heshmati (2024) The interaction between economics and politics in rentier states. Qalaai Zanist J 9(3):1101–1125. https://doi.org/10.25212/lfu.qzj.9.3.43

R. C. Biro, *Political Challenges of Economic Development in Rentier States*, Perspectives on Development in the Middle East and North Africa (MENA) Region, https://doi.org/10.1007/978-981-96-0563-7_1

inefficiencies; these inefficiencies affect economic performance and hamper growth while also raising service charges (Sümer and Joseph 2017).

The role of the holder and the held in rentier states is such that the government's primary responsibility is overseeing and distributing resource revenues. Engagement, accountability, and cohesion in society create a larger socio-political structure through interdependence (Amiri et al. 2019). It supports structures that negate growth in the economy, which is why it hinders the right structural change required for growth. This is a problem to seek control over the influence concerning the oil-rich region in Iraqi Kurdistan, and it requires those who are local and global. This matter exposes political factors that constitute the region's economic praxis with a view into how political and economic parameters cohabit in KRI.

Thus, the focus on oil and gas exports implies certain economic and political effects within the framework of the rentier. Fluctuations in the price of oil lead to sharp changes in the economy and shift the focus of various businesspeople to look for oil-related revenues. In the political aspect, it centralizes the leadership, whereby most of the powers are vested with the few political leaders, often to the detriment of the entire country. Economic and political coupling in the process of building the rentier state has structural effects on the path of development and the emergence of socio-cultural arrangements. The decisions that are made in terms of management of resources, division of the money, and the governance structure bear great consequences that can promote only sustainable development, or on the other hand, result in corruption and instability (Eklund et al. 2021).

This research aims at covering the relations of Iraqi Kurdistan, particularly in the period after the year 2003. This period was characterized by the exit of Saddam Hussein together with the establishment of the Ministry of Natural Resources in 2006, which paved the way for the KRI oil industry. More specifically, the following study objectives can be outlined to contribute to the present state of knowledge in this field: Our study aims at providing an understanding of and explanation for the diverse and complex issues in this region to fill the literature based on pooled ordinary least squares (OLS), fixed-effect, and random-effect models for quantitative analysis. Thus, it is necessary to critically discuss the political and economic conditions for sustainable development in KRI.

In this way, by carrying out historical research and empirical analysis, this book tries to reveal the multifaceted connection between politics and economics in Kurdistan. Looking at the case of the Kurdistan Region, such a study will try to assess how the political obstacles provided by the rentier state model have influenced economic development in the region. While conducting this research, it is crucial to underline crucial problems affecting political processes and the possibilities of economic development. Therefore, our goal is to contribute to stimulating further academic research and formulating state policies aimed at sustainable economic development of the analyzed regions, especially Kurdistan.

1.2 Research Problem and Significance

This book has important implications as it examines the complex relationship between politics and economics within Iraqi Kurdistan. By breaking down variables like political risks, corruption, and oil reliance, it explains what hampers the process of diversification and crucial changes. By collecting data after 2003 and employing methodologies such as OLS models, this study will endeavor to paint a wider picture on how political instabilities affect the economic growth of Kurdistan. It will enlighten scholars and policymakers and provide evidential approaches to work for sustainable development not only in Kurdistan but in other such regions of the world as well.

1.3 Aims and Objectives

This politics entrenched the political issue that has emerged during the development of the Kurdish Regional Government (KRG). It will particularly concentrate on calling for local, national, and regional agents to contribute toward enhancing the region. These political challenges can be of the following nature: Suspected of not being directly governed by the constitution, it is slow in reform, has instances of perceived corruption, is intricate and absurd, and it violates and blurs the divide between public and private spheres. Nevertheless, the KRG and the Federal Government of Iraq remain in conflict as well as make other issues for the development of the economy of the area. The Kurdistan Region also faces issues related to falling oil prices and the long-term consequences of the international war on the Islamic State of Iraq and Syria (ISIS). Previous studies have explored the effect of oil, gas, and natural resources' reliance on the political and economic evolution of Kurdistan; however, this research seeks to offer a broader perspective, assessing with precision the political factors that constrain economic growth in the region.

There are further objectives of this study as listed below:

- Investigating how political and economic connections influence Iraqi Kurdistan, focusing on obstacles to diversification and reform. It will emphasize challenges such as disrupted connections between the public and private sectors, instability, corruption, and reliance on oil. Additionally, it will analyze barriers to economic diversification, such as opposition from powerful political groups, social factors, and difficulties in privatization efforts.
- Find the impact of geopolitical influences on economic stability. Investigate the consequences of geopolitical factors, particularly the strategic dominance over territories abundant in oil resources, on the economic environment of Iraqi Kurdistan. Evaluate how domestic and international attention affects the stability and expansion of the economy.

1.4 Methodology

By employing a mixed method of quantitative and qualitative techniques of research methodology, this research will collect data and analyze them to address the research questions and link the literature review, aims and objectives, and research questions to generate the expected results. Atkinson (2017) stated that a mixed methodology method in research strengthens the value and usefulness of a study. Moreover, it helps the researcher to grasp a better concept of the subject by using different and competitive methods allowing for sensitivity analysis of the results.

Most of the resource literature focuses on comparing different rentier states in the case of economic growth or oil management. Nevertheless, this two-phase research method will analyze Iraqi Kurdistan's political difficulties and development approach as a single case study. Thus, given the limited data available, it interprets the relative qualitative data to determine the political indicators of the region's development. Afterward, this research for the quantitative part employs econometric methods to analyze data for a specific period. Teddlie and Tashakkori (2003) stated that the mixture of the research methods would shed more light on understanding a single case study because it considers various perspectives.

Teddlie and Tashakkori (2009) categorized the mixed method into four different models: embedded, explanatory, triangulation, and exploratory. This study will use the exploratory type, also called (the sequential mixed method), which first focuses on the qualitative data and then will work on gathering the quantitative data. Firstly, this study gathers the qualitative data and relevant variables of rentier states and the Kurdistan Region and will analyze them. In the next step, we will work on collecting and elaborating the quantitative data to establish a relation between both types of data and achieve the goals of this research. The reason behind the selection of this model is the suitability and correspondence of the model with our research goals.

As mentioned earlier, the exploratory sequential method is the core research model of this research. In this model, qualitative investigations as phase one will enable us to find the relationship between political difficulties and economic growth in resource-rich states. Afterward, the panel data as phase two will allow for analyzing related data and variables to establish the institutional quality of certain rentier states. Subsequently, a comparative method will be applied to analyze similar data and find the same economic and political relations for the Kurdistan Region of Iraq. This combination of the research methods will increase the quality of the research and will decrease the weakness of either approach if they are conducted alone (Creswell 2003). Eventually, the quantitative method is conducted to validate the findings from the qualitative method, contributing to empirical and theoretical findings (Jefferson et al. 2014). A similar pattern is expected in the current research case.

Depending on the quality of the data, a suitable model will be specified, and regression analysis will be conducted to shed light on the effects of political challenges, economic freedom, and institutional quality on economic growth of rentier states in Chaps. 4 and 5, and in the Kurdistan Region in Chaps. 6 and 7. The data sources for the collection in this research are varied. Various national and international secondary databases help governments, academics, and scholars to conduct their research. Likewise, this study will take advantage of those databases. The national data banks include the Central Organization for Statistics in the Ministry of Planning of Iraq and the Ministry of Planning of Kurdistan Regional Government. The international databases include The World Bank's World Development Indicators (WDI), the International Monetary Fund's International Financial Statistics (IFS), and Fraser Institute for the World Economic Freedom (WEF). The different datasets are combined to extract the best forms of variables of interest at the country level used in the specification of models to analyze challenges that affect economic development in the Kurdistan Region.

1.5 The Outline

Using a structure that navigates the rather complex relation between the discovered political tensions and the economic development of Iraqi Kurdistan between 2003 and 2020, this research works as a frame and presents key points of interest along the shaded routes. The investigation also involves the correlation between the political obstacles and economic development, and this book seeks to reveal the interaction of this relationship in Iraqi Kurdistan during this period.

Chapter 1 mainly comprises a review of the study background, where more emphasis is laid on the research background and general research groundwork that would enable a comprehensive analysis of the political and economic processes of the KRI. The topic of analysis is chosen, and the relevance of the research is established, stressing the fact that the study is essential to contribute to the existing literature on the multifaceted connection between political issues and economic development in resource-rich states. The chapter is rather successful in presenting the main goals and some specific objectives, which provide readers with an idea of what further research will concern. The specific research questions are stated briefly to guide the study as follows: While the clear explanation of the chosen method, as well as the methods of data collection and analysis, enhances the trustworthiness of the study. Finally, the chapter briefly concludes the study outline so that the readers can have a tip of what to expect from the subsequent chapters. Thus, in Chap. 2, the audience will learn more about the historical and geopolitical situation of the Kurdistan Region of Iraq. This forms the background that is critical in establishing the peculiarities of this part of the region. Moving to the literature review section, Chap. 2 aims at providing historical and geopolitical background of the Kurdistan Region of Iraq. These findings lay the foundation for evaluating specific factors that contribute to this area's difficulties. The literature review delves into the intricate link between political issues and economic development, examining current research and highlighting key concepts and perspectives. The next parts of the investigation explore resource reliance in states that possess abundant resources, economic policy, and its connection to politics. Theoretical frameworks are presented and evaluated as the theoretical foundation for the following empirical study. The literature review finishes by effectively identifying deficiencies in current research, so setting the stage for the present study, and indicating prospective directions for future research initiatives.

Chapter 3 thoroughly examines the political and economic situation of the KRI. An in-depth analysis is conducted on the political system and economic circumstances, with particular emphasis on oil reserves, revenues, and macroeconomic variables that influence the KRI's economic dynamics. The interconnections between economic reliance, diversification attempts, and the convoluted relationship between the KRG and central authorities are explained in detail.

Chapter 4 explores the important topic of institutional quality in rentier regimes. An in-depth analysis is conducted on institutions, focusing on their quality and influence on economic progress. The chapter gives empirical evidence, examines the outcomes, and thoroughly analyzes the findings. A closing summary briefly summarizes the main points derived from this investigation, preparing for the subsequent Chap. 5.

Chapter 5 examines the relationship between economic freedom and development. It explains the concept of economic freedom and introduces the Economic Freedom of the World (EFW) Index, along with its related factors. This chapter systematically presents data, participates in a rigorous outcomes debate, and provides a detailed summary. Chapter 6 sets the context for exploring the complex relationship between political problems, institutional quality, and economic freedom in the KRI. The chapter thoroughly examines the obstacles faced by economic freedom and governance, the significance of institutions in economic progress, and the influence of political issues on economic freedom indicators in the KRG.

Chapter 7 examines the political obstacles that influence the economic growth of the Kurdistan Region of Iraq (KRI). The chapter thoroughly examines several factors, including political instability, reliance on oil, corruption, and the need for economic diversification, to fully understand the complex dynamics in action. The compact summary succinctly captures the main discoveries of the chapter, preparing for the final Chap. 8.

The last chapter, Chap. 8, presents detailed conclusions of the study. A summary of results succinctly presents the fundamental findings and insights obtained from the study. The study's conclusions are carefully analyzed, emphasizing the practical significance of the findings for policy decisions. In the end, the chapter explores the implications of the study for the existing body of knowledge while providing useful advice for subsequent efforts.

References

Abdullah S, Gray T (2022) White collar crimes and corruption at border crossings in the Kurdistan region in Iraq: causes, effects and challenges for reform. J Kurdistani Strat Stud. https://doi.org/10.54809/jkss.vi2.76. Last Access on 6 July 2021

Amiri H, Samadian F, Yahoo M, Jamali SJ (2019) Natural resource abundance, institutional quality and manufacturing development: evidence from resource-rich countries. Resourc Policy 62:550–560

Atkinson J (2017) Qualitative methods. In: Journey into social activism: qualitative approaches. Fordham University Press, New York, pp 65–98. Retrieved July 14, 2021, from http://www.jstor.org/stable/j.ctt1hfr0rk.6. Last Access on January 4th 2022

Creswell JW (2003) Research design: qualitative, quantitative, and mixed methods approach, 2nd edn. Sage, Thousand Oaks, CA

Eklund L, Abdi AM, Shahpurwala A, Dinc P (2021) On the geopolitics of fire, conflict and land in the Kurdistan region of Iraq. Remote Sens 13(8):1575

Jefferson T, Austen S, Sharp R, Ong R, Adams V (2014) Mixed methods research: what's in it for economists? Econ Labor Relat Rev 25(2):290–305. https://doi.org/10.1177/1035304614530819. Last Access on January 5th 2023

Sümer F, Joseph J (2017) Compatibility of the Kurdistan region of Iraq's institutions and economic development within Iraq. In: Anaid A, Tugdar EE (eds) Iraqi Kurdistan's statehood aspirations: a political economy approach. Palgrave Macmillan, pp 27–54

Teddlie C, Tashakkori A (2003) Major issues and controversies in the use of mixed methods in the social and behavioral sciences. In: Tashakkori A, Teddlie C (eds) Handbook of mixed methods in social & behavioral research. Sage, Thousand Oaks, CA, pp 3–50

Teddlie C, Tashakkori A (2009) Foundations of mixed methods research: integrating quantitative and qualitative approaches in the social and Behavioral sciences. Sage, London

Chapter 2
Literature Review

This chapter theoretically explores the complex interconnection between political issues and economic growth, paying special attention to the Kurdistan Region in the existing literature. In the chapter, the background of the Kurdistan Region and the politics of the Kurds' struggle to gain the separate governing administration since World War I are stated. It points to principal events such as the uprisings against Saddam Hussein, the formation of the Kurdistan Regional Government (KRG), and the creation of the governmental system of the region. The discussion goes further to take a look at the complex relations between various countries in the region and focus on the powerful countries such as the United States, Turkey, and Iran on how they help to influence the region's economic, security, and military affiliations. In general, it covers an analysis from a historical perspective, including problems in the past, the emergence of politics, and current geopolitical situations in the KRI. This chapter strongly engages with politics and policies and their profound impacts on the management and consequently the economic growth of the Kurdistan Region. This study focuses on the arrangements for this use of resources in resource-rich states considering metamorphosing political-economic profiles. In this context, a theoretical stance is carefully synthesized to evaluate various impacts that are involved in the formation of the Kurdish economic environment. Furthermore, this chapter deeply examines the deficiencies in current literature, creating potential for unexplored research crucial for understanding the complex connections between politics and economic growth in the Kurdistan Region.

R. C. Biro, *Political Challenges of Economic Development in Rentier States*, Perspectives on Development in the Middle East and North Africa (MENA) Region, https://doi.org/10.1007/978-981-96-0563-7_2

2.1 Kurdistan Region of Iraq

The term 'Kurdistan' means the land of the Kurds where mountains surround it. Moreover, it shares borders with Iraq, Turkey, Iran, and Syria. The world knows the Kurds as the people who do not have their independent state despite a population larger than the average world country size. Most Kurds are Sunni Muslims; however, some are Shia, Alevi, and Yezidi Kurds. Therefore, Kurds are different ethnically from Arabs and Turks but related to Persians, who share their new year, which is called the *Newroz* (New Year) holiday at the beginning of the spring on March 21 each year (Park et al. 2017).

Michael says that the tendency of all Kurds for independence, or even cultural autonomy and political one, caused much Kurdish rebellion since the shaping of the new Middle East by the British–French Sykes–Picot agreement during the First World War, which left the Kurds with no independent state of their own. On the other hand, the states like Iran, Turkey, Iraq, and Syria, who rule the divided Kurdish land and extract their natural resources, fear their Kurdish minority because they think that Kurds are a threat to their source of revenues.

In 1991, Kurds in the Kurdistan Region in Iraq engaged in an uprising against Saddam Hussain; too many civilians were forced to leave Iraq and flee to Iran and Turkey. Later, during the First Gulf War, the United Nations Security Council passed Resolution 688 on March 1, 1991, establishing a "no-fly zone." This zone, enforced by the air forces of France, the UK, and the United States, was created to protect Kurdish refugees and facilitate their return to their homes. The Kurdish fighters "Peshmarga" continued to fight against the Iraqi army until Iraqi troops were forced to leave the Kurdish lands and the region became a de facto independent Kurdistan Region. On May 19, 1992, a new coalition between political parties of Kurdistan Region emerged, which held the first combined parliamentary election, and as a result, the first autonomous Kurdistan Regional Government in Iraq was established.

In 2003, the United States, along with its allied forces, invaded Iraq, leading to a significant overhaul of the country's political system; then the new era started for Kurds within Iraq. According to the new Constitution of Iraq in 2005, Kurdistan Region has formally been recognized as an autonomous region with its legislature and military forces. After the collapse of Saddam Hussain, the KRG has tried to play a major role in the reconstruction of new Iraq in cooperation with the federal government, but after a short time, the Kurds found that the cooperation did not work out properly for them (Simuziya 2023).

Furthermore, Erbil asked Baghdad to follow Article 140 of the Constitution, which states that "there should be conducted a census and conclude by referendums in Disputed areas such as Kirkuk according to the willingness of their inhabitants." This step should have happened before December 31, 2007, referring to the initial condition of completing a census across the country (Meier 2020). Although some Iraqi leaders believe the article has expired, Kurdish political parties not only regard Iraq's refusal to apply Article 140 as a violation of the constitution, but they also consider it as a sign of Iraq's failure as a federal state. Because of this significant issue and some others, Kurds believed that the partnership with Iraq had failed, and these issues forced them to do a referendum (International Crisis Group 2011).

Several political conflicts within Iraqi Kurdistan involve differences between political parties on various topics. The conflicts revolve around power allocation, governance, inter-party conflicts, electoral conflicts, Kurdish autonomy, and financial asset administration. The conflicting goals, beliefs, and perspectives on these matters often need to be revised to maintain the region's political balance and harmony.

Table 2.1 provides a comprehensive understanding of the Kurdistan Region's governmental branches and a broader picture of its governance.

2.1.1 Regional Interactions

The Middle East has seen significant and profound changes due to complex and diverse upheavals, such as the Arab Spring, internal wars, and interventions by global powers. These occurrences have fundamentally altered the composition of coalitions and structures of power. The region's geopolitical environment has been transformed by factors such as the U.S. shift toward Asia, weariness resulting from extended military involvements, and progress in local energy production. As a result, new alliances have formed, impacting the Kurdistan Region's connections with neighboring countries and international players. The shifts in the regional

Table 2.1 The Institutional Components of Kurdistan Region of Iraq

Branches	Institutions	Description
Executive	Kurdistan Regional Government (KRG)	The executive branch of the Kurdistan Region is called KRG, which drives the government.
	Kurdistan Presidency	The Presidency is the top administrative post, managing legislative, operational, and political duties crucial for regional administration, and serving citizens at both domestic and international levels.
Judiciary	Judicial Council	The judicial council is the highest judiciary power in the region, and it is one of the three fundamental branches along with legislative and executive power.
Legislative	Kurdistan Parliament	The Kurdistan Parliament is the legislative body governing the Kurdistan Region, responsible for enacting laws, overseeing regional administration, and representing the interests of the people in matters of governance.

actors' power concerns and affiliations impact the safety measures and diplomatic relations with the Kurdistan Region (Eklund et al. 2021).

America remains engaged in the Middle Eastern region despite having a very clear reduction in its activity level. It does not mean complete withdrawal, but it does point to a less interventionist but active involvement in regional affairs. This shift of America has implications for the Kurdistan Region, which has relied on the support of the United States for the assurance of stability in security and in politics. That is why it is crucial to get an intricate understanding of this growing relation to build a long-term perspective for the Kurdistan Region.

In addition to the prominent powers of the world, several regional actors hold their stake in the sphere of international relations. KSA, Iran, Turkey, Israel, Russia, and China are emerging as major powers able to shape the policies and trends in the region. Each of them carry their own objectives that are followed through actively, thus creating a web of alliances and antagonisms and conflicting interests. These engagements in the area squarely shape Kurdistan's economic relations, security partnerships, and political affiliations (Anaid 2018).

Heavy impact is observed on the GDP growth as the conflict in the Middle East, including the Syrian war and the emergence of ISIS, affects the region. They hinder the pace of social exchange, deny the freedom of conducting business relations across the border, and form problems leading to instability and developments in the region. Such conflicts lead to disruptions that offer threats to jobs, markets, and investment settings in the KRI.

Because the Middle East lies at a crossroad of continents, it has been considered a vital region of interest for global powers to protect resources and expand their influence. The current and past competitions and conflicts clearly influence the economic relations and political relations of the KRI. There is always conflict of interest in dealing with international players; however, the need to maximize the region's strategic importance is critical for the Kurdistan Region's growth and sovereignty.

Thus, comprehending the nature of these geopolitical processes is of vital importance for the Kurdistan Region. Thus, knowing all these complexities, the area could be able to handle issues, turn opportunities to its advantage, and develop sound and effective policies. This strategic outlook helps advance the economic agenda and create favorable long-term political conditions within the ever shifting and high-risk regional context (Sommer 2021).

In the past, Turkey has had a bad history with the Kurdistan Region, particularly because of concerns about Kurdish independence. However, from the beginning of the century, especially the early 2000s, Turkey has experienced a significant change in its role and participation and can be characterized as an active participant. The purpose of this reform was to build deeper and better relations and to reaffirm Turkey's premier economic power in the region. The relations between Turkey and the Kurdistan Democratic Party (KDP), which is one of the leading parties in the Kurdistan Region, have expanded cooperation for economic sectors. The focus has been given to trade, energy cooperation, and investment in construction that have highly boosted the economic growth in both regions (Demir 2019).

In general, it is possible to note that Iran's interests in the Kurdistan Region are extensive and multifaceted. Even as it is concerned with Kurdish independence within its borders, it also wants to play political power game in Iraq. Iran has always supported the other faction of the Kurds, namely the Patriotic Union of Kurdistan (PUK), and has politically aligned itself to create a complicated web of resource sharing. Iran has invested in the Kurdistan Region on an economic basis and not necessarily on a political basis in economic ventures. The trade contacts, especially in energy resources, have been massive. But often political and security issues have obscured such trade relations (Shamouli et al. 2020).

The civil war in Syria has had an impact on the relationships between the Kurdistan Region and Syria. Thus, the appearance of Rojava, which is under the control of the PYD, has changed the balance of forces in the region. Still, adopting these changes in geopolitical links of the Kurdistan Region, its access to Syria becomes limited. There are darker consequences of the recent elections in Iraq that can change the vector of Turkish–Iranian relations in the region. Therefore, it will affect the diplomatic relationship between the Kurdistan area and these nations and might even change the general dynamics of the area (Azizi 2022).

These systems of factors are geopolitical and interact in a complex manner that impacts the economy of the KRI in terms of growth and dependable stability. Changing involvement of Turkey, the diverse goals of Iran, and the developing dynamics in Syria after the civil war significantly impact the standing of the Kurdistan Region within the broader geopolitical framework. An in-depth knowledge of these interconnections is essential for accurately predicting future trends and overseeing local dynamics. In addition, weak management of domestic politics and foreign interference hinders the KRI's economic growth within complex geopolitical contexts.

2.2 The Nexus Between Political Challenges and Economic Development

Politics and economics are two critical drivers of the development of a country that form the pathway of success or failure. A state's economic, political, and societal forms are core elements of growth patterns. However, the political instability of a state is the critical component of an unsuccessful development outcome. The political form of government and institutional frameworks affect the economic growth of a state. Moreover, a state that provides easy access to its citizens to government organizations is more willing to develop than those countries with restricted policies for their citizens (McGovern 2016).

According to Anstey (2023), economic development is the structured process through which a country enhances the quality of life for its society, guided by governmental economic and social strategies. Robinson and Acemoglu (2012) argue that the advancement of a state is intricately linked to principles such as increased factor productivity, a robust political framework, and the protection of human rights, ensuring the equitable distribution of wealth among its citizens. These factors collectively shape a state's capability to govern its economy, politics, population, and governance effectively.

Political economics in Iraqi Kurdistan is consistent with the idea of a "rentier state" and its features. Like the characteristic traits of a rentier state, the Kurdistan Region heavily depends on oil earnings, mirroring the reliance on income from natural resources seen in rentier states. The management and allocation of these earnings, which are often consolidated within the hands of political elites (Muhamad and Heshmati 2021), have a significant influence on the economic and political frameworks in the area, resembling the control seen in rentier economies (Nuri and Karakır 2022). Moreover, the dependence on oil revenue might impact the political decision-making process, possibly hindering attempts to diversify the economy or distribute non-economic benefits within the region's governance.

There are dynamics in the rentier states that can lead to tensions between the country's leadership and the people; one of them is the attempt at diversifying the economy and seeking political mastery. These challenges are, however, curable through increasing the institutions' capacity and promoting economic liberalization. Measures to enhance standards of other institutions, such as fights against corruption, transparency, and strong regulatory structures, form one of the core precursors to economic diversification and development. The ability to enhance economic freedom is to focus on the use of market liberalization measures as strategies that strive to reduce the state's presence in the economy and expand the functioning of the private sector. Thus, in the following measures described, countries can manage their dependence on the outcome from rents and create a more sustainable economic setting. However, the application of such improvements can meet fierce resistance from special interest groups and the ruling elites who benefit from the current system (Kaya 2018).

Since both paths of increasing institutions and economic freedom present challenges to economic diversification and governance in rentier governments like Iraqi Kurdistan, it is imperative to strike a balance. In this context, it is necessary to implement such changes as fighting against corruption, increasing the transparency of the activity, and decreasing the influence of a state in the economy to achieve sustainable development. However, such changes pose significant challenges to revolutionary change because the current status quo is defended stringently by groups who gain from the current situation.

Politics and economy are two intertwined facets of human life, and thus, it is indispensable to distinguish the political hurdle to economic growth in Iraqi Kurdistan. The economic development of that region remains challenging because of its distinctiveness in the political structure, which greatly influences finances and decision-making processes. As Auzer (2017) explains, the political structures, methods, and general political culture of Iraqi Kurdistan play a very big role when it comes to economic analysis and formulation of policies. Moreover, there is opposition between political institutions to economic operations. Findings have shown that political bands and their beliefs in the Kurdish political system affect the rate of diffusion and both economic activities, possibly helping define the economy of the Iraq Kurdistan Region.

Consequently, the division and relationship between economics and politics in international relations influenced perspectives on economic development previously. This division, if often attributed to such doctrines as liberalism, has implications for the analysis of the degree of state involvement in fiscal activities (Yamada 2020). However, it is important to challenge this perspective, especially when the area in focus is, for example, Iraqi Kurdistan, that is torn by political realities affecting the economic processes and outcomes. It can be identified that political consideration is closely related to the financial market regarding the matters of economic challenges in Iraqi Kurdistan. Political players, legal structures, and policies affect the rewards and the risk of fluctuation in the financial investment markets (Auzer 2017). This, in turn, results in economic development and/or stability depending on the effects of the said inputs. It is critical to comprehend these overlaps to understand the economic challenges faced by Iraqi Kurdistan.

Democracy in theory enhances economic development through stability, transparency, and free-market policies principles. They attain higher quality of human capital, improvement of facilities, and increased quality of social services. However, one has to appreciate that this link is not always direct. Democracy interacts with other factors such as institutions, political stability, corruption, and policy implementation to determine whether a country will be economically developed or not. In this connection, it is possible to speak about the advantages of autocratic regimes for the achievement of economic development at the price of disregarding personal freedoms, as well as about the potential demerits of some democracies that may face severe financial problems because of inefficiency or political stalemate. Hence, it can be concluded that the impact of democracy on economic growth depends on several factors that define the socio-political and economic context of a country (Wang et al. 2021). Subsequently, investigating the correlation between democratic government and economic growth is significant. It is crucial to comprehend the complexity of the link between democracy and financial success in the KRI, despite the commonly held belief that they are positively correlated. Therefore there is a the need for a thorough examination of the influence of political systems, such as democratic processes, on the economic progress and advancement in Iraqi Kurdistan.

2.3 Resource Dependency in Resource-Rich States

According to Haig (2020), there are a few differences between the regular source of incomes like taxation, agriculture productions, and industrial goods and substantial rents from foreign parties. No big effort is required to receive the later amount of rent. Moreover, it does not push the labor market to be competitive and productive as the natural resources are extraction. Therefore, the individuals in a rentier state only see the outcomes and not the efforts, which make them over-reliant on this easily earned money like petrodollar extracted by foreign labor and capital.

Besides, Herb (2019) argues that the distribution of oil revenue to the economy of gulf states has led to their citizens being assured of high living standards. Foreign rents in the rentier states are distributed among individuals through public employment, annual payments, and other subsidies. These allocation plans increased the dominance of the regimes to run their countries. Furthermore, by wealth distribution, they have bought the loyalty of certain groups to face the rival groups within their territory. On one hand, as the quality of life was growing up, on another hand, the depletable oil reserve kept decreasing. Moreover, the fluctuation of oil prices hardened the governments' plans and the advancement of technology has the potential to weaken the world dependency on the oil of the Gulf states. These states have built a type of economy that cannot be reformed because the benefits of the political elites would be threatened. As a result of that, during the oil price shock, the Gulf states have decreased their spending instead of diversifying their economy to reduce their dependency on foreign rent.

In most of the Gulf states, there are social contracts between the regime and its population regarding the distribution of wealth. Thus, these social contracts determine the way foreign revenue is distributed among individuals. It is not only about paying salaries to individuals employed as public servants. It is more about several subsidies by the state to its citizens including free healthcare, free education, employment in the public sector, pension, and so forth. Therefore, the state starts to monopolize the whole economy and political structure of the country, which decreases the democracy indicators in a society (Beblawi 1990). In short, there is no proper taxation system to finance public services and development infrastructures, instead the state finances the public services using rentier income. At the same time, the alliance of politics and business uses the public service provision channel to transfer the public budget to the monopolized business sector as part of business development and not a part of the strategy for national interest development.

In determining the way political power and resources are distributed, Acemoglu and Robinson (2006) argued that different states prefer diverse political structures based on their interests, cultures, and beliefs. Similarly, Kuru (2014) believed that there are different aspects of governance in rentier states. He first said that foreign rents are not the main element of authoritarianism in the Muslim states, as the undeveloped and small states are authoritarian as well. Afterward, he argued that democracy and a high rate of natural resources interact positively in most of the states in Latin America. Lastly, he added that culture, patriarchy, religion, and institutional structures are the key points of the non-democratic feature of Muslim rentier states.

In 1993, Auty introduced the term "resource curse" to describe a phenomenon where countries endowed with abundant natural resources, particularly petroleum, struggle to effectively harness this wealth for sustained economic growth. He noted that these nations often face slower economic development compared to those with fewer natural resources. A review of Badeeb et al. (2017), Boutilier (2017), Venables (2016), and Frankel (2012) shows that the resource curse hampers the economic development of the country. It is accompanied by problems like expectations of an appreciation of the real exchange rate detrimental to industries that are geared toward exports and escalation of economic risk. But they still argued that a given country's availability of non-renewable resources is related to the inclination for civil conflict.

In (2015), Almaz presented an argument that indicates why some countries endowed with natural resources are either performing poorly economically or have encapsulated democratic issues. He stated that he indeed thought that the resource curse approach is usually a helpful method for determining how the availability of natural resources impacts institutions, governance, as well as the economic performance in the resource-endowed nations. He thought that the resource-rich countries are at a higher frequency facing various issues such as a lower level of democracy, unsustainable development, and domestic or international conflicts, all of which are the results of improper management of resources.

Speaking of the presented dynamics, it is possible to state that they describe the situation in the Kurdish Region appropriately, the analyzed processes indeed impact political and economic relations through the dependence on resources. Analyzing these similarities in view of the peculiarities of Iraqi Kurdistan highlights different prospects of the political challenges and opportunities within this context while considering the general framework of the economic development.

2.4 Economic Policy and Political Dynamics

The negative implications of the type of institutional quality where there is ineffective institutional quality in the management of the oil revenues in extractive nations produce inequality and societal conflict. Due to differences in the economic and political systems in Petro-states, there is an inverse relationship in which one party is blamed for and gains strength from injustice and tyranny (Martorano 2018; Bjorvatn and Naghavi 2011). It was further emphasized that the primary cause of socio-political instability in rentier states lies in the absence of transparency and accountability in income management. In such environments, rent seekers seek to maximize their profits from oil revenues, leading to unequal distribution of oil income, which can potentially provoke social unrest and even civil conflicts in countries rich in natural resources.

The labor market in resource-rich countries does not distribute the human capital development in a rentier economy since the exploitation of resources does not require advanced human resources (Turan and Yanıkkaya 2020). These points highlight the disparity between the fluctuations in the job market and the growth of people's skills and knowledge in economies that rely on income from rents. The presence of these complexities highlights the need for a more profound comprehension of how institutional frameworks influence economic results and social welfare in countries that rely on natural resources.

In addition, North (1981) states that high political officials should not set up the governmental institutions because they will arrange the institutions according to their own interests. Similarly, Robinson (1997) explained the dictators' desires to protect their power by their greedy habits. Furthermore, Acemoglu and Robinson

(1999) promoted a relevant theory of growth, which argued that economic threats and opportunities that challenge statemen determine the entity framework and economic structures. However, it is the main element to determine whether technological progress is promoted or gets blocked. In fact, if political elites who have a high position in oppressive regimes feel any kind of losing their position will block the advancement.

Besides, scholars explored that a regime in which a set of individuals has a political monopoly and provides public services. These political groups provide rooms for every single person to get engaged in the economic activities in the given states but do not let the individuals enter the political arena. In fact, they monopolize the political positions in the state and will provide public services with a higher price to populations to receive personal profits. Thus, these actions make inequal distribution of wealth among individuals, which means that the elites receive a higher portion of the state wealth (Sanghera and Satybaldieva 2021). Also, Omeje and Omeje (2021) argued that absolute regimes with no constitutional limits witness political monopoly and lower economic growth, which in general decrease national interests. They also added that autocratic regimes would not tax their citizens to prevent people demanding their civil rights.

States with a low level of macroeconomic policies such as budget shortage, sustainable inflation, and inconsistent exchange rates, experience large macroeconomic fluctuations and low levels of economic growth and performance (Acemoglu et al. 2004). Furthermore, they argued that macroeconomic volatility may represent poor "institutions" in nations with inefficient fiscal policy. Poor governmental systems that do not control political elites, inadequate protection of investors' intellectual property, massive corruption, and a significant level of political instability are among them.

They also have highlighted that the market economy is one of the key elements to increase the living standards from the beginning of the Industrial Revolution, particularly in resource-rich states that also have powerful institutions like the United States, Australia, New Zealand, and Iceland. Additionally, Radu (2015) states that although the market factors are important for assessing the economic performance of a state, other economic freedom and political elements should be considered, including the political struggle for macroeconomic policies, technology development, and innovations.

As described by Aikins (2009), with no powerful economic framework and solid institutions, it is impossible to have a sustainable economic development, which leads the situation to a dilemma and will threaten the stability of the whole economy. Furthermore, other scholars like Adams and Mengistu (2008) and Pradhan and Sanyal (2011) believed that economic development is highly linked to government policies whether the government follows the instructions directly or indirectly. Subsequently, Acemoglu et al. (2003) stated that the outcome of good governance is human development and subsequent economic growth.

Moreover, McGovern (2016) argues that there is a tight association between development, politics, and economics. However, the unpredictability of the political environment and the shaky economic structure and organization will decrease the speed of development. Ainous (2018) states the there is a clear relationship between macroeconomics, inequality of income, and poverty rate. Nafziger and Yoder (2021) shed light on the socio-political factors of development such as capital accumulation and economic development, instability of political administration, political freedom and democratic organizations, and distribution of wealth among individuals. However, they added that macroeconomic administration is the outcome of certain political conversations in an organizational entity.

There is a link between development and wealth distribution. Moreover, economics is primarily concerned with running the economy, whereas politics is concerned with making decisions that influence people's lives (Birdsall 2007). Also, Erb (2001) argues that although politics is about the framework of government and economy, it refers to trade, production, and distribution of wealth, there is a strong interaction between these two disciplines. In line, Aristotle (384–322 B.C.), in his book named *Oikonomikè* defined economics as the management of the household (Crespo 2010). Likewise, because economics engages with the distribution of wealth by companies, individuals, administrations, and political concerns, the influence of political systems on various communities, and the connection between economics and politics are obvious.

Incomes from resource-dependent states should be the main elements of long-term economic growth. Diversification methods might include increasing positive contribution within the petroleum sector, expanding new advanced goods into new international markets, and gradual migration from the oil and gas sector entirely) Sachs and Warner 2001). Furthermore, Gelb (2011) asserts that unlike the extractive industry, the manufacturing sector offers significant potential for creating new jobs, fostering capacity building, and driving innovation. The non-resource sectors are viewed as crucial drivers of economic and technological progress, as well as modernization.

To prove that IMF (2016) argued that the process of economic diversification requires skilled personnel and well-developed facilities. Political responsibility and institutional quality, on the other hand, could be critical determinants in the efficacy of diversification programs. When a governing élite's monopolistic power is threatened, diversification may be tough to accomplish. Various initiatives might be hampered by a lack of political will and poor quality of institutions. Checks and balances may strengthen the openness and accountability attributed to resource-rich states. Lack of qualified personnel and well-developed development infrastructure are two more reasons that might block economic diversification efforts (Miniaoui 2020).

The dynamics emphasized here are particularly significant in relation to Iraqi Kurdistan's political and economic situation. Within this framework, the interplay between politics and economics influences the path of growth in the KRI. The importance of governance, institutions, and policies in promoting economic diversification, effectively managing resources, and facilitating sustainable development is of utmost importance for an area such as Iraqi Kurdistan, particularly given its abundant natural resources. The Kurdish Region's distinctive socio-political architecture is severely affected by the problems of reconciling political interests with economic success, ensuring institutional stability, and managing the intricacies of diversification attempts. Developing an in-depth grasp of these dynamics is essential for building a strategy to achieve sustained economic growth in Iraqi Kurdistan.

2.5 Theoretical Frameworks

2.5.1 Dutch Disease Theory

The *Dutch Disease* is the principal, albeit not unique, definition offered by economists. In 1977, the phrase invented by the economists, which attributed to the harmful impacts of natural resources on the manufacturing sector of Netherland after discovery of gas in Groningen (Alssadek and Benhin 2021). According to the Dutch disease theory, resource-rich countries have a poor level of economic growth since income inflows drive exchange rate increases. This may have an impact on the manufacturing sector due to expenditure and capital transfer impacts, causing a reduction in manufacturing's proportion of the economy (Asiamah et al. 2022).

According to the theoretical framework, a rise in resource exports is associated with many interrelated consequences. Initially, the increase in income generated by the exportation of resources bolsters the nation's currency, thereby reducing the competitiveness of its non-resource industries, such as agriculture or manufacturing, in the international marketplace. The phenomenon of "crowding out" is observed when the flourishing resource industry attracts workers and assets, leading to a downturn in the other industries. Subsequently, the rise in resource-generated income typically results in a rise in the value of the currency. The increase in currency valuation causes export expenses, impeding non-resource industries' competitive edge (Vasquez et al. 2024).

Other scholars believe that governments can reduce the threat of Dutch Disease by saving the windfall or investment abroad like what Venezuela, Kuwait, and Norway have already executed (Taguchi and Khinsamone 2018). Gelb et al. (2002) also argued that state authorities can decrease the obstacles against the improvement of the tradable sector in two directions. Either they can implement strategic industrialization plans like what Indonesia and Algeria have done, or they may develop the rural areas like what Indonesia and the Islamic Republic of Iran have concluded.

The political system in a rentier state is characterized by several factors impacting negatively the performance of the rentier economies. These include governance, institutions, corruption, and politics/business versus national interest driven development strategies which affect economic development. Good governance affects political stability, which leads to organized production and economic development. Besides, stability is the fuel of organizational improvement and economic growth (Mohamadifar and Sadeghi Amroabadi 2020).

Cammett et al. (2019) argued that one of the features of resource-rich states is the low level of interaction between individuals and government combined with mistrust, which makes the regime less responsive and authoritarian. Therefore, it lessens the transparency and accountability of the government and widens corruption. The oil and gas sector, known for its relatively low labor intensity compared to other sectors, may not be capable of providing adequate employment opportunities to accommodate the labor force relocated from industries experiencing a decline. The mentioned circumstance has the potential to result in joblessness or insufficient employment, specifically in remote regions or among individuals with lower levels of expertise.

Besides, Castillo (2021) stated that the abundance of the petrodollar that comes through rent highly alters the attitude of political elites who come to power. Moreover, capital gain from resource rents might encourage politicians to take dominance via pressure or limit election participation. The Dutch disease theory posits that the reliance on exporting natural resources can result in instability in government incomes due to the unpredictable fluctuations of resource prices in the global marketplace. The presence of volatility can lead to an uncertain fiscal setting, posing challenges for governments in devising and executing sustainable development plans over extended periods.

Political instability poses a hindrance to economic growth in rentier states, as highlighted by Auzer (2017). The absence of transparency and accountability regarding oil revenue perpetuates enduring political conflicts. Moreover, rentier states try to increase their oil revenue by selling it, which generates inequality within a society that leads to deepening social distrust of the government. Dutch disease theory indicates that political instability harms the economy of a resource-rich state, due to the wrong management of the oil revenue and ignorance of non-oil sector.

2.5.2 *Resource Curse Theory*

The "resource curse," often referred to as the "paradox of plenty" is an economic theory that contends that nations with abundant natural resources seem to have less efficient economic development, greater levels of inequality, and weak governance than those with less abundant resources. The theoretical framework emphasizes the adverse outcomes that are linked to the ignoring or improper distribution of natural resource assets (Moritz 2020).

Erum and Hussain (2019) highlighted that corruption is a subcategory of the recourse curse. Corruption is the outcome of weak governance that spoils the economic development in a rentier state. The affluence of natural resources boosts corruption due to the low performance of government institutions and it leads to a decrease in government productivity, performance, and poor democracy. Šumah (2018) stated that corruption has impacts on both economic development and society. In his view, this phenomenon has the power to prevent economic development, investment, employment, and will reduce tax income due to lacking accountability, transparency, a decrease of trust in the law and regulations and their enforcement.

Transparency is a critical component in reducing the negative consequences of the resource curse. Corruption and favoritism may be reduced if organizational performance is improved via transparency, which simply makes facts on resource income gathering and expenditure publicly available. As a result of the development of multiple global efforts, extractive governments may be forced to enhance their institutional performance, encouraging transparency and accountability. Furthermore, as a foundation of economic development, strong and efficient governmental entities might improve human resource development to support productivity and growth (Bak 2020).

Natural resources are the main element of decrement in accountability, which leads to a low rate of economic development in a rentier state (Yamada 2020). Developed states tax their population, which needs accountability and transparency, but in rentier states, taxation either does not exist or at a low level applied to public servants as saving to finance their pension. Therefore, this issue leads to political violence and will threaten the regime stability, and may lead to domestic violence, terrorist activities, and in some cases revolutions with radical regime changes as an outcome (Barma 2021). Höltge et al. (2021) highlighted that oil revenue makes political officials dominate the resource sector and increase their power in politics and economy of the state. Therefore, in the rentier states, the need for taxation is low as taxation will decrease the power of the ruling elites and their profits generated from taxable business revenues.

2.6 Gaps in Literature and Research Opportunities

The discussion about the relationship between politics and economics in Iraqi Kurdistan highlights several crucial elements, although it needs enhancement in terms of study. First and foremost, examining the intricate relationship between political acts and economic outcomes should include specific empirical investigations into economic indicators impacted by politics, such as GDP growth or the effects unique to industries. Moreover, it suggests strategies to foster economic diversification and enhance institutions. However, it must meet the test of implementing such measures within the setting of the Kurds. In addition, there is a call for the analysis of the functional activities of political institutions and their consequences for economic policy. Furthermore, it is possible to carry out a comparative evaluation of various systems of governance to determine the adverse economic consequences caused by them. Previous research should also consider the effects of external factors like conflicts in its neighboring regions or political alliances that the KRI may be part of.

However, more quantitative research is needed to provide more evidence about the relationships that are presented between political interests and economy. This naturally underlines the necessity of carrying out evidence-based analysis to understand the direct relationship between political activities and the economy in the KRI. Appreciation of these weaknesses will foster an enhanced understanding of the relation between politics and economics concepts, hence the formulating of better strategies that would enable sustainable development in the region of Iraqi Kurdistan.

This chapter provides extensive information on the operations of the resource-dependent economies and the affected rentier administrations' complexities and multiple problems. Nevertheless, it also reveals a few issues that require further exploration, particularly in the context of Iraqi Kurdistan. Firstly, it focuses on the impact of rentier income on societies; this shows how excessive rents could hamper labor market competitiveness and productivity, though they do not focus on certain specifics of the economies or reduced specificity of certain factors. Further, there is a specific need to obtain research evidence regarding the impact of distribution plans for key sociocultural entities in Iraqi Kurdistan. This will assist in acquainting ourselves with the locations socio-political attributes in relation to political dominance and the dissemination of money in rentier states.

Besides, it emphasized the fact that business governance and its relation to institutions and agencies and their effects on economic development involve multiple layers of decision-making. However, it does not include the concrete examples concerning the situation in Iraqi Kurdistan. Thus, it is imperative to focus on the intensified analysis of the political institutions of the regions under consideration and their financial impacts.

Furthermore, prior studies show the difficulties in the diversification of economic activity, although there is a need for more specific working methodologies or examples regarding Iraqi Kurdistan (Muhamad 2022). This is an opportunity to evaluate the possibilities of diversification activities and how successful they are likely to be, among other aspects. Thus, this research primarily focuses on exploring the link between politics and the economy of Iraqi Kurdistan. However, these correlation results must be supported by additional empirical data and quantitative reasoning. This will improve practical knowledge of the economic problems and opportunities in the region. Had these shortcomings been addressed, I could elaborate on the understanding of the subtle relationship between governmental actions, fiscal systems, and social consequences in Iraqi Kurdistan. This will offer important viewpoints that form the basis of sustaining economic development over the long term.

Dutch disease and resource curse theories lack sufficient analysis regarding the specific impact of both theories on Iraqi Kurdistan. Despite frequent references to the effects on industrial industries and shifts in governance, it offers no cases or real numeric values. It is the nature of these problems and requires further comprehensive introduction to the methods of addressing them but briefly states them and the need to highlight their importance in the context of Iraqi Kurdistan. However, most of the time, for the discourse on corruption or any issue of a supreme resource, particular occurrences or facts from the homestead need to be provided. Thus, the specific targeting of Iraqi Kurdistan allows us to further our knowledge and offer strategies to counteract its economic problems.

2.7 Summary

The literature review chapter discusses the economic performance of the Kurdistan Region with regards to the period 2003 to 2020 with the aim of establishing the relationship between political and economic growth patterns. This work takes an action-oriented approach to analyzing political actions regarding economic outcomes to address the gap between political actions and concrete financial outcomes. The study continues repeating the message of the importance of empirical findings in the effect of politics on GDP growth and specific effects on industries. It contains suggestions for diversification of economic development and institutions enhancement regarding the challenges that have been encountered in Kurdistan to guarantee the effective conceptualization and implementation of the recommendations.

The focus is to understand the effects that many political systems have on general economic policy. Moreover, while capturing the financial stability of the KRI, it focuses on the external factors, which may include conflicts in a certain region. By applying reality and experimenting with the case studies local to the country in question, the arguments behind the existing theories like Dutch disease and resource curse could be made stronger. These ideas are crucial when understanding the interaction of political determinations, economic platforms, and their effects on the public overhaul in Kurdistan.

References

Acemoglu D, Robinson A (1999) Political origins of poverty and prosperity. Unpublished manuscript, Massachusetts Institute of Technology

Acemoglu D, Robinson JA (2006) Economic origins of dictatorship and democracy. Cambridge University Press

Acemoglu D, Johnson S, Robinson J, Thaicharoen Y (2003) Institutional causes, macroeconomic symptoms: volatility, crises, and growth. J Monet Econ 50(1):49–123

Acemoglu D, Johnson S, Robinson JA (2004) The rise of Europe: Atlantic trade, institutional change and economic growth. Working Paper, Department of Economics, MIT

Adams S, Mengistu B (2008) Privatization, governance and economic development in developing countries. J Dev Soc 2:415–438

Aikins SK (2009) Global financial crisis and government intervention: a case for effective regulatory governance. Intl Publ Manag Rev 10(2):23–43

Ainous R (2018) Macroeconomic, income inequality, and poverty relationship: a review of research perspectives. Rev Black Polit Econ 45(2):123–146

Almaz A (2015) Testing the rentier state theory: the case of Azerbaijan. J Global Anal 5(2):60–72

Alssadek M, Benhin J (2021) Oil boom, exchange rate and sectoral output: an empirical analysis of Dutch disease in oil-rich countries. Resourc Policy 74:102362

Anaid A (2018) The nature of political economy challenges of the Kurdistan region of Iraq. In: Iraqi Kurdistan's statehood aspirations: a political economy approach. Springer, Cham, pp 9–26

Anstey V (2023) The economic development of India. In: Women's economic writing in the nineteenth century. Routledge, pp 84–92

Asiamah O, Agyei SK, Ahmed B, Agyei EA (2022) Natural resource dependence and the Dutch disease: evidence from sub-Saharan Africa. Resourc Policy 79:103042

Auty R (1993) Sustaining development in mineral economies: the resource curse thesis, 1st edn. Routledge. https://doi.org/10.4324/9780203422595. Last Access on May 16th 2022
Auzer KA (2017) Institutional design and capacity to enhance effective governance of oil and gas wealth: the case of Kurdistan region. Springer. https://doi.org/10.1007/978-981-10-4518-9. Last Access: April 22nd 2022
Azizi H (2022) Turkish and Iranian involvement in Iraq and Syria: competing strategies, rising threat perceptions, and potentials for conflict
Badeeb RA, Lean HH, Clark J (2017) The evolution of the natural resource curse thesis: a critical literature survey. Resourc Policy 51:123–134
Bak M (2020) (Rep.). Transparency international. Retrieved September 2, 2021, from http://www.jstor.org/stable/resrep24898. Last Access: February 22nd 2023
Barma NH (2021) Do petroleum rents fuel conflict in developing countries? A case study of political instability in Timor-Leste. Energy Res Soc Sci 75:102018
Beblawi H (1990) The rentier state in the Arab world. In: Luciani G (ed) The Arab state. University of California Press, Berkeley and Los Angeles, pp 71–100
Birdsall N (2007) Income distribution: effects on growth and development. SSRN Electron J. https://doi.org/10.2139/ssrn.1003252
Bjorvatn K, Naghavi A (2011) Rent seeking and regime stability in rentier states. Eur J Polit Econ 27(4):740–748
Boutilier RG (2017) Raiding the honey pot: the resource curse and weak institutions at the project level. Extract Indust Soc 4(2):310–320
Cammett M, Diwan I, Leber A (2019) Is oil wealth good for private sector development? Economic research forum working paper (1299)
Castillo VZ (2021) Authoritarianism and the Rentier State-Venezuela and Nigeria
Crespo R (2010) Aristotle on the economy. Philosophia, 39–68. Retrieved 2 September 2021, from http://file:///Users/ribazbiro/Desktop/Thesis%20/Literature%20Review/v%202/Dialnet-AristotleOnTheEconomy-4970318.pdf. Last Access September 29th, 2021
Demir M (2019) The geopolitics of Turkey–Kurdistan relations: cooperation, security dilemmas, and economies. Rowman & Littlefield
Eklund L, Abdi AM, Shahpurwala A, Dinc P (2021) On the geopolitics of fire, conflict and land in the Kurdistan region of Iraq. Remote Sens 13(8):1575
Erb S (2001) Party politics and economic policy in the New Germany. German Politics 10(3):191–206. https://doi.org/10.1080/714001157. Last Access June 13th 2022
Erum N, Hussain S (2019) Corruption, natural resources and economic growth: evidence from OIC countries. Resourc Policy 63:101–429. https://doi.org/10.1016/j.resourpol.2019.101429. Last Access May 12th 2022
Frankel JA (2012) The natural resource curse: a survey of diagnoses and some prescriptions. HKS faculty research working paper series RWP12-014, John F. Kennedy School of Government, Harvard University
Gelb A (2011) Economic diversification in resource-rich countries. Mimeograph, Center for Global Development, Washington, DC
Gelb A, Eifert B, Tallroth NB (2002) The political economy of fiscal policy and economic management in oil-exporting countries. Policy research working paper 2899, The World Bank, Washington, DC
Haig RM (2020) The concept of income—economic and legal aspects. In: Forerunners of realizable values accounting in financial reporting. Routledge, pp 140–167
Herb M (2019) Introduction: the politics of rentier states in the Gulf. [online] Project on Middle East Political Science. Available at https://pomeps.org/introduction-the-politics-of-rentier-states-in-the-gulf [Accessed 12 June 2021]
Höltge J, Theron L, Jefferies P, Ungar M (2021) Family resilience in a resource-cursed community dependent on the oil and gas industry. Fam Process 60(4):1453–1469
IMF (2016) Economic diversification in oil-exporting Arab countries. International Monetary Fund, Manama, pp 5–29

International Crisis Group (2011) The disputed territories stalemate. In Iraq and the Kurds: confronting withdrawal fears, International Crisis Group, pp 6–13. http://www.jstor.org/stable/resrep36833.5
Kaya Z (2018) Gender equality in Iraq and Iraqi Kurdistan. LSE Middle East Centre Blog (January 5). https://blogs.lse.ac.uk/mec/2018/01/05/gender-equality-in-iraq-and-iraqi-kurdistan/. Last Access on April 7th 2023
Kuru A (2014) Authoritarianism and democracy in Muslim countries: rentier states and regional diffusion. Polit Sci Quart 129(3):399–427. Retrieved August 21, 2021, from http://www.jstor.org/stable/43828435. Last Access on April 7th 2022
Martorano B (2018) Taxation and inequality in developing countries: lessons from the recent experience of Latin America. J Int Dev 30(2):256–273. https://doi.org/10.1002/jid.3350. Last Access on January 19th 2023
McGovern A (2016) Beyond model answers: a new approach to the relationship between economics and politics. Juncture 22(4):334–339
Meier D (2020) 'Disputed territories' in northern Iraq: the frontiering of in-between spaces. In: In-between border spaces in the Levant. Routledge, pp 79–99
Miniaoui H (ed) (2020) Economic development in the gulf cooperation council countries: from rentier states to diversified economies, vol 1. Springer Nature
Mohamadifar N, Sadeghi Amroabadi B (2020) Analysis of the interactive effects of good governance and the rentier state on the political instability of OPEC member states by GMM. J Econ Regional Dev 27(19):165–196
Moritz J (2020) Rentier political economy in the oil monarchies. In: Routledge handbook of Persian gulf politics. Routledge, pp 163–186
Muhamad GM (2022) Private sector development analysis in post-conflict Kurdistan region of Iraq. UKH J Social Sci 6(2):19–32
Muhamad GM, Heshmati A (2021) Dependency on natural resources and diversification of economies in MENA. Retrieved from https://urn.kb.se/resolve?urn=urn:nbn:se:hj:diva-55122. Last Access August 1st 2024
Nafziger EW, Yoder JC (2021) The economics of development. In: Mennonites and post-colonial African studies. Routledge, pp 114–127
North DC (1981) Structure and change in economic history. Norton, New York
Nuri ZM, Karakır İ (2022) The impact of 'rentier state' on economic development: the case of Kurdish regional government (KRG) of Iraq. Türkiye Politik Çalışmalar Dergisi 2(1):1–17
Omeje K, Omeje K (2021) Natural resources and rentier capitalism. The failure and feasibility of capitalism in Africa, pp 85–116
Park B, Jongerden J, Owtram F, Yoshioka A (2017) Field notes: on the Independence referendum in the Kurdistan region of Iraq and disputed territories in 2017. Kurdish Stud Transnat Press Lond 5(2):199–214
Pradhan RP, Sanyal GS (2011) Good governance and human development: evidence from Indian states. J Social Dev Sci 1(1):1–8
Radu M (2015) The impact of political determinants on economic growth in CEE countries. Procedia Soc Behav Sci 197:1990–1996. https://doi.org/10.1016/j.sbspro.2015.07.579. Last Access on March 10th 2023
Robinson A (1997) When is a state predatory? Unpublished manuscript, University of California-Berkeley. Available at SSRN: https://ssrn.com/abstract=273022. Last Access on June, 20th 2022
Robinson JA, Acemoglu D (2012) Why nations fail: the origins of power, prosperity and poverty. Profile, London, pp 45–47
Sachs J, Warner A (2001) The curse of natural resources. Eur Econ Rev 45(4–6):827–838. https://doi.org/10.1016/s0014-2921(01)00125-8. Last Access on March, 24th 2022
Sanghera B, Satybaldieva E (2021) Rentier capitalism and its discontents. Springer

Shamouli H, Zargar AR, Pazokian A (2020) Explaining the geopolitical challenges of Iraqi Kurdistan and its impact on the security of the borders of the Islamic Republic of Iran. J Border Stud 8(1):97–107

Simuziya NJ (2023) The (il)legality of the Iraq war of 2003: an analytical review of the causes and justifications for the US-led invasion. Cogent Social Sci 9(1):2163066

Sommer F (2021) Geopolitics of Iraqi Kurdistan: a role of external and internal actors in Kurdish issue

Šumah Š (2018) Corruption, causes and consequences. Trade Global Market. https://doi.org/10.5772/intechopen.72953. Last Access on July, 19th 2023

Taguchi H, Khinsamone S (2018) Analysis of the 'Dutch disease' effect on the selected resource-rich ASEAN economies. Asia Pacific Policy Stud 5(2):249–263. https://doi.org/10.1002/app5.233. Last Access on December 19th 2021

Turan T, Yanıkkaya H (2020) Natural resource rents and capital accumulation nexus: do resource rents raise public human and physical capital expenditures? Environ Econ Policy Stud 22:449–466

Vasquez C, Carpenter N, Blessing C (2024) Rentier states and the transition away from oil: Oman, Kuwait, and Saudi Arabia. Macalester Street J 1(2)

Venables AJ (2016) Using natural resources for development: why has it proven so difficult? J Econ Perspect 30(1):161–184

Wang QJ, Feng HL, Chang CP (2021) The impacts of democracy on innovation: revisited evidence. Technovation 108:102333

Yamada M (2020) Can a rentier state evolve to a production state? An 'institutional upgrading' approach. Br J Middle Eastern Stud 47(1):24–41

Chapter 3
Political and Economic Landscape of the KRI

This chapter examines the interacting factors that determine the political and economic context of the Kurdish Region of Iraq (KRI) in detail. The chapter thus scrutinizes the evolution of the role of political forces on the economy in the region by revealing both the positive and negative sides that characterize the region. Also, it focuses on the complex interaction between Erbil and Baghdad and describes the conditions that determine collaboration and conflict in their activities. In this respect, applying a rich and diverse data set, the chapter is devoted to revealing a wide range of political and economic prerequisites of the KRI's efficiency and steady development at both regional and national levels. Conflicts in the distribution of revenue, the exportation of petroleum, and the supervision of resources have implications for both economic expansion and regional self-governance. Comprehending the complex relationship between political conflicts and economic liberty is crucial to investigate advancing economic variety, enhancing financial establishments, and establishing a setting that fosters sustainable growth in the Kurdistan Region of Iraq.

3.1 Political System of Kurdistan Region

Specifically, the question of establishing a united, politically stable, and modern political structure as an autonomous area has been a major issue for Iraqi Kurdistan. Over the past three decades, the Kurdistan Region has been dominated by two main political entities: the main parties are the Kurdistan Democratic Party (KDP) and the Patriotic Union of Kurdistan (PUK). While their contestation was already strong since the 1970s, it intensified between 1994 and 1998 and was characterized as fierce, destructive, and occasionally brutal. In the early 1990s, when the region achieved sovereignty, specific bureaucracies to meet the needs of each party existed;

R. C. Biro, *Political Challenges of Economic Development in Rentier States*, Perspectives on Development in the Middle East and North Africa (MENA) Region, https://doi.org/10.1007/978-981-96-0563-7_3

the KDP administered Erbil and Dohuk provinces while the PUK controlled Sulaymaniyah province.

In the subsequent general elections that were held in the year 2009, other forms of political players, including Change Movement (Gorran), among others, have risen as serious contenders in the region's political realms. Subsequently, the Alliance for Democracy and Justice, New Generation, and several Islamic groups have also become prominent players (Abdullah 2018; Rafaat 2018).

Leezenberg (2015) said that Kurdish sovereignty was acknowledged by the Iraqi constitution in 2005, following the US-led Iraqi war in 2003. The two major ruling parties of KDP and PUK had to set aside their longstanding antagonism and reconstitute the KRG's unitary institutions to preserve American backing and secure a significant level of autonomy. Moreover, Hama (2018) argued that the settlement between KDP and the PUK settlement was introduced as a new 50:50 influence. The deal made in January 2006 recreated the united KRG government and specifically outlined the division of significant political appointments between the two parties. The KDP and PUK maintained direct authority over their separate *peshmerga* troops, which were never integrated and commanded by their respective party leaderships.

The Kurdistan Region has developed a unique political structure that incorporates a recognizable form of governance. While many characterize the KRI's political system as presidential, Parliament has historically possessed the authority to vote on whether the President remains in office or is removed. Political disagreements among parties have emerged as a substantial barrier to the region's political advancement and the establishment of a cohesive political framework. Moreover, the absence of a formal constitution in the KRI has sparked ongoing debates over the extent of the President's powers and the procedures for electing the President (Stansfield 2017).

Ala'Aldeen (2016) argued that the Kurdish political system is split between two distinct ideologies of Erbil and Sulaymaniyah. These cities have remained different since the Ottoman Empire's Kurdish Emirates, but they have also developed divergent political environments, which shows that Erbil is conservative and Sulaymaniyah is liberal. Importantly, these confrontations were extensions of significant partisan political debates and interpersonal rivalries among officials dating back to the 1960s, if not earlier.

Albeit with a fashionable political order, the Kurdish political landscape gradually shifts, mostly super reflective and reactionary, tribal-colored initiatives toward a more advanced, democratic structure. In the KRI, decision-making in the political process lacks trust and transparency. Another major issue to address is the hidden task played by the KDP and the PUK; this became practically hard to determine who had the power to represent the KRI in a global context (Rubin 2016).

The KRG was authorized to receive 17 percent of Iraq's hydrocarbon income as a federal state and share 83 percent of extractions from the Kurdistan Region fields with Baghdad. This tremendous rent had been used to reinforce the current class structure. The KDP and PUK elites ranked highest of the governing class in the area, with prominent leaders dominating pyramid-shaped client systems.

Nevertheless, this injection of funds and the region's political stability provided a volatile economic boom. The main objective of Kurdish officials was to imitate the behavior of affluent rentier economies instead of employing these assets to reconstruct the Kurdish economy via the growth of its key sectors (Shukor et al. 2017). KRG failed to promote self-sufficient incapacity to reconstruct, further develop the region, and participate in the reconstruction of neighboring regions inhabited by Kurds.

The dominant group utilized an opportunistic accumulation strategy, directing a substantial share of the KRG revenue into funding government service wages, pensions, and various subsidies. In the lack of a macroeconomic perspective, the populace became reliant on government assistance, increasing the system's clientelism nature and causing the difficulty of public criticism of the political system. These resources would save the citizens of the region from financial difficulty. In essence, the KRG's public employment policy was an expression of the region's existing cultural attitudes toward state interdependence and a significant cause for the inefficient connection between the KRG and its citizens (Hasan and Perot 2021). The long-term effects of the failed policies are evidenced by recent years of massive youth migration, which further harms the Regions recovery and development and increases its dependency on foreign labor force and material import.

3.2 Economic System of Kurdistan Region

Agriculture, industry, and services are the three major economic sectors, subdivided into a series of sub-sectors. Capital, labor, plants, land, energy, water, mining, natural resources, infrastructure, and other resources are used to produce commodities and services in an economy. The labor, capital, land, and equipment costs are covered by output gains in wages, return to capital investment, capital accumulation, land rental, energy, and material and intermediate commodity purchases (Heshmati et al. 2012). However, after March 25, 2023, things have changed. The Paris Arbitration Court's decision resulted in the Kurdistan Region of Iraq (KRI) losing its ability to sell oil directly. Accordingly, the KRI's operational budget is now provided by the federal government in Baghdad, rather than being financially independent (Karim and Aziz 2024).

The semi-independent Kurdistan Region of Iraq has an autonomous economy disconnected from the Iraqi economy. The economy of Iraqi Kurdistan relies predominantly on revenues generated from the oil industry, agriculture, and tourism sectors. Due to high security and political stability compared to the rest of Iraq, the economy of Kurdistan has enjoyed a high rate of growth. The situation changed concerning the budget dispute and relation crisis with the central government and the ISIS attack in 2014 (Heshmati 2010).

3.2.1 Oil Reserves and Revenues in Kurdistan

Official figures indicate that the KRI possesses estimated oil reserves of 45 billion barrels and natural gas reserves of almost 200 trillion cubic feet (Ministry of Natural Resources 2022). Based on these statistics, if Kurdistan were an independent nation, it would rank among the top ten countries globally in terms of oil reserves. To prove that, look at Table 3.1; the tenth position is occupied by Nigeria that has only 37 billion barrels, eight billion barrels less than Kurdistan (Amereller and Zamel 2021).

In developing states with high oil dependency, the most vital sector to consider for more investment is the energy sector; that is why the government should concentrate more on this sector to achieve growth and development targets. The investment policy of the KRG in the oil industry provides plenty of job opportunities in the private sector for local workforce (Ministry of Planning 2015). As a result of this investment policy, investment in the oil industry of KRI also increased the national income of the region (Ministry of Planning 2015). Furthermore, Kurdish petrodollars (see Fig. 3.1) also were distributed by the Ministry of Natural Resources to boost several economic sectors in addition to financial resources. According to the KRG Ministry of Natural Resources (MNR 2022), Kurdistan Region has started its oil export from 100,000 barrels per day (BPD), now about 300,000 BPD. The KRG had already planned to export about two million BPD by 2020, but it was not able to accomplish the plan because of ISIS wars and the departure of most of foreign companies from the war zone for security reasons.

3.2.2 The Macroeconomic Conditions of Kurdistan

In macroeconomics, various economic indexes are used to evaluate the size and level of the economy. Generally, economists and officials use economic indexes such as production, demand, money supply, exchange rate, labor force, GDP,

Table 3.1 World liquid petroleum reserves (billion barrels)

World rank	Country	Oil reserves in 2020
1	Venezuela	303,800
2	Saudi Arabia	297,500
3	Canada	172,350
4	Iran	157,530
5	Iraq	147,245
6	Russia	107,800
7	Kuwait	101,500
8	United Arab Emirates	97,800
9	Libya	48,400
10	Nigeria	37,070

Source: Worldometers.info

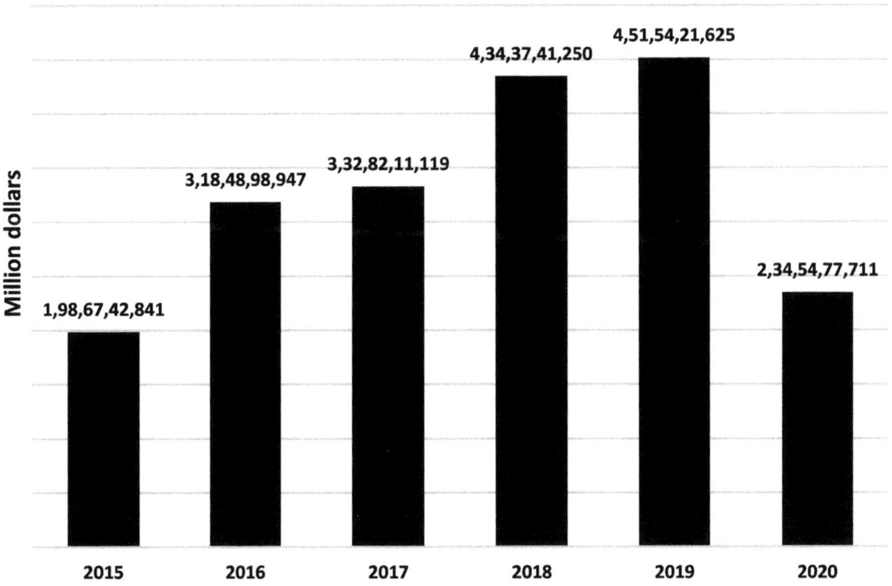

Fig. 3.1 KRI oil revenue between 2015 and 2020. Source: Open Data, KRG 2022

economic development, employment, unemployment rate, saving, investment, and inflation rate. These kinds of economic factors could be profitably used in the economy of KRI. The Kurdistan Region needs to create a data bank including these indexes and collect data on farms, firms, and households covering all-economy subsectors. This mission is an obligation element for KRI to have balanced and sustainable economic growth because in Iraq and the Kurdistan region, there is no accurate statistic, and if there is some information that exists, it is unreliable and inadequate (Heshmati 2010). The Kurdistan Region, despite 30 years of autonomy and the large size of natural resources revenues, is the only place in the world that it has no bureau of statistics, no national bank, no national account, no firm and household registers, no national research and economic policy institute, and hardly any functional or practice economic plan. On top of all these limitations, the top 500 positions are nominated with little consideration for the abilities of the nominees.

The financial regulations, government expenditure, and taxes in Kurdistan are different from that of an advanced economy. The government expenditure includes classical public activities like building infrastructure and providing public services. The taxation system in KRI does not work correctly, and if it works, it is old-fashionably developed in 1960 and remained the same due to all wars and misallocation of resources. To meet its public expenditure, the KRG depends highly on its share of oil and gas incomes. There is also some additional income for the government, which is uncountable compared to the oil incomes, such as import tariffs, vehicle registration, payments on permission for construction, and so forth (Muhamad 2020). The foreign labor force operates the oil and gas industry. It means the Kurdish population has almost no contribution to the local production and revenue generation, but only to the distribution of imported goods and consumption.

There is a monetary policy of the regions that is controlled by the Iraqi Central Bank. The economic policy is restricted to fiscal policy in public employment, providing public services, leisure infrastructure, healthcare, electricity generation, distribution, water supply utilities, and education. The government authorities who are responsible for the economic sector do not practice any stabilization policies to maintain the actual output close to its capability and reduce unemployment or create a balanced current account. The budget of KRG has been used for public employment, import of production materials, support of consumer products, and cash and in-kind transfer (Al Mihya 2017). The local production is managed by imported labor. Education in the middle east in general and oil-rich countries was designed to produce bureaucrats. The graduate is expected to be nominated and placed in public employment. The public servants' daily effective labor hours of work are almost zero (Minnis 2006).

In a standard economy, a central bank is autonomous and oversees the monetary policy, money supply, interest rate, inflation rate, exchange rate, banking, financial institutions, and current account, while the government is responsible for fiscal policy. The central bank and government roles in the Kurdistan region are mixed, and the central bank more or less functions as a commercial bank for business. Tabaqchali (2018) argued that the central bank plays a vital role in fiscal policy, which affects the money supply and regulates interest rates in the economy with several policy tools. Investment demands and consumption are affected by interest rates and money supply. Even though the Central Bank of Kurdistan Region depends on the Iraqi Central Bank to create its fiscal policies and their implementation, it must be able to provide appropriate processes to improve credit channels for the regional financial market.

The inflation in KRI is supposed to be lower than the rest of Iraq, and instability does not have a massive impact due to the high level of stability in KRI. The KRG does not have direct authority on the money supply and interest rate to lower the inflation rate. Increasing government expenditure on infrastructure, which depends on oil income, does not eliminate the private expenditure concentrated on automobiles, housing, household appliances. Besides, the region enjoyed a dual currency, which protected foreign direct investment (FDI) from the high inflation and local currency depreciation risks. The rebuilding process in KRI has led to an increase in combined inflation due to the rising of factor prices and high employment but consists of elements of eliminating domestic labor. The priority for foreign and domestic clients is to hire foreign employees. Kurdistan confronts structural unemployment due to the mismatch of the skilled workforce and job opportunities between skilled workers. Unemployment is due to the high salary of a skilled worker, which exceeds equilibrium wage level and is not in parity with their productivity, and unable to compete with foreign imported workers (Ismael 2022).

Although there are no official and accurate empirical data regarding economic indexes, some general data demonstrate economic growth. The Kurdistan Region of Iraq's GDP data is currently only accessible for a handful of years and their accompanying GDP figures. According to Fig. 3.2, the KRG's GDP for 2007 was $8.52 billion. This represents the total dollar worth of all products and services generated inside the region's boundaries that year. The graph illustrates the scope and production of the local economy during the period. The GDP rose significantly in 2008 and peaked at $20.9 billion. This significant development suggests that commerce in the Kurdistan Region has dramatically increased. Increased investments and better infrastructure, boosting other sectors like oil and gas, tourism, and services, all contributed to this boom.

Unfortunately, there is a gap in the information currently accessible for 2009 and 2010. During those years, limitations in data collection or reporting procedures may have been caused by corrupt authorities and a poorly educated workforce. The GDP reached $23.6 billion in 2011, continuing its rising trend. This suggests that the Kurdistan Region's economy was continuing to grow. Improved foreign investment, development of infrastructure, or progress in other economic sectors were all outcomes of this rise.

The GDP numbers for 2012, reported at $23.52 billion, indicate a slight decline from the prior year. Unfortunately, the information currently accessible from 2013 to 2017 still has a gap. It's essential to remember that during those years, Kurdistan had to deal with ISIS, which led to a lack of available GDP data for the KRI. The newest data from 2018 shows that the KRI's GDP was $25.74 billion. This signals potential growth and development within the area and a future rise in economic production (KRSO 2023).

According to Fig. 3.3, the GDP per capita growth in 2005 started from $762 and increased to $1,532 in 2006. At the end of the following year, in 2007, the GDP per

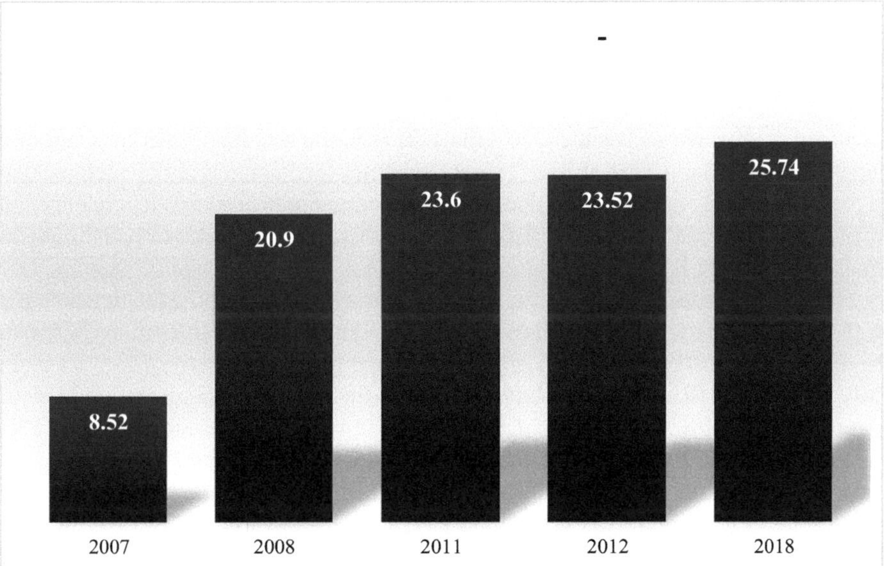

Fig. 3.2 KRI GDP growth between 2007 and 2018. Source: KRSO, KRG 2023

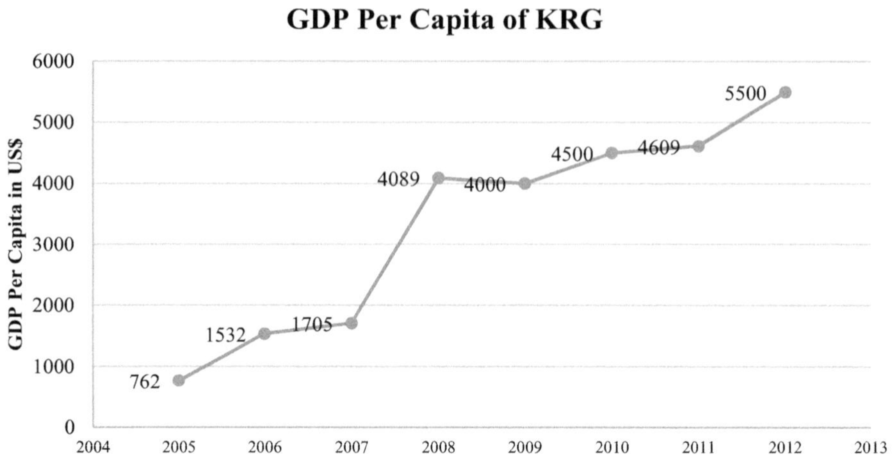

Fig. 3.3 Growth of GDP per capita in USD from 2005 to 2012. Source: KRSO, KRG 2012

capita growth in KRI scored $1,705. Since 2008, GDP per capita growth has boosted remarkably, and it reached $4,089, but it decreased to $4,000 in 2009. Moreover, in 2010 the individual per capita was $4,500, the year after, in 2011, it reached up to $4,609. After all ups and downs, GDP per capita growth stood at $5,500 in 2012. The annual growth rate of the eight-year period was 28.03 percent. In general, this discovery also shows that personal income growth is 8 percent per year, with an overall growth of 5.2 percent (KRSO 2012).

3.2.3 Economic Dependency in Kurdistan

As noted by the World Bank (2016), the KRI exhibits a certain level of economic dependency similar to that of Iraq. This dependency is characterized by factors such as heavy reliance on the oil industry, a dominant public sector, dependence on imports, significant reliance on cash transactions, and underdeveloped financial institutions. There is some clarification about these dependencies discussed below.

First, high dependency on the oil industry: Directly or indirectly, the dependency of the economy of KRI on the oil industry is inevitable. Available disputes between Baghdad and Erbil regarding the oil revenues and the budget shares have not been fully solved yet (Roberts 2016). Furthermore, the estimated percentage share of employment in this sector is just 1 percent of the region's total employment. This high dependency, particularly oil dependency, can cause a huge problem for an economy when the oil price decreases or if the economy is exposed to an external/internal shock to the industry (Heshmati 2010).

Given the generally challenging environment for private sector development, skill development has not kept pace with demand. There is a strong emphasis on incentivizing employment in the public sector, further weakening the private sector's competitiveness with other sectors in the market. These actions have limited the private sector's potential to improve and increase local production investment in tradable segments to reduce imports dependency and increase exports. Relying heavily on oil has transformed the Kurdistan Region into a rentier state, marked by cycles of economic boom and bust and an unstable business environment. During periods of rapid growth, underlying structural issues within the KRG were overshadowed. However, over the past decade, fueled by oil revenues, the KRG has acknowledged and attempted to rectify these structural deficiencies. Nevertheless, the sharp decline in oil prices in recent years exposed these problems, prompting the government to unveil new economic reforms in 2016 (Auzer 2017).

Secondly, the public sector wields significant influence over the economy of the KRI. Government expenditure by the KRG surpasses 50 percent of GDP, a figure lower than the 61 percent observed for Iraq as a whole. The KRG serves as a major employer in the region, with over 50 percent of total employment tied to government roles, including significant sectors like defense and security, which account for 24 percent of the workforce. Like other parts of Iraq, expenditures on salaries, social benefits, pensions, and subsidies (such as electricity, fuel, water, and agriculture) constitute more than 50 percent of the public budget. Tax revenues contribute a mere 4.7 percent of the total income, primarily allocated to public employee pensions. Consequently, public expenditure plays a crucial role in shaping economic development (Middle East Research Institute 2016a, b).

According to the Middle East Research Institute (2016a, b), a major issue is the high volatility of public spending, which leads to unpredictability in economic development through the fiscal multiplier effect. This volatility stems primarily from the unpredictable nature of KRG income, which fluctuates widely due to variations in oil prices, disruptions in oil production and transportation caused by conflict, and ongoing disputes with the Iraqi government over the mechanism for sharing oil revenues.

Despite the region's strong entrepreneurial spirit and potential, the dominance of the public sector in the KRI's economy hinders the growth and development of the private sector, keeping it small and underdeveloped in the Kurdistan Region of Iraq.

Third, dependency on imports: Because of the nature of the economy of Iraq, which is not diversified, in KRI, the demand for local production and size of this production are not equal (export of hydrocarbons constitutes 95 percent of Iraqi exports). The space between demand and production fills by imports, which consists of almost 90 percent of non-oil GDP. In Iraq, domestic production is limited to retailing of imported goods, the small size of the trade, and other expanded public services. An ordinary character of a rentier economy is the limitation of exports of local products, which exists in Iraq. However, there is no strong border and trade policy and import restrictions to protect local products. After all these problems, it is very tough for local producers to diversify and improve due to competing with foreign manufactured goods and imports (Manis 2016). The inability of the local industry to organize production and competition is drastically limited by the highly positioned government employees and leadership of import companies, banking, financial institutes, and retail businesses.

Fourth, there is a significant reliance on cash and a weak financial infrastructure in the KRI, which is critical for fostering private sector growth. A robust financial system is essential for facilitating larger investments and broader access to capital for more individuals. However, the KRI's financial system is characterized by inadequate infrastructure and limited availability of capital, particularly for small and medium-sized enterprises (SMEs). Commercial transactions heavily prioritize cash, with only about 3 percent of businesses utilizing the banking sector for financial operations. This preference for cash is reinforced by widespread distrust in the banking system, exacerbated by frequent financial disruptions and instability in the KRI (Mark and DeWeaver 2015). The major cause of distrust and dysfunctionality in the financial system is that the leaders own the banking, and they are the main channels of money laundry, corrupt behavior, and illegal transactions.

3.2.4 Economic Diversification in Kurdistan

For the long term, the agriculture sector has been far away from the economic development of Kurdistan, while the oil and gas industry has incredibly driven the economy of Kurdistan. Nevertheless, a decline in the price of crude oil pushed KRG, like all other oil-dependent states, to diversify its economy. In this case, the agriculture sector of KRG has a great potential to play a significant role in the economic diversification plan of the KRG (Eklund et al. 2017). However, agriculture is very primitive and far from being able without massive support to modernize and compete with the Turkey's agricultural products, which dominates the market.

Since 2011, Kurdistan's productive industries, such as agriculture and manufacturing, have shown no increase in their share of GDP. Analyzing the proportional contributions of economic sectors within the KRG reveals that the service sector, encompassing public administration and other services, constitutes 50 percent of GDP, while agriculture contributes 17.5 percent and manufacturing 9.4 percent (refer to Fig. 3.4). As indicated by sources on economic diversification in Kurdistan (Heshmati et al. 2012), the industrial and agricultural sectors exhibit significantly slower growth rates compared to the service sector. Moreover, infrastructure spending and investments by the KRG are crucial drivers of GDP development, playing a pivotal role in enhancing outputs across multiple sectors.

To draw a broader picture of the KRI's GDP compositions, it is important to compare them with the GDP composition of Iraq. By examining Fig. 3.5, we can observe that the primary sector driving the Iraqi GDP is services, which encompass public administration and other related services, accounting for a significant 51 percent of the GDP. On the other hand, the industrial sector contributes 45 percent to the overall GDP. However, it is noteworthy that the agricultural sector contributes a mere 4 percent to Iraq's GDP, indicating underestimation of agriculture industry in Iraqi economy and a high level of dependency on an oil industry.

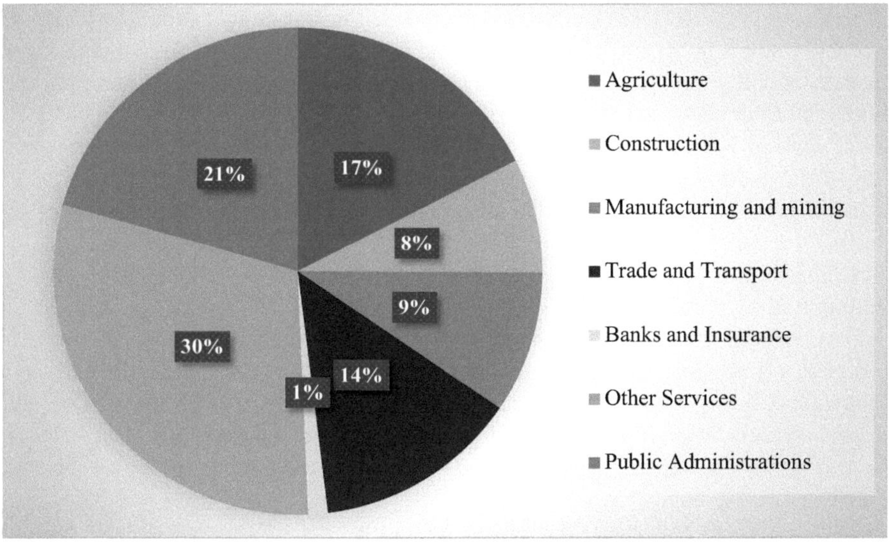

Fig. 3.4 Estimation for sector-wide value added to the GDP of KRI. Source: Ministry of Planning, KRG 2015

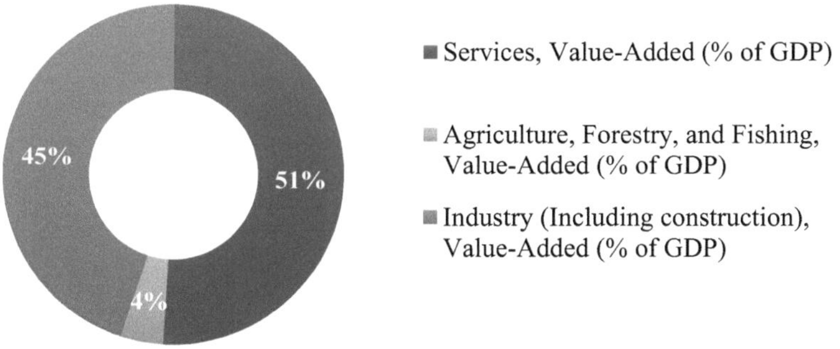

Fig. 3.5 Sector-wide value added to the GDP of Iraq, 2015. Source: World Bank 2015

In another study, Eklund et al. (2016) argued that there had been considerable changes in the agriculture industry of Kurdistan; this shows the possibility of this sector as a significant player in the economic growth of the region. Because of that, the KRG prioritized the agriculture industry's improvement to attract more international investment. Iraqi Kurdistan possesses 1.5 million hectares of irrigated lands, a very efficient environment, natural habitat, and different livestock that help Kurdistan have so many different agricultural products. Although this industry contributes only 10 percent of GDP growth, under optimal plan and policy conditions, the agriculture industry has a bright future to affect the KRI's development.

The Kurdistan Parliament enacted an investment law in July 2006 that gave international investors an unusually high level of independence and capital gain. However, it promoted collaboration with local merchants linked with the KDP and

PUK. From 2006 to 2012, the KRG attracted $22 billion in investment, which had a considerable impact on KRG income and employment due to the exceptionally investor-friendly structure. Moreover, Hansen et al. (2014a, b) highlighted that the most visible impacts of the FDI inflow were on the real estate sector that elevated the skyline of Kurdistan's towers. The KRG was pushed to pursue such strategies due to the worldwide dominance of the free-market economy and the desire to attract capital inflow. According to Biro (2019), the KRI enhanced its security in conflict zones by bolstering trade and economic relations with neighboring countries. This strategy was so effective that Turkey surpassed Iran to become the KRG's leading trading partner.

Diversifying investment and source of income is necessary to speed up self-sufficiency and sustainable economic development of the region. There are always connections between investment sectors to one another in the economy; the growth of one sector through spillover effect enhances the growth of other sectors. According to Fig. 3.6, private investments are distributed to 13 economic sectors in Kurdistan's economy.

Between 2006 and 2021, the KRI attracted a total investment of $59 billion, comprising 76.77 percent from national sources ($45.35 billion), 16.93 percent from FDI amounting to $9.9 billion, and 6.31 percent from joint ventures totaling $3.72 billion (see Fig. 3.7). The investment law encompasses all economic sectors except for oil and gas, with priority sectors identified as agriculture, industry, and tourism.

The tourism industry is a crucial sector for the sustainable economic development of KRG; that is why the government has initiated development goals to enhance the engagement of the tourism industry. The industry appears as an

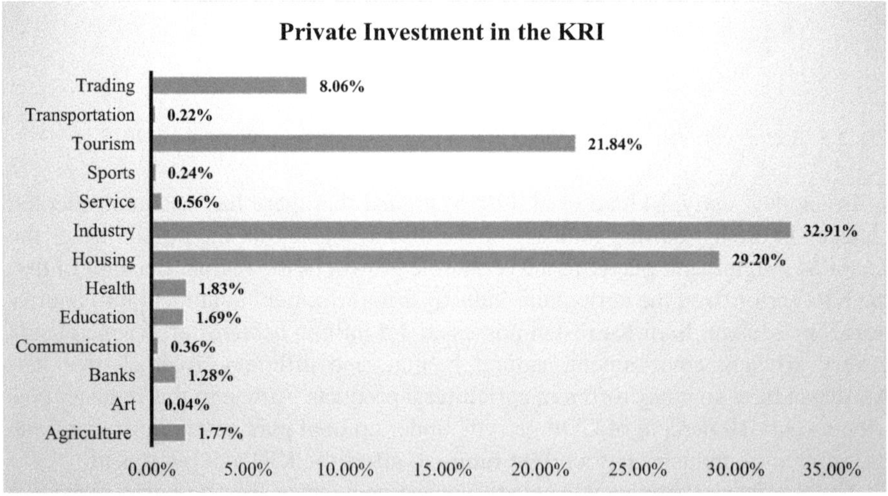

Fig. 3.6 Distribution of private investment to the various economic sectors in KRI. Source: Board of Investment, KRG 2022

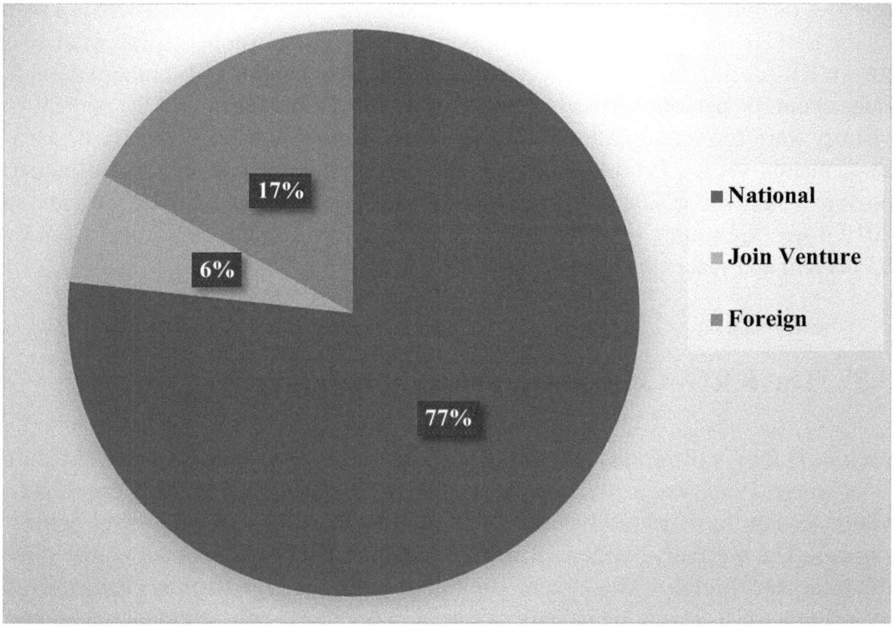

Fig. 3.7 Total percentage of private investment by investors. Source: Board of Investment, KRG 2022

essential sector to help with the diversification plans. The consequences of these objectives are positive. A tremendous amount of capital has been invested in infrastructure, accompanied by a comprehensive renovation of urban areas that have helped with the region development (Zebari and Ibrahim 2016). The stability and peace in the region encouraged the Iraqi Arab population who are subject to traveling restrictions to visit Kurdistan Region with a different climate, scenery, and leisure activities for holidays. The temporary return of Kurds living abroad, many refugees and international nongovernmental organizations (NGOs), foreign arm forces, and foreign consulates have also increased the flow of tourism.

Altaee et al. (2017) stated that the international community dramatically acknowledges the diversity of people, traditions, and landscapes of KRI. In 2011, *The New York Times* featured the KRI in an article titled “41 Places to Go,” ranking it 34th. That same year, National Geographic included KRI in its “20 best trips,” describing it as the “oasis of peace and stability in a historically volatile region.” By 2014, Erbil, the capital of KRI, was designated the 2014 Arab tourism capital by the Arab Council of Tourism. Apart from its unique composition of beautiful nature and stability, almost 3500 historical landmarks are placed in the Kurdish governorates of Iraq that make Kurdistan a tourist destination for domestic and international tourists.

Asaad (2018) indicates that in 2007, the number of tourists was only 377,397 visitors, while it increased in 2012 and reached 2.2 million visitors, and by the end of 2013, the number of tourists reached almost three million visitors. There is a plan by the KRG to attract about seven million tourists in 2025. About 66 percent of visitors in KRI during the previous years have come from central and southern parts of Iraq, about 14 percent of tourists were locals (KRI's citizens), and 20 percent of visitors were foreigners. Many foreigners who came to the KRI came to do business, mainly visited Erbil because it is the capital and most prominent businesses operate from Erbil. Eventually, the tourism industry created about 6000 jobs, and in 2012 it was the source of $650 million in income for the KRI, then it increased by 53 percent and reached $1 billion in 2013.

3.3 The KRG–Central Government Relations

Politics in Iraq is sectarian and sentimental, and ties between Baghdad and Erbil are even worse. Psychological variables, such as rapport and confidence between individual leaders, have primarily determined whether this interaction improves or deteriorates. The normative system of ties Iraq and the KRI has remained unmet since the Iraqi constitution was adopted. The relationship between them is characterized by a continuously changing balance of forces rather than a constitutional rule of law. The tensions between Erbil and Baghdad have varied over the recent years, imitating the ties between a highly autonomous area and a weak central authority and regional–federal connections (Gunter 2010).

Crocker and Younis (2017) expressed several tensions between Erbil and Baghdad, but the most significant is the dispute over natural resources. It looks at Iraq's constitution text on hydrocarbons, which led to its diverse approaches to developing oil reserves based on various ideas on federalism, the KRI's budgets, and oil production from 2003. Furthermore, Erbil and Baghdad have consistently expressed their commitment to resolving the dispute over the KRI allocation in the national budget and its oil production, adhering to the provisions outlined in the Iraqi constitution of 2005.

Furthermore, both stakeholders have different opinions on the core of constitutional articles 111 and 112, which concentrate on exploring and exporting natural resources. The central bone of disagreement is the power dynamic between the center and the sub-regional bodies. Iraqi officials insist that only the federal government decide on natural resource production. In contrast, Kurdish officials argued that regions and governorates within Iraq could decide their natural resources' extractions based on the Iraqi constitution. In the continuing conversations on the installation of a national government in Iraq, the context of Article 112 has been a crucial sticking point between the Regional and Central governments in Iraq (Tabaqchali et al. 2021).

Moreover, they added that the vagueness of the phrase "with" in Articles 112–1 and 112–2 is the source of controversy. The central administration views the "with" as admitting a place for provincial and district entities—albeit a minor one; the KRG, on the other hand, sees it differently and references it to the regional government. According to the provisions, in collaboration with the producing districts and regional authorities, the central government will handle oil and gas derived from present sites.

However, Article 112–2, which stipulates that "managing natural resources in a manner that maximizes profit for Iraqi citizens through the use of modern market methods and the promotion of investment," is subject to varying interpretations. Each party has viewed this section to enable implementing oil development initiatives with international oil companies (IOCs) that are suitable for their oilfields exporting obstacles. Concerning the power to sell oil provided by these IOCs, there are almost no legal clauses concerning hydrocarbon exports or if they are under the power of regional or central governments. Therefore, these ambiguities in the legal framework arise more conflicts when it is time for legislators to use the articles in the official hydrocarbon debates (Knights 2020).

Pergolizzi (2014) states that both parties established their respective understanding of the constitutional articles and negotiated oil production deals with IOCs that were contradictory. After enacting its natural resources law, the Kurdistan region signed a type of contract that covers oil exploration and export from A to Z called Production Sharing Contracts (PSC), which was never recognized by the central government or non-Kurdish MPs in Baghdad. Thus, this rejection to approve the PSCs resulted in a conflict over KRG's portion of the national budget in exchange for its oil production strategies. In countries rich in natural resources, a national or regional oil company is expected to manage the extraction and export of resources. Rarely, private interest is formulating and operating the nature of the long-term profit-sharing contracts, which are clearly in private interest and violating the national interest.

Following that, subsequent national budget regulations left KRG with no credit for the region's oil and gas production expenses, thus forcing the KRG to pay for the IOCs working in Kurdistan out of its ordinary yearly budgetary allotment. These exclusions worsened tensions between the two parties, leading to a breakdown in the cooperation that resulted in Baghdad blocking the KRG's portion of the national budget in 2014. The Kurdistan Regional Government (KRG) responded by pursuing the heavy step of its sales to generate sufficient cash. The IOCs working in Kurdistan increased their exploration, which reached 450,000 barrels per day in 2020 (Tabaqchali et al. 2021).

In 2013, Asadi explains the tension between both parties in the disputed areas. He argued that the tension on disputed territories between Iraq and Kurdistan Region remains another crucial issue between the two parties. Based on article 140, a census must be conducted, backed by a referendum, to decide the status of the contested regions. This problem will have to be resolved, as the headcount has been postponed, and it continues to be a source of contention between the two administrations. According to US official sources, the possible primary threat to Iraq's security is the likelihood of Arab–Kurdish violence over the disputed areas. This is certainly relevant when the gap is attributed to the lack of an agreed-upon political and legal structure for Iraqis to handle opposing views to these critical territories.

After 2003, Erbil and Baghdad failed to reach an agreement on running the disputed territories. Alternatively, each has tried to regulate its control by a mix of pressure, corruption, and favoritism to establish reality on the ground. Furthermore, both parties have embraced a zero-sum attitude that causes political failure rather than reaching an agreement. This atmosphere has intensified local conflicts and generated economic, social, and political cracks that terrorist groups have eagerly seized (Gunter 2011).

According to Ala'Aldeen (2020), there is a possibility of solving the issues between both parties. Iraq has wasted significant chances to get back on the rails, has shed trillions of dollars to corruption, and has seen its people grow increasingly militarized and separated. The state has squandered its autonomy, legitimacy, and any chance of proper recovery. Moreover, with the emergence of the COVID-19 pandemic and reduced oil prices, both Erbil and Baghdad sought to increase their revenues. In addition, the emergence of ISIS as a common challenge for both sides, the military activities of Turkey within the northern borders of Iraq, and the new debate between Iraq and the United States to reach a strategic partnership agreement deliver no adequate opportunity for greater cooperation between Baghdad and Erbil, and, inevitably, the exploration of a win–win outcome. Remarkably, both sides' new foreign involvement and common difficulties hardly provide any excellent chances to repair Iraq in the long run while also improving Erbil–Baghdad relations. The United States has never supported opposition to a central government unless it was a communist regime. In critical situations, the United States has supported opposition to partially change the government policy in line with US regional policy, but not overthrow the central government. The experience can suggest that the US–Baghdad relations will not be gainful or favorable to Kurdistan Region.

3.4 Summary

The political landscape of the Kurdistan Region of Iraq is grappling with challenges in achieving cohesion and stability. Being mainly dominated by KDP and PUK with other political parties contributing to the dynamics, the region's power balance risks being overridden after the recognition of Kurdish statehood was given. Even though KDP and PUK have serious power-sharing deals, still some controversies remain valid regarding the President of Iraq. Sulaymaniyah and Erbil are divided on ideological lines; trust and social distances are widening in the political area, which is dominated by the KDP and PUK. These are problems that should be solved to bring on unity, stability, and general progress in the region, as this chapter stresses.

Economic improvement, on the one hand, is not inclusive of the population's general wellbeing; rather, it is inclusive of the ruling elites, which militates against KRI development. Employment policies and government support are of the main responsibility for the establishment of the clientelism system and decrease of critical perception of the political system. This has resulted in a culture of dependency and hampered the efforts of rebuilding and developing the region, cutting down on the use of foreign labor and imported goods. The outcomes of these negative policies are revealed in the high level of youth emigration, which complicates the region's restoration and development even more.

This chapter provides insight into the area's economy, which heavily depends on oil and gas, mostly public employment, high import share, a preference for cash-based transactions, and limited financial infrastructure in the KRI. Crude oil as a powerhouse is one of the significant income earners for the region. Additionally, its monotonous income source based on oil revenues may prove to be a problem in one way or another due to either fluctuations in the oil market or other outside factors.

There is a significant presence of the government; expenditure stands at over 50 percent of GDP, and employment is a core facet. Yet instability in public expenditure and a strong position of the public sector in many countries negatively affect private business development. Also, the KRI has other constraints in the financial system under which SMEs struggle to access capital, and the populace lacks confidence in the financial institutions.

In the end, the Baghdad–Erbil relationship is quite complicated, particularly in managing oil resources and territories in dispute. Conflicts and breakdown of cooperation have been because of differing opinions as to the way the constitutional articles are to be implemented. The status of territory remains questionable, which poses a challenge to its stability. Although there are some chances of compromise; to bring about a win–win situation and foster better relations, the involvement of foreign elements and overbearing complications make it difficult to do so.

Thus, it is significant to understand the elements of a KRI to comprehend the political environment of the Kurdish population. It has shown that the region's governance branches, the KRG, the Presidency, the Kurdistan Parliament, and the judiciary contribute to the formation of the future of this region and the response to the desires of the Kurdistan development. However, the political and economic factors entail power-sharing, entailing major challenges in relation to the distribution of power, competition between political parties, and the central government in Baghdad. Despite the achievements of the Kurds of Iraq seeking self-administration and recognition, challenges are present in the desire of the Kurds to establish more autonomy as well as receive proper protection for their civil liberties. The region's economy depends much on the oil factor and the predominance of the public sector with problems of import coefficient and the underdeveloped financial system. In this aspect, the political system can be described as polarized and therefore not fully stable. To realize growth and development, there is a need to reform on handling central government relations crises as well as economic issues.

References

Abdullah FH (2018) The political system in Iraqi Kurdistan: party rivalries and future perspectives. Asian Affairs 49(4):606–624

Al Mihya S (2017) The economic crisis in Kurdistan region and its impact on foreign investment. Intl J Econ Manag Sci 06(05). https://doi.org/10.4172/2162-6359.1000453
Ala'Aldeen D (2020) The status of Erbil-Baghdad relations. Middle East Research Institute. http://www.meri-k.org/publication/the-status-of-erbil-baghdad-relations/. Last Access November 14th, 2021
Ala'Aldeen D (2016) State-building in a fragmented Kurdistan region of Iraq. Middle East Res Inst 3(13):1–3
Altaee A, Abdulkadhim H, Tofiq A, Jamel M (2017) Promoting the tourism industry of Kurdistan region of Iraq (Halabja Province as a case study). J Tourism Hospital Manag 104–110. https://doi.org/10.15640/jthm.v5n1a11
Amereller F, Zamel D (2021) The oil and gas law review: Iraqi Kurdistan. Retrieved February 11th, 2022, from https://thelawreviews.co.uk/title/the-oil-and-gas-law-review/iraqi-kurdistan#:~:text=The%20Kurdistan%20Region%20Ministry%20of,tcf%20of%20largely%20unproven%20gas. Last Access on January 14th 2023
Asaad M (2018) Foreign direct investment and its impact on development of the tourism sector in Kurdistan region—Iraq. J Univ Human Dev 4(1):80–90
Asadi A (2013) The territorial conflict between the central Iraqi government and the Kurdistan regional government. In: Wahlers G (ed) Elections and transitions in the Islamic world. Konrad Adenauer Stiftung, pp 50–80. http://www.jstor.org/stable/resrep10105.6. Last Access on April 8th 2022
Auzer KA (2017) Institutional design and capacity to enhance effective governance of oil and gas wealth: the case of Kurdistan region. Springer. https://doi.org/10.1007/978-981-10-4518-9. Last Access: April 22nd 2022
Biro R (2019) Political stability and security status. UKH J Social Sci 3(1):11–13. https://doi.org/10.25079/ukhjss.v3n1y2019
Crocker R, Younis N (2017) Mediating between Baghdad and the KRG. In: Report of the task force on the future of Iraq: achieving long-term stability to ensure the defeat of ISIS. Atlantic Council, pp 18–19. http://www.jstor.org/stable/resrep03713.8. Last Access July 17th, 2022
Eklund L, Persson A, Pilesjö P (2016) Cropland changes in times of conflict, reconstruction, and economic development in Iraqi Kurdistan. Ambio 45(1):78–88
Eklund L, Abdulhakim A, Mine I (2017) From producers to consumers: the challenges and opportunities of agricultural development in Iraqi Kurdistan. Land Publisher 6(2):44–50
Gunter MM (2010) Kurdish-Arab tensions and Irbil-Baghdad relations. J South Asian Middle Eastern Stud 33(3):40–47
Gunter MM (2011) Arab-Kurdish relations and the future of Iraq. Third World Q 32(9):1623–1635
Hama HH (2018) Partisan armed forces of Kurdistan regional government. J South Asian Middle Eastern Stud 41(2):38–51
Hansen ML, Howard JS, Louay C (2014a) Strategies for private-sector development and civil-service reform in the Kurdistan Region-Iraq. Rand Corporation
Hansen ML, Shatz HJ, Constant L, Smith AC, Kumar KB, Krull H, Usanov A, Dogo H, Martini J (2014b) Fostering private-sector development: taking advantage of private investment and reforming the enabling environment. In: Strategies for private-sector development and civil-service reform in the Kurdistan region—Iraq. Rand Corporation, pp 17–38. http://www.jstor.org/stable/10.7249/j.ctt6wq8hc.12. Last Access on December 23rd 2021
Hasan Q, Perot K (2021) Production sharing contracts and rentierism: reforming transparency gaps in Kurdistan's oil and gas contracts. Extract Indust Soc 8(2):1–7. https://doi.org/10.1016/j.exis.2021.100899. Last Access on November 27th 2022
Heshmati A (2010) The economy of southern Kurdistan. Nova Science, Hauppauge, NY
Heshmati A, Dilani A, Baban S (2012) Perspectives on Kurdistan's economy and Society in Transition. Nova Publishers, New York, pp 308–315
Ismael AA (2022) The effect of inflation on financial and accounting data's ability to reflect profitable gains reported by financial statements

Karim BM, Aziz PH (2024) Legal disputes between Iraq and Turkey over the KRG's oil fields and the implications of the ICC Court's ruling on them. J Islam Asia 21(1):166–190. E-ISSN 2289-8077
Knights M (2020) Iraqi Kurdistan: priority issues for international mediation. Middle East Research Institute. http://www.jstor.org/stable/resrep25306
KRSO (2012) Socio-economic monitoring system report. Kurdistan Region Statistics Office, Erbil, Iraq. https://krso.gov.krd/en/indicator/. Last Access March 4th 2022
Kurdistan Region's Statistics Office (2023) GDP. Kurdistan Regional Government. https://krso.gov.krd/en/statistics/gdp#. Last Access on May 4th 2023
Kurdistan Regional Government (2022) Government Open Data. Deloitte Reports. https://gov.krd/english/information-and-services/open-data/. Last Access March 5th 2022
Leezenberg M (2015) Politics, economy, and ideology in Iraqi Kurdistan since 2003: enduring trends and novel challenges. Arab Stud J 23(1):154–183. http://www.jstor.org/stable/44744903. Last Access on April 12th 2022
Manis A (2016) The KRI's faltering economy: causes and relevance of possible solutions, in averting an economic meltdown in the Kurdistan region of Iraq: aligning political objectives with economic necessities. Middle East Research Institute, pp 10–14. http://www.jstor.org/stable/resrep13621.5. Last Access on April 18th 2022
Mark A, DeWeaver (2015) Kurdistan's great recession: from boom to bust in the rentier economy. IRIS-American University of Sulaimani. Retrieved November 8th 2021, from https://auis.edu.krd/iris/sites/default/files/IRIS%20Iraq%20Report%20IIR_Mark%20DeWeaver_Inside%20Iraq%E2%80%99s%20Cash%20Economy_2016_0.pdf. Last Access on January 12th 2022
Middle East Research Institute (2016a) Making Kurdistan competitive again: away from the rentier state. In: MERI economic forum. Middle East Research Institute, pp 11–12. http://www.jstor.org/stable/resrep13624.6. Last Access on December 8th 2022
Middle East Research Institute (2016b) Structural weaknesses of Kurdistan's economy, in the Best of Times and The Worst of Times: addressing structural weaknesses of the Kurdistan Region's economy. Middle East Research Institute, pp 24–32. http://www.jstor.org/stable/resrep13633.6. Last Access on January 12th 2022
Ministry of Natural Resources (2022) Production report. Kurdistan Regional Government. https://gov.krd/mnr-en/publications/. Last Access March 1st 2022
Ministry of Planning (2015) All capital investment projects report 2007–2014: Kurdistan Regional Government, Ministry of Planning, Erbil
Minnis J (2006) First nations education and rentier economics: parallels with the Gulf states. Canadian J Educ/Revue Canadienne De L'éducation 29(4):975. https://doi.org/10.2307/20054207
Muhamad MG (2020) Private sector development in Kurdistan region of Iraq: lessons learnt from the role of the government in emerging economies. University of Kurdistan at Hewler, Erbil, Kurdistan Region of Iraq, Defended on July 9th 2020
Pergolizzi E (2014) Energy crossroads: shifting dynamics in the troubled triangle between Ankara, Erbil and Baghdad. Global political trends center (gpot). Http://www.jstor.org/stable/resrep14130. Last Access on February 13th 2023
Rafaat A (2018) Kurdistan in Iraq the evolution of a quasi-state, 1st edn. Routledge, London, pp 148–165
Roberts J (2016) The reliance of the Kurdistan regional government and the regional economy on oil and gas, in Iraqi Kurdistan oil and gas outlook. Atlantic Council, pp 8–10. http://www.jstor.org/stable/resrep03675.6. Last Access on June 18th 2022
Rubin M (2016) What form of government will Kurdistan embrace? In: Kurdistan rising?: considerations for Kurds, their Neighbors, and the region. American Enterprise Institute, pp 56–63. http://www.jstor.org/stable/resrep03254.7. Last Access on May, 26th 2022
Shukor A, Klazinga N, Kringos D (2017) Primary Care in an Unstable Security, humanitarian, economic, and political context: Kurdistan region of Iraq. BMC Health Serv Res 17(1):590–599

Stansfield G (2017) The evolution of the political system of the Kurdistan region of Iraq. Between State and Non-State, 61–76. https://doi.org/10.1057/978-1-137-60181-0_4

Tabaqchali A (2018) Statehood in the Kurdistan Region of Iraq, Through an economic Lens. IRIS-American University of Sulaimani. Retrieved November 14th 2021, from https://www.auis.edu.krd/iris/sites/default/files/Statehood%20in%20KRI%20through%20an%20Economic%20Lens_%20FINAL_March2018_0_1.pdf. Last Access on April, 14th 2023

Tabaqchali A, Al-Shadeedi H, Absullah S (2021) Breaking the impasse: the Baghdad-Erbil budget divide. Institute of Regional and International Studies-American University of Iraq. https://auis.edu.krd/iris/sites/default/files/20210516-IER2-Final_0.pdf. Last Access November 14th 2021

World Bank (2015) The Kurdistan region of Iraq: assessing the economic and social impact of the Syrian conflict and ISIS. The World Bank

World Bank (2016) The Kurdistan region of Iraq – reforming the economy for shared prosperity and protecting the vulnerable: executive summary (English). X. Washington, DC: World Bank Group. http://documents.worldbank.org/curated/en/708441468196727918/Executive-summary. Last Access on May 18th 2022

Zebari H, Ibrahim R (2016) Methods & strategies for sustainable architecture in Kurdistan region, Iraq. Proc Environ Sci Improv Sustain Dev Countr (ISCDC) 34:202–211

Chapter 4
Institutional Quality in Rentier States

Based on the previous chapter's findings, the KRI exhibits characteristics of a rentier state, which faces several challenges in terms of its governance and institutional quality. Moreover, this chapter explores the institutional quality of 51 rentier states by assessing various political and economic determinants. This chapter aims to enhance knowledge of the political determinants that impact economic advancement in the given rentier states and the resulting outcomes. Therefore, it aims to present essential findings as a basis for comparing the context of institutional quality between 51 rentier states and KRI in Chap. 5, which aligns with the primary research question and aims of this study.

4.1 Institutions

With the advent of the prosperous era in the oil industry and the growth of the emerging Gulf oil-producing nations, the notion of a rentier state has garnered significant attention. Adam Smith, a renowned economist, drew a noteworthy distinction between rent and other forms of revenue, namely salaries and earnings. He posited that rent, in contrast to salaries and profits, assumes a distinct position in the valuation of a product. The determinants of high or low prices are, in fact, the corresponding levels of remuneration and earnings, which subsequently influence the cost of rent (Lamb 1973. It is worth mentioning that rent often acts as compensation for the control over natural resources, extending beyond a mere source of income for owners. According to Samuelson (1977), land and mining operations typically pay royalties to their landlords, and this payment, coupled with the land's rent, is an outcome that does not lead to increased output. This phenomenon holds true for various natural resources and unique assets, including geographical location, climatic conditions, and other factors. The term "rent" is generally employed to denote

R. C. Biro, *Political Challenges of Economic Development in Rentier States*, Perspectives on Development in the Middle East and North Africa (MENA) Region, https://doi.org/10.1007/978-981-96-0563-7_4

the financial gains derived from natural endowments. In this broad sense, all economies experience rents, albeit to varying degrees (Aslaksen and Torvik 2006).

There is already a comprehensive discussion on how natural resources have affected economic development. Although resource availability would enhance income and increase per capita, others contend that economies that focus on extracting and trading natural resources flourish at slow rates (Schwarz 2008). The notion that having an excess of mineral wealth may be more harmful than advantageous for some nations has received significant recognition in the literature. Literature has tried to explain this widely recognized dichotomy, called the "natural resource curse." A fundamental problem is why certain nations with abundant natural resources, like Chile and Botswana, experience significant socioeconomic development while others, like Nigeria and Venezuela, struggle with poor economic development yet own vast natural resource reserves (Bjorvatn and Naghavi 2010).

Several factors describe the curse connected with the rent from natural resources. First, the extraction procedures of natural resources use financial capital that would direct to sustainable and productive sectors, such as industry or services. Besides, unstable petroleum prices globally undermine the stability of rentier economies (Atkinson and Hamilton 2003). Furthermore, the concentration of rent inputs makes it easier for non-inclusive authorities to collect rent instead of fostering economic development since their systems benefit the maintenance of political power. The resource curse also develops if a nation concentrates all of its efforts on just one sector, like mining, and ignores other significant economic areas. Moreover, other studies mentioned that the low quality of political and financial institutions is an essential factor that prevents economic advancement in rentier states (Malik 2017).

Countries become excessively reliant upon the cost of resources, leading to the unstable growth of the GDP. Likewise, when there is no sufficient resource privilege, the rule of law (hence, institutional quality (IQ)), and a national income structure in the community, corruption within the government typically leads to the resource curse, leading to unequal regulation of a particular sector (Auty 1993). The fact that resource-poor countries perform better than resource-rich economies is not surprising. Everything comes down to institutions and, even more crucially, if the resources were found before or after the institutions were set up. An instance is Norway, which had the institutions in place before its oil was discovered, in contrast to Organization of Petroleum Exporting Countries (OPEC), which discovered oil accidentally and are now struggling to create effective institutions while having nothing to demonstrate. Generally, countries with high-quality institutions performed better than those without institutions when they discovered their natural resource fields (Dellepiane-Avellaneda 2010).

Several studies found that in developing markets, raising IQ may treat a large spectrum of problems, including restricting capital inflows, violence, and fraud. Notwithstanding, there is a remarkable lack of knowledge of this concept among politicians and others who maintain economic growth. The dual benefits of raising IQ are that it encourages growth in the economy and democratization. Therefore, IQ is crucial in allowing resource-rich economies to have more influence on their livelihoods by influencing the most feasible strategies for fostering economic development. The wealth earned by rent tends to stop improving a nation's financial status and instead becomes a burden when that nation's economy is defined by low IQ (Glaeser et al. 2004; Levchenko 2007; Kunčič 2014; Chong and Calderon 2000).

Levchenko (2007) argued that it is not a novel idea that solid institutions have a significant role in a nation's economic prosperity. The link between the rate of GDP growth and IQ has been extensively researched, theorized about, and experimentally evaluated by several writers. Numerous economists have believed that solid institutions affect a nation's capacity to advance economically from the early 1990s. There is plenty of research on the vital element, which mentions that high institution quality promotes economic growth. Better institutional quality fosters an environment that supports wealth creation, as highlighted by Acemoglu et al. (2005) and Robinson and Acemoglu (2012). According to Runde (2017), low-level institutions harm economic growth because they may prevent possible market opportunities like increased public goods supply and the recruitment of highly skilled workers. De Haan (2007) claims that organizational capability can affect economic performance by redistributing resources. Resource misallocation may lead to ineffective expenditures, which can impede social prosperity.

While institutional quality has held a prominent place in classical institutional economic theory for a considerable period, its significance has somewhat receded in the wake of evolving industries and the increasing diversity and openness in investment and production locations. To address this gap in contemporary economic scholarship, this research embarks on a comprehensive examination of the impact wielded by institutional factors. To be precise, it delves into the six primary institutional factors as defined by the World Bank, investigating their intricate interactions with macroeconomic variables. This chapter endeavors to uncover their collective influence on per capita GDP, specifically within the context of 51 rentier states. The information was sourced from the World Bank's World Development Indicators Database. Our aim with this study is to underscore how institutional quality remains a crucial factor in driving economic growth, despite the continuous shifts in the economic environment.

4.1.1 Institutional Quality

Douglass North conducted pioneering research on institutional quality primarily in the 1980s. According to North, institutions are frameworks and regulations established by humans to govern social interactions. In North's theory, the quality of institutions improves when the power of the executive branch is constrained. These constraints can be formal laws or informal cultural norms, and their effectiveness depends on enforcement mechanisms. Limiting executive power aims to prevent leaders from arbitrarily asserting authority above legal frameworks. This ensures that individuals, business owners, and others investing in a transparent economic system are protected by law in their commercial activities, investments in human capital, and endeavors in adopting advanced technologies (North 1989, 1990).

These efforts are crucial for advancing technology through investments in research and development (R&D), especially in emerging innovations, and accelerating the adoption of cutting-edge technologies that are already widely used globally. Such initiatives challenge political and economic authorities due to their inherent uncertainty and disruptive nature. Therefore, robust institutions are essential to ensure that both authorities and competitors receive equal legal protection. Acemoglu et al. (2001, 2003, 2005) employ a broader view that considers de facto and de jure authority rather than focusing primarily on de jure executive power. Additionally, a difference is established between formal and informal power and political, institutional, and economic powers. Moreover, they identify the interaction between institutional quality and financial gains but insist that institutional quality is the leader in this dance.

To describe institutional quality by data, firstly, institutions should be regarded as a fundamental necessity for long-term development and economic prosperity. Second, there are many vital components of institutional quality, including some that are problematic to measure. It is best suggested to construct this indicator on fully public data that has been as fairly collected as possible for neutrality and reliability. Thus, Kaufmann et al. (2010) have articulated six specific governance indicators that measure an institution's quality by empirical data, and the World Bank collects the data annually. These indicators are allocated to three categories:

- The procedure of government selection, overseeing, and overthrowing.
- The government's potential for decision-making and imposing sound policies.
- Mutual respect between the state and people and their interaction.
- Each category has two dimensions, which equals to the abovementioned six dimensions. The dimensions are listed below for a brief description:
- The procedure of government selection, overseeing, and overthrowing is a measure based on the following two indicators:
- *Voice and accountability* (VA): This metric assesses citizens' perceptions of their ability to select their government, freedom of expression, civil liberties, and access to independent media.
- *Political stability and absence of violence/terrorism* (PV): This indicator measures the perceived likelihood of government destabilization or violent overthrow due to terrorism, political violence, or other illegal means.
- The government's potential for decision-making and imposing sound policies is determined by the following:
- *Government effectiveness* (GE): Where developing and implementing sound policies are concerned, and since political influences among governments can significantly impact its policies and public services, this criterion provides a basis for assessing a government's capability in maintaining policies and sticking to these policies.
- *Regulatory quality* (RQ): This parameter examines what the people think about the government's capacity to come up with good policies and legal frameworks that foster the development of the private sector.

- Mutual respect between the state and people and their interaction is assessed based on the following:
- *Rule of Law* (RL): This index gauges people's trust in the efficiency of legal frameworks and authorities, as well as the efficiency of contract rights, protection of property, the condition of law and order, police, courts, and the number of crimes and incidents of violence.
- Control of corruption (CC): This index measures the perception of corruption within the civil service, encompassing both petty and grand corruption, and the extent to which public office is exploited for personal gain by elites and private interests.

The relationships among these six governance indicators are strong and interconnected. For instance, it is logical to infer that stronger accountability systems are associated with lower levels of corruption. A government that operates effectively can establish better regulatory frameworks, while adherence to the rule of law can promote fairer electoral processes and reduce instances of public office misuse for personal gain. Our composite measures of these six indicators consistently show significant positive correlations across countries, even when considering these interconnections (Alsaleh et al. 2021).

4.1.2 Institutions and Economic Growth

In the most prestigious intellectual literature, this subject still ignites discussion. Acemoglu et al. (2005), who support the institution-driven advancement causality direction, and Glaeser et al. (2004), who strongly oppose the direction of causality, are the two research teams that best reflect the two sides of the argument. It is significant to observe that both sides of the argument support their positions with the historical case of Korea. Acemoglu et al. (2005) refer to the Koreas to highlight how small the two Koreas' economic assets or structural differences were at the end of the Second World War. The critical distinction has been in the later institutional structure decisions being made. A private ownership framework and an economic structure centered on market factors and commercial incentives were both retained in South Korea. Thus, South Korea developed by adhering to good governance, becoming one of the "Asian economic surprises" in the 1960s.

Stands in opposition, North Korea adopted a centralized economy and abolished private ownership following the communist paradigm. The North Korean leadership adopted extractive structures, and its economy has lagged its southern neighbor. It has also been moving backward since the 1990s regarding overall economic well-being. According to Acemoglu et al. (2005), the Korean "natural experiment" provides a compelling argument in favor of their contention that institutional quality is a crucial component of the enabling environment that fosters long-term economic success. It is worth mentioning that a large share of the difference in development between North and South Korea is attributed to the effects of economics, finance, trade, technology, and political sanctions imposed on North Korea by the United States and its Western allies.

Referring to the same experiment, Glaeser et al. (2004) noted that after the two Koreas split into two independent countries, the institutional quality gap between them was insignificant. Following economic growth, South Korea embraced a more democratic institutional structure. In essence, they believe that South Korea's financial success, not North Korea's, is to blame for the current gap in institutional quality between the two countries. In addition, but more crucially, they imply that nations may only allow themselves to develop in the openness of organizations once they have attained a minimal degree of economic development.

Acemoglu et al. (2007) state that private ownership-right entities are the primary forces behind long-term economic growth and financial advancement. Moreover, they demonstrated that the presence of the rule of law promotes economic growth in many nations. Moreover, the beneficial impact of institutions is determined by several variables, including the institutions, social standards, and citizens. Occasionally, organizations with comparable elements produce different results for various groups and locations.

4.2 Data Presentation

This work utilizes panel data spanning 51 rentier states from 2003 to 2020 to investigate how institutional quality impacts economic growth. Various political and economic factors are analyzed to explore the relationship between GDP growth and institutional quality. Data and variables are sourced from the World Bank's World Governance Indicators (WGI) and World Development Indicators (WDI) databases. The six institutional quality indicators, as previously described, are derived from the WGI database, graded on a scale from −2.5 to +2.5 (Kaufmann et al. 2010). Additional observations are obtained from the WDI database.

Our research places significant emphasis on both the dependent and independent variables to ensure the precision of its econometric models and findings. Drawing from theoretical frameworks and empirical data, a range of independent variables have been selected to influence the dependent variables in various ways. The primary objective of this research is to explore the interrelationships among these variables.

The central focus of the study is GDP per capita growth, which serves as the principal indicator of economic development. The independent variables encompass:

- Inflation rate (percentage change in prices).
- Net inflows of foreign direct investment as a percentage of GDP.
- Net outflows of foreign direct investment as a percentage of GDP.
- Size of the labor force.
- Trade openness, measured by the share of imports and exports in GDP.
- Percentage of merchandise exports accounted for by manufactured goods.

- Manufacturing value added as a percentage of GDP.
- Official exchange rate.
- Total natural resources rent as a percentage of GDP.

Assessing economic dependency on natural resources involves calculating resource rents as a proportion of GDP, a method advocated by scholars such as Auty (2007). This metric includes revenues from various natural resources such as coal, minerals, oil, natural gas, and forest resources (WDI 2018). Dummy variables are also utilized to differentiate between low-income (LowInc), middle-income (MidInc), and high-income (HigInc) country groups within the dataset. In 2008, a worldwide economic crisis affected every economy, and countries submitted negative growth (Kotz 2009); thus, it is a must to mention this recession with a specific variable (2008Cris). Moreover, to differentiate the rentier states that depend only on oil and gas from other rentier countries with different natural resources, a dummy variable of (OiGaPr) has been generated.

The 51 rentier states chosen for the survey are divided into low-, middle-, and high-income countries with various sizes, political systems, and levels of reliance on natural resources based on the World Bank country classification. These states receive different income levels from selling natural resources such as minerals, oil, natural gas, and other natural resources. The representative nations are divided into income levels based on their dependence on natural resources.

Missing unit values were found in the data collection. Several imputations, such as forward and backward trends, have been made to appropriately use the data and its possibilities. The country-specific mean values formed the basis for the imputations—this data collection benefits from offering a dataset for all states with abundant natural resources. Although the imputed data are produced using each country's mean, any deviation would not affect the estimation accuracy. The essential advantage is that accurate and reliable parameter estimations may be made using all available information in the estimating process.

This research employs the model represented by Eq. (4.1), which incorporates six institutional quality factors and various macroeconomic variables to analyze the impact of governance on per capita GDP. This model aims to estimate how governance influences economic growth while controlling for the economic conditions and relationships specific to the sample countries.

$$\begin{aligned}\text{GDPCap}_{\text{it}} = \beta_0 + &\begin{bmatrix}\beta_1\text{ConCor}_{\text{it}} + \beta_2\text{GovEf}f_{\text{it}} + \beta_3\text{PolSta}_{\text{it}} + \beta_4\text{RegQua}_{\text{it}} \\ +\beta_5\text{RolLaw}_{\text{it}} + \beta_6\text{VoiAcc}_{\text{it}}\end{bmatrix} + \\ &[\beta_7\text{Inflation}_{\text{it}} + \beta_8\text{GovCon}_{\text{it}} + \beta_9\text{FDINin}_{\text{it}} + \beta_{10}\text{FDINou}_{\text{it}} \\ &+\beta_{11}\text{LabFor}_{\text{it}} + \beta_{12}\text{TraOpe}_{\text{it}} + \beta_{13}\text{ManExp}_{\text{it}} + \\ &\beta_{14}\text{ManVad}_{\text{it}} + \beta_{15}\text{OffExc}_{\text{it}} + \beta_{16}\text{TotRen}_{\text{it}}] + e_{it}\end{aligned} \tag{4.1}$$

where GDPCap is the average per capita GDP. Countries and time are represented by subscripts i and t, respectively. β_0 is constant intercept-coefficient, and β_1–β_{16} is a vector of sloping parameter coefficients. ConCor is control of corruption,

GovEff is government effectiveness, PolSta is political stability, and RegQua is regulatory quality. Moreover, RolLaw is the role of law, VoiAcc is voice accountability, Inflation is the inflation rate, GovCon is government consumption, FDINin is foreign direct investment net inflows, and FDINou is foreign direct investment net outflows. Furthermore, LabFor is the labor force, TraOpe is trade openness, ManExp is manufactured exports, and ManVad is manufactured value-added. In addition, OffExc is the official exchange rate, TotRen is the total rent of natural resources, and lastly, e_{it} represents the random error term assumed to have a zero mean and constant (homoscedastic) variance.

The vector of control variables in the literature on rentier states economies is total rent of natural resources, official exchange rates, investment, trade openness, manufacture value-added, inflation, and size of government, which have been broadly discussed by Belbawi and Luciani (1987) and Acemoglu et al. (2005). The monetary values are measured in real USD values. For accurate estimations, choosing the right estimating approach is crucial. This study uses a panel data estimation approach to quantify how institutions affect economic development. Since it enables many cross-sections and periods and offers a more accurate and robust estimation, the panel data estimation approach is considered a practical analytical approach. Moreover, this research applies pooled OLS, fixed-effects (FE) model, and random-effects (RE) model and selects the appropriate model to analyze the results based on the Hausman test.

4.3 Results and Discussion

As already described in Chap. 2, the term "rentier state" first emerged in the 1970s. Mahdavy (1970) is one of the first users of this term as he used it in an article regarding the economic system of Iran and the concept of external rent with an article titled "The Patterns and Problems of Economic Development in the Rentier States". Mahdavy believed that rent is a gift given by nature through natural resources, which are available in all economies in a different way such as selling natural resources, FDI, and labor remittances. Moreover, Mahdavy highlighted that foreign rental incomes could also be paid by vessels that travel from the Suez Canal and payment to those countries that transit natural resources like gas pipelines and railway transportation of coal and minerals.

This chapter utilizes the research conducted by Mahdavy to identify and include 51 rentier states from a total of 162 countries to construct the empirical model estimation data set. The selection of samples for the following dataset is predicated on the extent to which foreign rents contribute to the economic growth of their respective countries. In the countries that have been chosen for this work, the criteria for determining inclusion are outlined as follows:

- Natural resources, encompassing commodities such as oil, gas, ores, and metals, substantially exceed 25% of a nation's overall export value.

- The proportion of exports derived from natural resources, expressed as a percentage of the GDP exceeds 10 percent.
- The aggregate value of natural resource rents surpasses 10 percent of their GDP.
- The proportion of personal remittances to the (GDP) exceeds 10 percent.[1]

These criteria are selected meticulously to guarantee that the sample encompasses nations in which foreign rents, such as revenue derived from natural resources and remittances, exert a substantial influence on the growth of their economies. For example, a country that meets the initial criterion may demonstrate a heavy reliance on petroleum exports. In contrast, another country that meets the third criterion may experience considerable advantages from foreign direct investments in its mining industry. Utilizing such selection criteria facilitates the comprehensive inclusion of various sources of foreign rents within rentier states. These elements can be identified and understood by categorizing the sample of countries into rentier states and non-rentier states, as the latter may lack these characteristics. We can acquire valuable insights into the unique economic dynamics linked to foreign rents by conducting a comparative analysis of these two groups.

Data on institutional quality indicators at the national level, inflation, FDI, manufacturing, and reliance on natural resources are all included in the model specification. The data is representative of each country's population and consists of all nations that derive income from natural resources. There are several benefits to panel data testing over traditional assumption testing (Hsiao 2022). Panel data also provides a high degree of freedom, lack of multicollinearity issues, and broad data coverage.

The descriptive summary statistics of the research data in Table 4.1 include measures such as means, minimum and maximum values, and standard deviations, which indicate the spread of the data. According to the results in Table 4.1, the average governance score during the study period was approximately 30 percent, suggesting that resource-rich countries generally exhibited lower-quality governance. There is notable variability among the sampled countries. For instance, in terms of the rule of law, the minimum score was 0.5 percent and the maximum was close to 100 percent, indicating significant disparities among countries. Similar variations were observed in the other two variables: regulatory quality ranged from 0.5 to 97.1 percent, and voice and accountability ranged from 0.5 to 100 percent.

The GDP growth in this set of countries is only 1.4 percent, with an average consumption of 15 percent and an inflation rate of 9.7 percent annually. Furthermore, these countries receive an average of 4 percent of FDI net inflows annually. They also have a high rate of trade openness (defined as the export plus imports share of GDP) based on results, which show almost 83 percent. Manufacturing has a small share of the 83 percent openness with a provision of only 18.4 percent, which means the rest of the trade openness is allocated to importing and exporting natural

[1] For additional information, please see Appendices A.1 and A.2, which provide references to sample selection of rentier states based on the Mahdavy (1970), Beblawi's (1990) work, and Yamada's (2020) study.

Table 4.1 Summary statistics of the variables 2003–2020, NT = 51*18 = 918

Variables	Variables Name	Mean	Minimum	Maximum	Std dev
GDPCap	GDP per Capita	1.4091	−50.7342	85.6880	7.0836
LowInc	Low-Income	0.5686	0.0000	1.0000	0.4953
MedInc	Middle-Income	0.2745	0.0000	1.0000	0.4463
HigInc	High-Income	0.1569	0.0000	1.0000	0.3637
Cris	Crisis of 2008	0.0556	0.0000	1.0000	0.2291
OiGaPr	Oil-Gas Producer	0.7059	0.0000	1.0000	0.4556
ConCor	Control of Corruption	31.3817	0.4739	99.5192	25.1800
GovEff	Government Effectiveness	34.3905	0.4808	98.5782	24.9134
PolSta	Political Stability	34.9594	−0.3175	97.5728	25.4413
RegQua	Regulation Quality	33.5295	0.4808	97.1154	25.3243
RolLaw	Role of Law	30.8644	0.4695	100.0000	24.2705
VoiAcc	Voice Accountability	29.2373	0.4085	100.0000	22.5161
Inflation	Inflation	9.7760	−8.0360	254.9485	25.1632
GovCon	Government Consumption	15.7747	0.9517	115.9324	10.4529
FDINin	FDI Net Inflow	4.2334	−13.6564	103.3374	8.3118
FDINou	FDI Net Outflow	1.2916	−10.5031	75.9995	5.0001
LogLab	Log of Labour Force	15.2562	11.9975	18.7589	1.5182
TraOpe	Trade Openness	82.9868	0.1933	290.4993	35.6157
ManExp	Manufacture Exports	18.4449	0.0001	96.2393	20.6909
ManVad	Manufacture Value-added	10.3358	0.2326	49.8794	6.5543
OffExc	Official Exchange	1534.3713	0.3760	42000.0000	4613.4913
TotRen	Total Rents	19.1664	0.5201	81.9129	14.1511
Trend	Trend	9.5000	1.0000	18.0000	5.1881

resources. Eventually, the results show that 19.16 percent of the income of these countries comes from the rent of natural resources.

The multicollinearity test determines whether the regression model's independent variables are correlated, which results in confounded effects. Inadequate information is the source of the multicollinearity issue, and multicollinearity problems can have various effects on estimating findings since they may vary the quantity, sign, and significance of the coefficients (Daoud 2017). According to Greene (2012), the factors are often firmly integrated. This produces several statistical issues, such as minor shifts in the data having a substantial impact on parameter estimations—also, the coefficients of the two correlated parameters being significant with a sufficiently high coefficient of variation. A high correlation coefficient suggests that the two variables' consequences may be confused. Changing any of the two parameter's types can avoid the confused effect, resulting in the absence of interaction (Khayyat 2013). It should be noted that the correlation coefficient captures the unconditional pairwise correlation relationship between the variables. The explanatory variables are expected to be uncorrelated but highly correlated with the dependent variable suggesting high explanatory power.

According to Spearman's rank order, the correlation from 0 to 0.3 is weak, 0.3 to 0.7 is moderate, and 0.7 to 1.0 is highly correlated. However, it allows correlation coefficient values lower than 0.59 because the difference would be endless, and the two parameters would be fully linked (Baskar et al. 2020). Green, nevertheless, proposes utilizing either more data or removing the irrelevant variables to address this problem. The selection of regressor variables that demonstrate a stronger association with the dependent variables is required for this study's definition of the estimation. The correlation coefficients were computed using the Pearson product–moment method. When the correlation coefficients between two predictors, X and Y, range from 0.7 to 1.0, they are deemed strongly associated, indicating a high degree of linear relationship. It's important to note that correlation exists only when it is non-zero.

In Table 4.2, all correlation coefficients among the explanatory variables are presented. The table highlights a positive relationship, with correlations of 0.90 observed between government effectiveness, political stability, and regulation quality.

To assess the impact of institutional quality on the economic development of 51 rentier states during the period spanning from 2003 to 2020, this research employs a comprehensive analytical approach. The examination of the model presented in Eq. 3 involves the application of three estimation methods: pooled OLS, fixed-effects, and random-effects. The selection of the appropriate model is determined through the Hausman test, a crucial tool in panel data analysis. This test scrutinizes whether a relationship exists between individual country effects and the model's regressors. Furthermore, it is essential to note that the test underscores the significance of a *p*-value less than 5 percent for rejecting the null hypothesis, as elucidated by Hahn et al. in 2011. Consequently, the probability associated with this model falls below the 0.05 threshold, indicating that the fixed-effects model is the most suitable for our analysis. Although fixed-effects estimation ensures consistency and unbiased results irrespective of correlation relationships, it may suffer from inefficiency.

In accordance with the fixed-effects model, our findings confirm a counterintuitive relationship between government efficiency and political stability and GDP growth in the selected states, running contrary to conventional growth literature predictions. Intriguingly, voice and accountability exhibit a statistically significant positive effect on GDP growth, with an increase of 0.1 percent.

Furthermore, the model incorporates various control (conditional) variables to evaluate their impact on the GDP per capita of these 51 rentier states. Our results reveal that government consumption exerts a negative influence on GDP growth, with a substantial decrease of 23 percent. This outcome aligns with prior research, indicating that larger government sizes tend to impede economic development, as evidenced by studies such as those conducted by Zhang et al. (2021) and Sabir et al. (2019).

Several reasons help to explain why institutions in these countries may not play a major role in the stability of the economy. This may be the case due in large part to political vulnerability, where often politicians and civil servants spend a great

Table 4.2 Pearson correlation coefficient of variables, NT = 918 observations

	GDPCap	Year	Trend	LowInc	MedInc	HigInc	Cris	OiGaPr	ConCor	GovEff	PolSta	RegQua	RolLaw	VoiAcc
GDPCap	1.000													
Year	−0.170	1.000												
Trend	−0.170	1.000	1.000											
LowInc	0.039	0.000	0.000	1.000										
MedInc	0.061	0.000	0.000	−0.706	1.000									
HigInc	−0.128	0.000	0.000	−0.495	−0.265	1.000								
Cris	0.062	−0.164	−0.164	0.000	0.000	0.000	1.000							
OiGaPr	−0.089	0.000	0.000	−0.215	0.011	0.278	0.000	1.000						
ConCor	−0.055	−0.010	−0.010	−0.580	0.087	0.683	0.002	−0.108	1.000					
GovEff	−0.041	0.033	0.033	−0.657	0.186	0.666	−0.010	−0.007	0.900	1.000				
PolSta	−0.011	−0.032	−0.032	−0.367	−0.003	0.503	0.008	−0.109	0.712	0.680	1.000			
RegQua	−0.040	−0.002	−0.002	−0.596	0.135	0.647	−0.001	−0.061	0.866	0.909	0.646	1.000		
RolLaw	−0.055	0.013	0.013	−0.560	0.068	0.680	−0.012	−0.115	0.938	0.919	0.746	0.905	1.000	
VoiAcc	0.044	−0.010	−0.010	−0.246	0.197	0.092	0.000	−0.349	0.575	0.514	0.393	0.558	0.553	1.000
Inflation	−0.045	0.089	0.089	−0.046	0.154	−0.127	−0.038	0.046	−0.200	−0.212	−0.177	−0.241	−0.212	−0.122
GovCon	−0.077	0.099	0.099	−0.081	0.006	0.104	−0.023	0.028	0.182	0.061	0.125	0.026	0.108	0.172
FDINin	0.091	−0.092	−0.092	0.122	−0.060	−0.093	0.057	−0.154	−0.049	−0.090	0.032	−0.044	−0.038	0.013
FDINou	0.006	−0.048	−0.048	−0.042	0.027	0.025	0.103	−0.014	0.058	0.012	0.042	0.027	0.023	0.061
LogLab	0.025	0.084	0.084	0.048	0.173	−0.278	−0.009	0.207	−0.269	−0.119	−0.463	−0.150	−0.255	−0.190
TraOpe	0.038	−0.093	−0.093	0.023	−0.220	0.239	0.036	0.021	0.138	0.115	0.260	0.094	0.159	−0.086
ManExp	0.048	0.036	0.036	−0.033	0.113	−0.094	−0.049	0.053	0.068	0.149	0.119	0.134	0.084	0.112
ManVad	−0.056	−0.041	−0.041	−0.308	0.260	0.100	0.010	0.181	0.134	0.199	−0.017	0.099	0.110	0.012
OffExc	0.069	0.087	0.087	0.109	−0.004	−0.143	−0.020	0.017	−0.085	0.020	−0.064	−0.138	−0.050	−0.167
TotRen	0.036	−0.243	−0.243	−0.002	−0.107	0.135	0.115	0.259	−0.171	−0.244	0.001	−0.225	−0.196	−0.393
	Inflation	GovCon	FDINin	FDINou	LogLab	TraOpe	ManExp	ManVad	OffExc	TotRen				

Inflation	1.000													
GovCon	−0.026	1.000												
FDINin	−0.045	−0.091	1.000											
FDINou	−0.026	0.030	0.434	1.000										
LogLab	0.110	−0.317	−0.163	−0.070	1.000									
TraOpe	−0.184	0.144	0.162	0.140	−0.395	1.000								
ManExp	−0.093	−0.068	0.079	−0.018	0.146	0.161	1.000							
ManVad	−0.022	−0.170	−0.135	−0.117	0.167	−0.140	−0.009	1.000						
OffExc	0.027	−0.099	−0.039	−0.068	0.345	0.034	0.236	0.114	1.000					
TotRen	−0.034	0.093	0.103	0.100	−0.209	0.319	−0.280	−0.105	−0.102	1.000				

deal of time rent-seeking and, in the process, stifle the development of institutions. Several works have shown that institutions perform poorly in weak democratized settings, as demonstrated by the work by Brinks et al. (2019) and Stasavage (2020). The other cause may simply lie in the inherent weakness of the institutional structure in rentier states. These institutions may not be very efficient in the achievement of success, and a constant manipulation of structures in the economy may not help in the expansion of the economy's growth. Additionally, institutions may not meet a universally accepted standard of performance. Mohammed et al. (2022) argue that systems are most successful when their standards surpass the global average. In general, countries with robust governance tend to experience more significant economic growth than those characterized by weak institutions.

Furthermore, trade and FDI emerge as critical catalysts for economic growth in emerging nations. FDI inflows often facilitate the transition from underdeveloped to industrialized economies, concurrently promoting the growth of host countries' institutions and human resources. Trade, recognized as a potent driver of economic expansion, enhances the efficiency of goods and services production by capitalizing on the competitive advantages of various nations (Hayat 2019). In our study, FDI net inflow is shown to increase the GDP growth rate by 0.06 within the 51 rentier states.

Finally, among the control variables impacting our model's dependent variable, GDP per capita, is manufacturing value-added. A one-unit increase in this indicator results in a 0.15 percent decrease in GDP, consistent with prior research findings. Many influential developing and emerging economies, including China, Vietnam, and Ukraine, are strategically shifting toward manufacturing, thereby enhancing the productivity of domestic businesses and delivering high-quality goods to their respective markets (Brown et al. 2019). However, the negative coefficient associated with manufacturing highlights a possible impediment to growth within rentier states. The fluctuation in commodity prices has impeded the expansion of the manufacturing sector in nations highly dependent on natural resources. This phenomenon, known as the "resource movement effect," has escalated the migration of labor from the traded goods sector to the non-traded sector, rendering the latter more appealing as a workplace (Amiri et al. 2019). As a result, this shift has detrimental effects on the development of other industries, underscoring the presence of a resource curse, as elaborated in Table 4.3.

A crucial indicator of whether a fixed effects model or random effects model is suitable for panel data analysis, is the Hausman test. According to the null hypothesis (H0), country effects and explanatory variables are uncorrelated, the random-effects model is more efficient and reliable. The alternative hypothesis (H1) argues that the random effects model contradicts because the fixed effects model, which allows correlation between country effects and explanatory variables ought to be used instead since unexplained specific influences could be related with predictors. This study computed its test statistic (chi2(16)) as 33.19 with 16 degrees of freedom given the number of variables under consideration. The null hypothesis is rejected because Prob > chi2 = 0.0070 < $\alpha = 0.05$ standard threshold for p-values. The large differences in coefficients between these two models, as shown by this rejection,

Table 4.3 Empirical results of panel data regression, dependent variable is GDP per capita

Variables	Pooled OLS (robust)			Fixed-effects			Random effects		
GDPCap	Coefficient	Std. Err.	*P* Value	Coefficient	Std. Err.	P Value	Coefficient	Std. Err.	*P* Value
MedInc	1.0220	1.2562	0.416	–	–	–	–	–	–
HigInc	−0.8290	1.6299	0.611	–	–	–	–	–	–
2008Cris	0.8439	0.6500	0.194	0.9595	0.9968	0.336	0.8321	0.9921	0.402
OiGaPr	−0.8434	0.5130	0.101	–	–	–	–	–	–
ConCor	−0.0098	0.0353	0.782	0.0412	0.0448	0.357	0.0104	0.0337	0.759
GovEff	0.0282	0. 0329	0.391	−0.0826	0.0499	0.098	0.0044	0.0362	0.904
PolSta	0.0106	0.0224	0.636	−0.0467	0.0278	0.093	−0.0009	0.0190	0.962
RegQua	−0.0042	0.0236	0.857	−0.0022	0.0508	0.965	−0.0067	0.0325	0.837
RolLaw	−0.0421	0.0366	0.250	0.0066	0.0569	0.908	−0.0418	0.0418	0.317
VoiAcc	0.0323	0.0117	0.006	0.1035	0.0595	0.082	0.0530	0.0188	0.005
Inflation	−0.0117	0.0089	0.189	−0.0068	0.0135	0.616	−0.0075	0.0107	0.481
GovCon	−0.0441	0.0347	0.205	−0.2318	0.0488	0.000	−0.0871	0.0306	0.004
FDINin	0.0381	0.0396	0.335	0.0615	0.0335	0.067	0.0501	0.0307	0.103
LogLab	0.1293	0.2492	0.604	−2.8193	2.1881	0.198	0.0513	0.2901	0.86
TraOpe	0.0087	0.0111	0.432	0.0173	0.0130	0.183	0.0072	0.0095	0.444
ManExp	0.0004	0.0142	0.973	0.0139	0.0307	0.652	0.0053	0.0164	0.747
ManVad	−0.0780	0.0373	0.037	−0.1567	0.0811	0.054	−0.0878	0.0478	0.067
OffExc	0.0001	0.0000	0.002	0.0001	0.0001	0.461	0.0001	0.0001	0.049
TotRen	0.0214	0.0287	0.456	0.0097	0.0333	0.771	0.0246	0.0245	0.317
Trend	−0.2030	0.0494	0.000	−0.0856	0.0747	0.252	−0.1906	0.0470	0.000
_cons	1.3444	4.3868	0.759	48.2770	33.2325	0.147	2.6648	5.0448	0.597
No. of observations		918			918			918	
R-Squared		0.0763			0.0092			0.0637	
Corr (*u*–*x*)		6.8874			−0.8342			0.0000	

Table 4.4 The Hausman test

	Coefficients			
Variable	*b* (fixed)	*B* (random)	(*b*–*B*) difference	Sqrt(diag(*V_b*–*V_B*)) S.E.
Cris	0.9595	0.8321	0.1274	0.0967
ConCor	0.0412	0.0104	0.0309	0.0294
GovEff	−0.0826	0.0044	−0.0870	0.0341
PolSta	−0.0467	−0.0009	−0.0458	0.0203
RegQua	−0.0022	−0.0067	0.0045	0.0391
RolLaw	0.0657	0.0148	0.0484	0.0386
VoiAcc	0.1035	0.0530	0.0504	0.0564
Inflation	−0.0068	−0.0075	0.0008	0.0028
GovCon	−0.2318	−0.0871	−0.1447	0.0381
FDINlin	0.0615	0.0501	0.0115	0.0136
LogLab	−2.8193	0.0513	−2.8706	2.1688
TraOpe	0.0173	0.0072	0.0100	0.0088
ManExp	0.0139	0.0053	0.0086	0.0253
ManVad	−0.1567	−0.0788	−0.0779	0.0655
OffExc	0.0009	0.0006	0.0003	0.0000
TotRen	0.0097	0.0246	−0.0149	0.0226
Trend	−0.0856	−0.1906	0.1050	0.0581

b = consistent under Ho and Ha; obtained from xtreg
B = inconsistent under Ha, efficient under Ho; obtained from xtreg
Test: Ho: difference in coefficients not systematic
chi2(16) = (*b*–*B*)′[(*V_b*–*V_B*)^(−1)](*b*–*B*) = 33.19
Prob > chi2 = 0.0070
(*V_b*–*V_B* is not positive definite)

indicate that rather than utilizing the random effects model, it will be appropriate to use fixed effects in line with Hausman's specification test results (Table 4.4).

4.4 Summary

In this chapter, a comprehensive discussion of how natural resources have affected economic development over the years has been discussed. Although resource availability would enhance income and increase per capita, it also can have the reverse impact of slow rates. The notion that having an excess of mineral wealth may be more harmful than advantageous for some nations is called the "natural resource curse." It is discovered that a significant fundamental problem is why certain countries with abundant natural resources, like Chile and Botswana, have important socioeconomic development while others, like Nigeria and Venezuela, struggle with poor economic development yet own vast natural resource reserves.

Through the provision of factors, this chapter identified that, first, the procedures of extraction of natural resources are expensive and can be used in other industries or services. Besides, unstable petroleum prices globally undermine the stability of rentier economies. Furthermore, the concentration of rent inputs makes it easier for non-inclusive authorities to collect rent instead of fostering economic development since their systems benefit the maintenance of political power. Moreover, this chapter figured out that the low quality of political institutions is a significant factor in preventing economic advancement in rentier states. Institutions have a crucial role in administering public life, including the social, educational, commercial, and bureaucratic spheres. However, it is demonstrated that more vital institutions are found in developed nations, while weaker institutions are located in underdeveloped countries.

This chapter presented six governance indicators of Kaufmann et al. (2010), including voice and accountability, political stability, government effectiveness, regulatory quality, law role, and corruption control, to describe institutional quality by data. Moreover, the beneficial impact of institutions is determined by several variables, including the institutions, social standards, and citizens. Occasionally, organizations with comparable elements produce different results for various groups and locations.

This project employs the panel data of 51 rentier states from 2003 to 2020 to determine the impacts of institutional quality on economic growth. Various political and economic factors are used in this research to find the relationship between GDPs per capita and institutional quality. In general, the econometrics model and estimation process have been applied to this chapter. The panel data investigated the issue of endogeneity and the dependency between some of the explanatory variables. Different levels of resource revenue dependency frequently exist amongst nations that produce the same rents. This chapter adjusts for many national factors, capturing all the data's heterogeneities in place of the country-specific fixed effects. According to the empirical results, government efficiency and political stability have negative impacts on GDP per capita in the selected states, and voice and accountability significantly impact the growth of the GDP per capita. Furthermore, results described that government consumption negatively affects the growth of GDP per capita.

Generally, several explanations exist for why institutions in such countries do not contribute much to economic stability. The poor political structures in these states might be one of the causes. They have become able to rent-seek more frequently due to politicians and other public servants. This restriction hinders the institution from promoting growth. As such, growth in this sense is stronger in countries that have better governance than in the institutions that are weaker.

References

Acemoglu D, Johnson S, Robinson JA (2001) The colonial origins of comparative development: an empirical investigation. Am Econ Rev 91(5):1369–1401

Acemoglu D, Johnson S, Robinson J, Thaicharoen Y (2003) Institutional causes, macroeconomic symptoms: volatility, crises, and growth. J Monet Econ 50(1):49–123

Acemoglu D, Johnson S, Robinson JA (2005) Institutions as a fundamental cause of long-run growth. In: Aghion P, Durlauf S (eds) Handbook of economic growth. North-Holland, Amsterdam. https://doi.org/10.1016/S1574-0684(05)01006-3. Last Access on 6 July 2021

Acemoglu D, Gelb S, Robinson JA (2007) Black economic empowerment and economic performance in South Africa. Cambridge, MA: Center for Economic Development, Working Paper, 2003.
Alsaleh M, Abdul-Rahim AS, Abdulwakil MM (2021) The importance of worldwide governance indicators for transitions toward sustainable bioenergy industry. J Environ Manag 294:112960
Amiri H, Samadian F, Yahoo M, Jamali SJ (2019) Natural resource abundance, institutional quality and manufacturing development: evidence from resource-rich countries. Resourc Policy 62:550–560
Aslaksen S, Torvik R (2006) A theory of civil conflict and democracy in rentier states. Scand J Econ 108(4):571–585
Atkinson G, Hamilton K (2003) Savings, growth and the resource curse hypothesis. World Dev 31(11):1793–1807
Auty R (1993) Sustaining development in mineral economies: the resource curse thesis, 1st edn. Routledge. https://doi.org/10.4324/9780203422595. Last Access on May 16th 2022
Auty R (2007) Natural resources, capital accumulation, and the resource curse. Ecol Econ 61(4):627–634
Baskar S, Dhulipala VS, Shakeel PM, Sridhar KP, Kumar R (2020) Hybrid fuzzy based spearman rank correlation for cranial nerve palsy detection in MIoT environment. Heal Technol 10:259–270
Beblawi H (1990) The rentier state in the Arab world. In: Luciani G (ed) The Arab state. University of California Press, Berkeley and Los Angeles, pp 71–100
Beblawi H, Luciani G (1987) The rentier state. Croom Helm, London
Bjorvatn K, Naghavi A (2010) Rent seekers in rentier states: when greed brings peace. SSRN Electron J. https://doi.org/10.2139/ssrn.1597135
Brinks DM, Levitsky S, Murillo MV (2019) Understanding institutional weakness: power and design in Latin American institutions. Cambridge University Press
Brown JD, Earle JS, Shpak S, Vakhitov V (2019) Is privatisation working in Ukraine? New estimates from comprehensive manufacturing firm data, 1989–2013. Comp Econ Stud 61(1):1–35
Chong A, Calderon C (2000) Institutional quality and income distribution. Econ Dev Cult Chang 48(4):761–786
Daoud JI (2017) Multicollinearity and regression analysis. In: Journal of physics: conference series, vol 949, No. 1. IOP Publishing, p 012009
De Haan J (2007) Political institutions and economic growth reconsidered. Public Choice 131(3):281–292
Dellepiane-Avellaneda S (2010) Good governance, institutions and economic development: beyond the conventional wisdom. Br J Polit Sci 40(1):195–224. http://www.jstor.org/stable/40649429. Last access on October 23rd 2022
Glaeser E, La Porta R, Lopez-de-silanes F, Schleifer A (2004) Do institutions cause growth. J Econ Growth 9(3):271–303
Greene WH (2012) Econometric analysis. Pearson Education, England
Hayat A (2019) Foreign direct investments, institutional quality, and economic growth. J Int Trade Econ Dev 28(5):561–579
Hsiao C (2022) Analysis of panel data, vol 64. Cambridge University Press
Kaufmann D, Kraay A, Mastruzzi M (2010) The worldwide governance indicators: methodology and analytical issues. Hague J Rule Law 3(02):220–246. https://doi.org/10.1017/s1876404511200046
Khayyat NT (2013) Exploring demand for energy in the South Korean Industries. Doctoral dissertation, SMC University, Zurich, Switzerland
Kotz DM (2009) The financial and economic crisis of 2008: a systemic crisis of neoliberal capitalism. Rev Radic Polit Econ 41(3):305–317
Kunčič A (2014) Institutional quality dataset. J Inst Econ 10(1):135–161
Lamb R (1973) Adam Smith's concept of alienation. Oxf Econ Pap 25(2):275–285
Levchenko AA (2007) Institutional quality and international trade. Rev Econ Stud 74(3):791–819

Mahdavy H (1970) The patterns and problems of economic development in rentier states: the case of Iran. In: Cook MA (ed) Studies in the economic history of the Middle East. Oxford University Press

Malik A (2017) Rethinking the rentier curse. In: Luciani G (ed) Combining economic and political development: the experience of MENA. Brill, pp 41–57. http://www.jstor.org/stable/10.1163/j.ctt1w8h356.10. Last access on 21/11/2022

Mohammed S, Desha C, Goonetilleke A (2022) Investigating low-carbon pathways for hydrocarbon-dependent rentier states: economic transition in Qatar. Technol Forecast Soc Chang 185:122084

North D (1989) Institutions and economic growth: an historical introduction. World Dev 17(9):1319–1332

North D (1990) Institutions, institutional change, and economic performance. Cambridge University Press, Cambridge. https://doi.org/10.1017/CBO9780511808678. Last Access on February 12th 2022

Robinson JA, Acemoglu D (2012) Why nations fail: the origins of power, prosperity and poverty. Profile, London, pp 45–47

Runde DF (2017) Quality infrastructure: ensuring sustainable economic growth. Center for Strategic and International Studies (CSIS). http://www.jstor.org/stable/resrep23247. Last access on 19/11/2022

Sabir S, Rafique A, Abbas K (2019) Institutions and FDI: evidence from developed and developing countries. Financ Innov 5(1):1–20

Samuelson PA (1977) A modern Theorist's vindication of Adam Smith. Am Econ Rev 67(1):42–49

Schwarz R (2008) The political economy of state-formation in the Arab Middle East: rentier states, economic reform, and democratization. Rev Int Polit Econ 15(4):599–621. Retrieved September 2, 2021, from http://www.jstor.org/stable/25261988. Last Access on January, 19th 2023

Stasavage D (2020) The decline and rise of democracy. In: The decline and rise of democracy. Princeton University Press

World Development Indicators, WDI (2018) Natural resource contribution to GDP. Retrieved 11/11/2022, from World Bank

Yamada M (2020) Can a rentier state evolve to a production state? An 'institutional upgrading' approach. Br J Middle Eastern Stud 47(1):24–41

Zhang D, Mohsin M, Rasheed AK, Chang Y, Taghizadeh-Hesary F (2021) Public spending and green economic growth in BRI region: mediating role of green finance. Energy Policy 153:112256

Chapter 5
Economic Freedom and Economic Development

Free markets and growth act as important functions in highlighting and defining the destiny of each country. Market economy or monetization implies financial freedom of citizens and legal persons, as well as companies and organizations. It comprises concepts like property rights, free trade, non-intervention of the government, and the supremacy of the law. On the other hand, economic development has been defined as a process of progressive improvement of a country's finances, usually through measurable aspects of per capita income, employment, and general standards of living.

Indeed, economic freedom and development are complexly linked since improving financial freedom heavily enhances the chances for creating innovation, investment, and entrepreneurship, thus effectively boosting the economy. This introduction elaborates on the interactional effect of economic freedom and development as factors that affect the economic status of countries.

5.1 Economic Freedom

Over the last few years, scholars have started to focus on the noneconomic factors that affect the GDP growth rate. Seeing it academically, two nations having the same resource base will have disparities in the rates of any economic growth if the noneconomic business aspects are not similar. The Fraser Institute and the Heritage Foundation are the two most important measures of economic liberty (Gwartney et al. 2021). Gamble (2021) examined both and found that, while considering kind of different measures of economic freedom, they rated economies equally. The neoclassical economics theory, which emphasizes component availability and technological capacity, has historically been the foundation for investigating the growth cycle and the variables influencing the approach. Experts have understood and

R. C. Biro, *Political Challenges of Economic Development in Rentier States*, Perspectives on Development in the Middle East and North Africa (MENA) Region, https://doi.org/10.1007/978-981-96-0563-7_5

accepted that noneconomic causes also significantly influence economic progress. Everyone agrees that capital and workforce are more potent in nations or situations where the noneconomic drivers of economic development are adequately established.

Economic growth is difficult to anticipate and manage, and economists have spent ages trying to comprehend the fundamental variables that promote development. The father of economics, Adam Smith, challenged the mercantile view of high protectionist policies in 1776 by arguing that open markets were essential for economic prosperity. The public perception of trade protectionism and liberalization has fluctuated since Adam Smith's time. The economic turmoil Latin American nations were experiencing in contrast to the open Asian economies has contributed to the current shift in public opinion, which is moving back toward views that accessibility and economic freedom are the primary forces behind economic progress (Miller et al. 2022).

The only reason free societies have developed and survived, according to Milton Friedman, is because economic freedom is more effective than alternative techniques for governing economic activity. In 1996, Block and his colleagues were among the first to describe economic freedom; scholars interpret the term in various ways, which stated that the right of people to engage in national economies without intervention from the government is the basis of economic freedom (Gwartney and Lawson 2003). The government should preserve property rights and the free trade of products, keep inflation and market prices steady, and stay out of its people's business to foster the national economy. Economic freedom will be reduced, and constructive economic activity will be discouraged by any policy that hinders it, such as costly transactions, abuses of property rights, extreme restrictions, and measures that lead to increased uncertainty (Brkić 2020).

Sustainable economic growth depends heavily on political and economic institutions. These organizations provide economic development and growth models alongside the laws and policies that regulate wealth creation. Political and economic frameworks contribute to the creation of a system that is reliable for investors and entrepreneurs. They offer a dependable policy structure, secure property rights, and execute agreements. Such reliability is vital to bring in investment and encourage economic expansion.

However, political and economic players may make the competitive market even better by minimizing the monopoly and encouraging innovations. Where competition is high, creativity is enhanced, prices are lowered, and generally, customer value is enhanced. Also, bearing in mind that the current political and economic systems are strong and might play a role in persuading both international and domestic investors into investing. This funding may create employment, may encourage start-up companies, and may promote economic growth (Acemoglu et al. 2005).

Economic liberalization means the amount of freedom people and organizations have in the economy; in other words, the level of state non-interference. Many works and topical debates in the literature of economics focus on the question of the relationship between economic freedom and economic development. Using the data, the nature of the findings regarding higher levels of economic freedom appears to significantly enhance the growth rates. This is so because economic independence may lead to higher creativity, investment, production, competitiveness, and performance levels in the market. For instance, decentralized or self-organizing individuals and corporations are more liable to respond to customers' demands and create new value and advanced ways of production (Ott 2018).

Paired with the said is, however, the understanding that there are quite a number of factors that can influence a nation's economic growth and development despite the fact that there is a combination between these two that may some way modify the correlation between the two. However, others believe that some policy measures are sometimes required to address shortcomings and advance well-being and that unlimited economic freedom might result in unfavorable outcomes like the wealth gap and the destruction of ecosystems. In conclusion, although there is evidence that suggests economic freedom may have a good effect on economic growth, it is crucial to consider the larger economic, social, and political environment in which it is applied (Malanski and Póvoa 2021).

The first is broad consensus in the research that less regulation would boost economic expansion. It is common knowledge that a publicly accessible market gives companies more chances to test out novel ideas with untapped marketplaces. Moreover, it stimulates enterprises to participate in experimental initiatives like FDI-related operations for better capital appreciation. On the other hand, if the market is heavily controlled, it harms how assets are distributed in that setting (Singh and Gal 2020). Furthermore, employment rules could potentially have an impact on spillovers from FDI. Suppose recruitment and termination policies are less strict. In that case, it is more likely that former employees of multinational corporations (MNCs) can transfer their skills and knowledge of emerging innovations to local industries, resulting in indirect impacts through labor mobility. Lastly, another component of economic freedom is the preservation of property rights. Siegan (2017) asserts that since MNCs may draw FDI with a higher technical quality, governments that offer superior property rights enforcement should demand to gain more significant benefits from their involvement. Lastly, international trade openness might boost local businesses in entering international markets. Moreover, higher institutional standards and improved governance often enhance the beneficial effects of FDI on economic expansion. Thus, governments in rentier nations must maintain their investment in social infrastructure while enhancing the standard of their institutions and governance since this will support them in preventing the problems they have experienced (Mahon 2018).

5.2 Description of EFW Index and Variables

Several scholars, including Adam Smith, David Ricardo, John Stuart Mill, Ludwig von Mises, F.A. Hayek, and Milton Friedman, have argued that an economic system grounded in private property, competitive markets, and free trade yields positive outcomes. Adam Smith maintained that if nations adopted policies supporting a "system of natural liberty," now known as economic freedom, the "wealth of the country" would grow. Adherents of this viewpoint believe that economic freedom fosters financial prosperity and overall human happiness.

However, other academics, such as Karl Marx, J.M. Keynes, Abba Lerner, and Joseph Stiglitz, have contended that economic independence can have significant, or at least undesirable, impacts, especially on business cycles and wealth distribution (Carlsson and Lundström 2002).

5.2.1 Fundamental Growth Variables

In studies evaluating the link between economic freedom and further economic developments, the GDP, a generally used indicator of a nation's economic success, is often employed as a dependent variable. The measure by which people and firms may conduct an independent financial activity without interruption from the state or other external factors is referred to as economic liberty. Economic independence is often believed to encourage economic growth and development, which may result in greater GDP.

GDP can be considered a dependent variable since various variables, notably economic freedom, influence it. Increased investment, creativity, and entrepreneurship are all linked to better economic freedom standards and may all help to raise the GDP rate. However, it can also be argued that economic freedom is one of the indicators of ability in the economy of a given country. Furthermore, a relationship between economic freedom and other economic variables mainly employs GDP as a dependent variable (Brkić 2020).

Overall, the FDI reflects the total investment made by the concerned international companies in a particular country. It is commonly employed as a measure of economic liberty's impact on international investment, which is used under circumstances where the dependent variable must be quantified. Research related to the relationship between economic self-sufficiency and other aspects of economic well-being, such as economic growth and development, typically uses FDI as the variable of interest. However, because factors such as economic liberty can affect it, FDI may be regarded, in this perspective, as a dependent factor. Based on tables such as low corruption practices, favorable property rights, and lesser hurdles to investment, countries with higher economic openness are usually more attractive to foreign investors. Also, the literature review provides evidence of a positive relationship between FDI and economic freedom, they suggest, meaning that the freedom may have a large and perhaps decisive role to play in a country's ability to attract foreign investment (Dkhili and Dhiab 2018).

Economic freedom is highly linked with economic development and FDI due to its role in fostering economic prosperity and FDI inflows. Moreover, the efficiency of spending is higher where the level of economic freedom is higher as well as the rates of economic growth. For instance, the Economic Freedom of the World Index by the Fraser Institute shows that countries with high economic freedom achieve higher GDP per head. The same findings have been conducted by the Index of Economic Freedom of the Heritage Foundation, which has concluded that the countries belonging to this list gain higher rates of economic growth (Ciftci and Durusu-Ciftci 2022).

Moreover, an analysis of economic freedom and FDI receptions shows a high level of positive connection between both variables. Potential investors are interested in countries that have fewer regulations controlling the amounts of money one can invest and legislation protecting businesses. The International Monetary Fund (IMF) conducted research that revealed that nations with greater degrees of economic freedom often draw more FDI. Generally, economic freedom, economic growth, and FDI are all positively correlated. Economic freedom fosters economic development and draws foreign investment, resulting in higher wealth for nations prioritizing measures promoting economic freedom (Singh and Gal 2020).

The Fraser Institute Index of Economic Freedom, developed by Gwartney, Lawson, and Block in 1996, is the source of "economic freedom." Over several conferences, the writers formulated the idea of economic freedom in collaboration with Milton Friedman and other well-known economists worldwide. According to the authors, "free decision, preservation of private ownership, and openness of trade" are the three pillars of economic freedom (Block et al. 1996). Five factors that measure economic freedom comprise the index: the size of government, legal system and protection of property rights, sound money, freedom to trade internationally, and regulation. Together, these factors have 24 subfactors. The index's data originates from outside sources; they are not based on the writers' opinions. On a scale ranging from 0 to 10, each section is graded. The aggregate average of economic freedom is the mean of the five dimensions, and the value for each element is the mean of its subcomponents.

5.2.2 *Government Size*

The rationale for the "size of government" factor is that citizens' autonomy would be hampered if the government significantly redistributes wealth, products, and services in society—rather than leaving that to individuals and businesses. High government spending and subsidies indicate a big, controlling government that limits citizens' freedom of choice. As a result, this will result in a poor score for this item. The third element involves checking for the presence of state-owned businesses with the potential to cause market disruption because of their ownership and investment structures. Finally, the highest marginal income tax rate is used to calculate the tax rate. In addition, since taxes divert funds from people's incomes, they are considered inconsistent with individual liberty. The subfactors are public spending, transfers, subsidies, state businesses and investments, and top marginal income tax. On a range from 0 to 10, each sub-element is graded. The average of its subcomponents is used to rate the size of the public sector (Bergh and Karlsson 2010).

5.2.3 The Legal System and Property Rights

There are at least nine subcomponents reported in this category. Protecting property rights is the government's most crucial duty and the foundation of a flourishing free market. Small businesses will participate in meaningful work if they cannot believe that obligations will be maintained, and their capital will be secured from loss. The Fraser Institute considers the legal system and property rights the most crucial factor in the index and predicts that low-scoring nations would not succeed even with good scores in the other factors. The subfactors are judicial autonomy, unbiased courts, safeguarding property rights, military involvement in politics and the rule of law, honesty of the judicial framework, legal implementation of obligations, regulating expenses of real estate sales, police dependability, and charges of crime. A range spanning 0–10 is used to evaluate each sub-factor. The combination of the legal system's core elements determines its ranking (Siegan 2017).

5.2.4 Sound Money

This section focuses on the importance of people's funds to purchase and sell items. The circulating currency must rise slowly and steadily, regardless of whether the public or a private organization is the funding source. Inflation generally refers to an imbalance between the quantity of money in circulation and the variety of products and services accessible for purchase. Since buyers and sellers must be fully aware of the worth of money, if the government finances its activities by creating additional cash, the currency's value would decline, eroding cash reserves and raising price fluctuations. In the end, the nation's economic freedom declines. This factor is assessed using inflation over the most recent year, inflation variance, and money growth. To get good marks in Sound Money, inflation has to be managed at a low and steady pace. Also, it determines how free individuals are to have bank accounts overseas and utilize other currencies. In addition, factors include monetary expansion, inflation volatility, year-on-year inflation, and the ability to open accounts in other currencies. From 0 to 10, evaluations are assigned to each component. The meaning of its subcomponents determines the grade of this variable (Gamble 2021).

5.2.5 Freedom of Trade Internationally

Countries with underdeveloped sectors receive advantages from global commerce in a globalized economy. Some nations continue to benefit from trade because they may concentrate on their most competitive sectors while importing more products. All commercial limitations, including tariffs, exchange controls, and regulations, are collected in this component. Furthermore, it discusses the methods used to regulate the flow of money and individuals, including the freedom to exchange currencies and the extent of foreign ownership.

The elements include tariffs (foreign ownership/investment limitations, capital controls, and liberty of foreigners to visit), regulatory trade restrictions (non-tariff trade barriers, and compliance costs of imports and exports), black market exchange rates, and control systems of the flow of cash and individuals. A score between 0 and 10 is assigned to each aspect. The meaning of its subcomponents determines the trade freedom grade (Razmi and Refaei 2013).

5.2.6 Regulation

The index's fifth factor is the government's control over the economy's enterprises, job market, and financial markets. According to the concept, government intervention in any market limits people's autonomy. Bank ownership and interest rate regulation are two sub-elements of the credit market. This category assesses a variety of labor laws, including those governing salary, staffing and dismissal practices, hours worked, and collective bargaining. Regarding the business sector, the index assesses license charges, start-up expenses, bribery trends, and administrative expenses. A high ranking in this element is produced by less restriction of the assets, workers, and markets, a large percentage of privately owned banks, and low levels of corruption. There is a 0-to-10 rating used to evaluate each element. The overall score for a set of rules is calculated by averaging its fundamental elements (Graafland 2020).

5.3 Data Presentation

Drawing from the literature, this chapter utilizes GDP per capita as the key growth indicator, or dependent variable. Data for this analysis, covering 162 countries from 2003 to 2020, was sourced from the World Bank's online World Development Indicators. The chapter also incorporates the five components of economic freedom and a time trend as independent variables, with data for these variables obtained from the Fraser Institute for the same set of countries and time frame. To estimate the relationship between economic freedom and economic growth, the study applies various versions of the specified model and presents the findings in tables.

$$\mathrm{GDPCap}_{\mathrm{it}} = \beta_0 + \begin{bmatrix} \beta_1 \mathrm{SizGov}_{\mathrm{it}} + \beta_2 \mathrm{LegPro}_{\mathrm{it}} + \beta_3 \mathrm{SouMon}_{\mathrm{it}} \\ +\beta_4 \mathrm{FrTrIn}_{\mathrm{it}} + \beta_5 \mathrm{RRegula}_{\mathrm{it}} \end{bmatrix} + e_{it} \tag{5.1}$$

where GDPCap is the average per capita GDP. Countries and time are represented by subscripts i and t, respectively. β_0 is intercept constant-coefficient, and $\beta_1 - \beta_5$ are slope parameter coefficients. SizGov is the size of government, LegPro is the legal system and property rights, SouMon is sound money, FrTrIn is the freedom to trade internationally, and Regula refers to regulations. Finally, *eit* is the random error term assumed to have zero mean and constant or homoscedastic variance.

For accurate estimations, choosing the right estimating approach is crucial. The current chapter employs a panel data estimation strategy to estimate the impact of economic liberty on economic development. Panel data testing has certain advantages over the test of assumptions generally known as assumption testing (Hsiao 2022). Another advantage that lies in using panel data is a higher degree of freedom, less multicollinearity problems, and a wide range of data collection. Hence the specification of the panel data estimation approach as a practical analytical approach because it allows for many cross-sections and periods besides offering a more accurate and robust estimation. Furthermore, this research adopts the fixed-effects model (FE) and the random-effects model (RE) and determines which model provides the best results given the Hausman test.

$$\mathrm{GDPCap}_{\mathrm{it}} = \beta_0 + \begin{bmatrix} \beta_1 \mathrm{SizGov}_{\mathrm{it}} + \beta_2 \mathrm{LegPro}_{\mathrm{it}} + \beta_3 \mathrm{SouMon}_{\mathrm{it}} \\ +\beta_4 \mathrm{FrTrIn}_{\mathrm{it}} + \beta_5 \mathrm{RRegula}_{\mathrm{it}} + \beta_6 \mathrm{trend}_{\mathrm{it}} \end{bmatrix} + e_{it} \tag{5.2}$$

In this model, Eq. (5.2), the time trend variable is also added. A trend variable used in the linear regression represents time and holds information about the trend or pattern in the data over the time span. It is most used in time series regression analysis that explains the impact and relationship of these variables by using data collected at different times. Trend in comparison with yearly time dummies use only one parameter but the effect unlike time dummies with year-specific effects is constant. The trend indicator is often demonstrated as a continuous variable that assumes time-related fractional or serial integer values. The next step involves adding it as a separate variable in the regression model to detect recurring changes or patterns in the data as time progresses. This time trend accounts for the impact of unseen, time-related variations that differ over time but remain consistent across countries annually.

The dataset used for the final empirical model estimation of economic independence consists of 2916 observations spanning 162 nations from 2003 to 2020. Data on all elements of economic freedom, GDP per capita, and FDI are all included in the model specification. The data is representative of each country's population and consists of all nations in the Fraser Institute database.

The descriptive summary statistics of the research data provide key metrics such as means, minimum and maximum values, and standard deviations as indicators of data dispersion. Table 5.1 reveals that, on average, the economic freedom components measured over the study period were approximately 6 percent, suggesting that the selected countries generally exhibit moderate economic freedom. There is significant variability among the sampled countries, with substantial differences observed across nearly all variables. The range between minimum and maximum levels spans from 1 percent to 90 percent for most variables, highlighting the diversity and disparity within the dataset.

Table 5.1 Summary statistics of the variables between 2003 and 2020, NT = 162*18 = 2916

Variable names	Mean	Minimum	Maximum	Std dev
GDP per Capita	415870.6000	355.9600	1.9907	1624661.0000
FDI net Inflow	5.7933	−104.0590	449.0809	18.7375
Size of Government	6.6680	0.1200	9.3500	1.2906
Legal System and Property Rights	5.2603	1.7000	9.0000	1.5869
Sound Money	8.1276	1.2500	9.9200	1.3489
Free Trade Internationally	7.0140	1.0000	9.6600	1.2935
Regulation	6.9617	0.4739	3.0400	9.4300
Trend	9.5000	1.0000	18.0000	5.1890

The GDP growth in this set of countries is only 41 percent, with a receiver of an average FDI of 5 percent. Furthermore, these countries' government size is 6 percent, and legal protection is 5 percent. They also have a high rate of sound money based on results, which show almost 8 percent. In the case of international free trade, the population submitted an average of 7 percent, which is relatively good. Eventually, the results show that regulations affect economic growth by an average of 6 percent in the chosen countries.

The correlation coefficient, ranging from −1 to 1, quantifies the strength and direction of the linear relationship between two variables. A coefficient of −1 indicates a perfect negative correlation, where one variable decreases as the other increases proportionally. Conversely, a coefficient of 1 signifies a perfect positive correlation, where increases in one variable correspond directly to increases in the other. A coefficient of 0 suggests no linear relationship between the variables, meaning changes in one variable do not predict changes in the other. These coefficients are crucial for understanding how variables relate in statistical analysis (Ames and Reiter 1961).

Based on the currently available data, the correlation matrix table illustrates the bilateral or pairwise relationships among seven factors: GDP, FDI, SizGov, LegPro, SouMon, FrTrIn, and Regula. According to Table 5.2, the correlation matrix reveals the following:

With GDP, FDI has an insignificantly poor −0.0417 association. SizGov has a slight negative connection with a GDP of −0.0374 and a slight positive association with an FDI of 0.0363. LegPro's moderately positive relation with GDP is 0.2377; its weak positive association with FDI is 0.1127; and its weakly negative relation with SizGov is −0.0934. Furthermore, SouMon has a medium positive link of 0.1738 with GDP, 0.0765 with FDI, a low level of relation with SizGov 0.0171, and a high positive relationship with LegPro 0.5659, which indicates the countries with the higher legal protection have a stable monetary system.

Concerning FDI and GDP, FrTrIn shows a marginally strong association of 0.1305 and 0.1126, respectively. However, it has a robust correlation with LegPro and SouMon of 0.6358 and 0.7318, respectively. This high correlation proves that a high level of legal protection and economic stability positively affects the international trading of individuals and businesses. The poor positive association between

Table 5.2 Correlation coefficient of variables, NT = 2916 Observations

	GDP	FDI	SizGov	LegPro	SouMon	FrTrIn	Regula	Trend
GDP	1.000							
FDI	−0.0417	1.000						
SizGov	−0.0374	0.0363	1.000					
LegPro	0.2377	0.1127	−0.0934	1.000				
SouMon	0.1738	0.0765	0.0171	0.5659	1.000			
FrTrIn	0.1126	0.1305	0.0398	0.6358	0.7318	1.000		
Regula	0.1353	0.0656	0.0240	0.6513	0.5349	0.6339	1.000	
Trend	0.0366	−0.0486	0.0258	0.0455	0.1220	−0.0298	0.0627	1.000

Table 5.3 Variance Inflation Factor (VIF) for the EFW factors

Variables	VIF	1/VIF
FrTrIn	2.81	0.356370
SouMon	2.25	0.445206
LegPro	2.15	0.466195
Regula	2.04	0.489534
SizGov	1.03	0.968365
FDI	1.02	0.976942
Mean VIF	1.88	

Regula and GDP is 0.1353, and the weak positive association between Regula and FDI is 0.0656. In contrast, the Regula has a robust positive relationship with LegPro, SouMon, and FrTrIn to the extent of 0.6513, 0.5349, and 0.6339, respectively. These robust relationships confirm that countries with high legal protection, stable monetary system, free international trade, and high-quality regulations tend to attract more foreign direct investments that can directly affect economic growth.

High correlation between variables not only indicates strong relationships but can also pose a collinearity issue. When pairwise correlation coefficients are below 0.50, it generally suggests there is no serious multicollinearity problem. The variance inflation factor (VIF) serves as a statistical measure to assess the degree of multicollinearity among predictor variables used in a regression model. VIF values below 5 or 10 are typically considered low, indicating that multicollinearity is not a substantial concern (Cheng et al. 2022). An analysis of VIF values in Table 5.3 reveals that all predictor variables in the model exhibit VIF values below 5, confirming minimal multicollinearity. Particularly, VIF values around two or lower indicate very low correlation between predictors. For instance, the VIF for the variable "FrTrIn," which is equal to 2.81, is relatively small compared to the threshold. This goes further to support the fact that "FrTrIn," as established by the previous analysis, has little statistical association with the other variables, thereby eliminating the possibility of large multicollinearity problems in the regression model.

Hence, based on the outcomes of the VIF test, it can be postulated that the predictor factors within the proposed model are sufficiently independent from each other to not be severely impacted by multicollinearity. The discovery is considered positive since high coefficients and levels of multicollinearity may prevail in unreliable estimates and decreased understanding in the results of regression analysis. If variance inflation factor values are less than 5, then it can be said that there is a higher level of confidence over the regression analysis and the coefficient projections.

5.4 Results and Discussion

This study employs a rigorous analytical framework to thoroughly investigate the impact of economic freedom on the economic development of 162 states from 2003 to 2020. The investigation starts by testing the model outlined in Eq. (5.1) using both fixed-effects and random-effects estimation methods. The selection of the appropriate estimation method is guided by the Hausman test, a critical tool in the analysis of panel data. The Hausman test assesses whether a relationship exists between individual country effects and the model's regressors. It is crucial to note that the p-value should be less than 5 percent to reject the null hypothesis, as established by Hahn et al. in 2011. In our analysis, the probability associated with this model falls below the 0.05 threshold, indicating that the fixed-effects model is the most suitable for our investigation. Fixed-effects estimation provides consistent and unbiased results irrespective of correlation relationships, although it may be less efficient. Conversely, if country effects and explanatory variables exhibit correlations, the random-effects model can yield inconsistent and biased results.

As illustrated in Table 5.4, our empirical results reveal that specific components of economic freedom significantly impact the GDP per capita of the examined states. Notably, a well-functioning legal system, secure property rights, a stable monetary system, and effective regulations exert positive influences on the growth of GDP per capita. These findings align harmoniously with the insights derived from growth literature, emphasizing the pivotal role of these factors in fostering robust economic growth.

In Table 5.5, where Eq. (5.2) is estimated, the fixed-effects model (validated by the Hausman test) provides robust evidence that two parameters—international free

Table 5.4 Empirical results of panel data regression (Eq. 5.1)

Variables	Fixed-effects			Random-effects		
GDP	Coefficient	Std. Err.	*P*-Value	Coefficient	Std. Err.	*P*-Value
SizGov	0.0255	0.0187	0.174	0.0252	0.0187	0.177
LegPro	0.1485	0.0463	0.002	0.1566	0.0458	0.001
SouMon	0.0766	0.0135	0.000	0.0770	0.0135	0.000
FrTrIn	−0.0210	0.0194	0.281	−0.0200	0.0193	0.302
Regula	0.0710	0.0235	0.003	0.0701	0.0234	0.003
_cons	8.8666	0.3171	0.000	8.8227	0.3379	0.000
No. of Observations	2916			2916		
R-Squared	0.1764			0.1782		
Corr (u–x)	0.2717			0 (assumed)		

Table 5.5 Empirical results of panel data regression (Eq. 5.2)

Variables	Fixed-effects			Random-effects		
GDP	Coefficient	Std. Err.	*P*-Value	Coefficient	Std. Err.	*P*-Value
SizGov	0.0117	0.0012	0.365	0.0116	0.0128	0.366
LegPro	0.0392	0.0274	0.155	0.0440	0.0275	0.110
SouMon	0.0114	0.0099	0.254	0.0117	0.0099	0.237
FrTrIn	0.0410	0.0131	0.002	0.0414	0.0131	0.002
Regula	0.0240	0.0180	0.185	0.0237	0.0179	0.187
trend	0.0334	0.0023	0.000	0.0333	0.0023	0.000
_cons	9.6388	0.2059	0.000	9.6106	0.2341	0.000
No. of observation	2916			2916		
R-Squared	0.0887			0.0948		
Corr (u–x)	0.1943			0 (assumed)		

trade and trend—has a statistically significant impact on GDP per capita within the selected states, with an increase of 0.04 and 0.03 percent, respectively. This outcome is in line with earlier studies where authors such as Profiroiu et al. (2020) pinpoint at trend elements as critical in determining national economies in the long run. According to this estimation, the model parameters reflecting changes in SizGov, LegPro, SouMon, and Regula do not demonstrate a statistically significant influence on GDP per capita.

Thus, it emerged from these empirical findings that a fundamental function of economic freedom is to influence economic development trajectories of nations. The business legal environment, particularly a legal system that effectively protects property rights, sound management issues, and open international trade circuits, become the necessary and sufficient conditions for economic growth to occur. Furthermore, the consideration of the trend elements in the study points to the need in addressing the principles of efficiency and elective, in addition to analyzing economic growth for longer horizons. In general, Tables 5.4 and 5.5 give an insight into our regression analysis with the general influence of economic freedom on the GDP growth in the states regarding the analysis. These empirical findings echo the need to ensure that matters that induce economic freedom are the ones to be politicized, making them important catalysts for the growth and development within the global economy.

5.5 Summary

In this chapter, we have further explored the seemingly complex correlation between economic freedom and economic growth of 162 countries in the time frame of 2003–2020. Our search has unveiled some crucial findings that seem to define how much economic freedom impacts a country's level of success. The chapter began by acknowledging the fact that there has been an increased understanding among scholars that noneconomic factors play a crucial role in determining the GDP of a country. We underlined the Fraser Institute and the Heritage Foundation as the landmark indicators of economic freedom and stressed the relevance of the concept of economic freedom in modern theories of economics.

The findings show that economic freedom, which includes factors like sound laws, secure property rights, a sound monetary system, and sound regulation, is positively and significantly related to GDP growth. These results are in conformity with the economic theories and the growth literature, hence highlighting the significance of these elements in spearheading economic development.

In addition, we explored the relationship between economic freedom and sustainable economic development, identifying that while economic freedom is a powerful catalyst that triggers higher levels of wealth, this process needs to be seen in the context of the economic, social, and political environment. We agreed that having too much economic liberation is not really good because it leads to issues such as income distribution and exploitation of the environment. Hence, the key issue and the area of major relevance is to find the right balance and stimulate the process, designing the policies that affect economic freedom but do not neglect the societal objectives.

The results of our empirical analysis, based on the statistical analysis of many quantitative indicators and specifications, demonstrate the potential of economic freedom as a factor for stimulating economic growth. Confirming these assumptions, the fixed-effect estimates indicated that these findings were robust; further, the utilization of trend variables displayed the significance of analyzing economic growth in the long run.

Thus, in general, this chapter provides support for the importance of economic freedom as a determinant of the economic trajectories of countries. Thus, analyzing the trends for the further development of the world economy, it is possible to conclude that the concept of economic freedom combined with the proper implementation of policy measures can help to achieve high levels of economic development. All in all, it is our hope that these findings help enrich dialogues and policies resulting in better and more fair economic development worldwide. These outcomes form a basis for the upcoming chapter in which a quantitative comparison of these results with the historical data on the Kurdistan Region from 2003 to 2020 will be provided.

References

Acemoglu D, Johnson S, Robinson JA (2005) Institutions as a fundamental cause of long-run growth. In: Aghion P, Durlauf S (eds) Handbook of economic growth. North-Holland, Amsterdam. https://doi.org/10.1016/S1574-0684(05)01006-3. Last Access on 6 July 2021

Ames E, Reiter S (1961) Distributions of correlation coefficients in economic time series. J Am Stat Assoc 56(295):637–656

Bergh A, Karlsson M (2010) Government size and growth: accounting for economic freedom and globalization. Public Choice:195–213

Block W, Gwartney J, Lawson RA (1996) Economic freedom of the world: 1975–1995

Brkić I (2020) The relationship between economic freedom and economic growth in EU countries
Carlsson F, Lundström S (2002) Economic freedom and growth: decomposing the effects. Public Choice 112(3–4):335–344
Cheng J, Sun J, Yao K, Xu M, Cao Y (2022) A variable selection method based on mutual information and variance inflation factor. Spectrochim Acta A Mol Biomol Spectrosc 268:120652
Ciftci C, Durusu-Ciftci D (2022) Economic freedom, foreign direct investment, and economic growth: the role of sub-components of freedom. J Int Trade Econ Dev 31(2):233–254
Dkhili H, Dhiab LB (2018) The relationship between economic freedom and FDI versus economic growth: evidence from the GCC countries. J Risk Financ Manag 11(4):81
Gamble A (2021) The free economy and the strong State1. In: After Brexit and other essays. Bristol University Press, pp 91–112
Graafland J (2020) When does economic freedom promote well being? On the moderating role of long-term orientation. Soc Indic Res 149(1):127–153. https://www.jstor.org/stable/48731558. Last Access 2nd August 2024
Gwartney J, Lawson R (2003) The concept and measurement of economic freedom. Eur J Polit Econ 19(3):405–430
Gwartney J, Lawson R, Hall J, Murphy R (2021) Economic freedom of the world-2021 annual report. Institute of Economic Affairs Monographs, Forthcoming
Hahn J, Ham JC, Moon HR (2011) The Hausman test and weak instruments. J Econ 160(2):289–299
Hsiao C (2022) Analysis of panel data, vol 64. Cambridge University Press
Mahon JE (2018) Rentier states, international finance, and governance. Intl Financ Govern (August 25, 2018)
Malanski LK, Póvoa ACS (2021) Economic growth and corruption in emerging markets: does economic freedom matter? Intl Econ 166:58–70
Miller T, Kim AB, Roberts JM (2022) Economic freedom. The Heritage Foundation, 490
Ott J (2018) Measuring economic freedom: better without size of government. Soc Indic Res 135(2):479–498
Profiroiu MC, Radulescu CV, Burlacu S, Guţu C (2020) Changes and trends in the development of the world economy. In: Competitivitatea şi inovarea în economia cunoaşterii, pp 324–330
Razmi MJ, Refaei R (2013) The effect of trade openness and economic freedom on economic growth: the case of the Middle East and east Asian countries. Int J Econ Financ Issues 3(2):376–385
Siegan BH (2017) Economic liberties and the constitution. Routledge
Singh D, Gal Z (2020) Economic freedom and its impact on foreign direct investment: global overview. Rev Econ Perspect 20(1):73–90

Chapter 6
Political Challenges Impacting Institutional Quality and Economic Freedom in the KRI

This chapter integrates a combination of quantitative and qualitative research techniques to assess the impacts of economic freedom and political and economic institutions on the economic development of the KRI. It focuses on the institutions for sustainable development and looks at the empirical relations between financial liberalization and institutions as well as their measures in the context of KRI. Thus, the chapter entails an evaluation of the KRI's financial freedom based on the EFW-adopted variables, such as government size, legal structure, and property rights; currency stability; trade openness; and business/regulatory climate. Furthermore, the chapter compares the current levels of economic freedom in KRI, Iraq, and around the world, encompassing detailed methodology and results that can help in understanding the direction and approach toward sustainable economic growth.

6.1 Challenges to Economic Freedom and Governance in the KRI

As stated by many researchers, it is now estimated that the first civilization was in Mesopotamia with a free-market production method. Iraq and the KRI are in the region known as Mesopotamia, which currently experiences weak organizational, legal, and socioeconomic structures (Sanandaji 2018). According to Gwartney et al. (2020) and Transparency International (2020), Iraq's economy is positioned as one of the least robust in terms of economic freedom and is widely regarded as highly corrupt on a global scale. The establishment of institutions that supported economic freedom was hampered by several indicators, such as historical constraints stemming from the colonial legacy, the regulations of subsequent Iraqi authorities, political and financial turmoil, and sociocultural and religious constraints.

R. C. Biro, *Political Challenges of Economic Development in Rentier States*, Perspectives on Development in the Middle East and North Africa (MENA) Region, https://doi.org/10.1007/978-981-96-0563-7_6

The KRI enjoyed solid economic development following the liberation of Iraq in 2003, which decreased poverty rate to 3 percent in 2013, and helped to raise living standards. However, the process of economic transformation has been complex, and the Kurdish community was not fully prepared to adopt significant changes and implement a free-trade system. The transition to a market economy has been unstable, and market forces have not provided a viable path forward without prior socioeconomic development. Consequently, the region entered the global economy without a solid foundation of sustained growth (Marr 2018).

Since becoming a constitutionally recognized region in 2005, the KRI has experienced significant economic growth driven primarily by oil exports. The oil industry has been the main engine behind this growth. While reliance on natural resources like oil can stimulate economic expansion, it also restricts diversification into other industries. The core challenges facing the KRG's economy include over-reliance on oil revenue and uneven wealth distribution, which hinder rather than facilitate economic growth.

The economy of the KRI is structured around two distinct sectors. The first sector, dominated by oil production and related activities, represents the more advanced segment. The KRI leases its oil extraction operations to international firms through agreements that involve production and revenue sharing. Oil production and its derivatives constitute over 90 percent of exports, government revenues, and more than half of the GDP. The second sector encompasses all non-oil activities, including agriculture, manufacturing, construction, industry, tourism, commerce, and services, among others. However, this sector remains underdeveloped (Wahab 2014).

The KRI's society is mainly dependent on government spending. The region's primary employer is the public sector, which employs 70 percent of the KRI's labor force. The private sector has made a tiny contribution (employs 20 percent of the labor force) to the region's macroeconomic stability. The KRG implements spending policies since it is responsible for most of the population's access to facilities like water, power, roads, and other necessities because of its similarities to oil rent states (Muhamad 2022; Sherwani and Ahmad 2023).

Oil price volatility, military invasions, and refugee movements are just a few reasons that have hampered the KRI's economic progress in recent years. World economic developmental discourse emphasizes the significance of good governance for long-term economic prosperity. A representative democracy is created by inclusive political structures, where different groups and values are included, and these structures may use political channels to reflect their needs. As a result, the region's institutions, including those established by the constitution, are not structured to enhance checks and balances, foster accountability among politicians and government officials, or improve transparency in public financial management (World Bank 2015). It is of utmost importance to move away from the present scenario where the requirements of various communities are not being fulfilled and political responsibility is absent. An all-encompassing administration is vital for maintaining long-term economic well-being. To establish a more robust economy, KRI can prioritize the expansion of the private sector, implement modifications in governance, and take cues from successful models employed in other areas. Thus, a more equitable and flexible economic environment can be achieved.

6.2 Role of Institutions in the Economic Development of KRI

Economic development surveys have shown that efficiency of governance is now widely considered as the key factor for long-term sustainable economic enhancement. Anti-discriminatory ones safeguard the property of citizens, recognize contractual relations, and show non-discrimination toward businessmen. Integrated political structures, which can reflect social categories and their preferences and state expectations in terms of political acts, form a representative democracy. These methods then define compromise and turn these into regulations for the following requirements. Besides providing public goods and services, they support the rule of law, prevent organizations and people from enslaving others and exploiting them, and ensure sufficient regulation and protection (Jakšić 2018).

As rightly said by Prasetyo and Kistanti (2020), political and economic institutions are the most important aspect for sustainable economic development. These institutions define the fundamental prerequisites for obtaining economic growth and development and the regulation of how economic procedures are undertaken. The fact that political and economic institutions are important for sustainable economic development can also be explained by several factors, namely, stability; political and economic institutions ensure that there is stability, hence allowing businesses and investors to thrive. Also, they generate certainties in regulations, defend property, and ensure contracts are adhered to. This stability is relevant for the interests of investors as well as for the encouragement of economic development. They give competition; political and economic institutions can encourage competition through checking the monopolies and encouraging the establishment of businesses. Positive aspects of this contest can be innovation that can lead to lower prices for the final consumer and improvement of modern consumer goods and services. Also, the institutions enable transport; political and economic institutions can enable transport by laying down some standards for ensuring free and fair transport. This can assist in the extension of the market and access to raw materials and, thus, the stimulation of economic growth.

Stakeholders that promote investment; the economy point of view of the stakeholders comprise political and economic institutions that can facilitate investment by the local and international investors. It can go a long way in providing capital needed to start up new enterprises or fund existing projects, thus creating employment and hence economic development. In addition, political and economic institutions enable the adoption of environmentally social responsibilities and policies that support sustainability. Moreover, these institutions can also assist in the improvement and growth of people's well-being by funding education, health facilities, and other necessary social needs (Holmes et al. 2013).

One concept that has received support from scholars is the factor that mainly determines the success or failure of a country in question—the quality of its political institutions. Specifically, countries with efficient institutions that exhibit political and economic openness, legal and property rights, and social mobility fare better than countries with extractive institutions that favor a specific club. Whereas institutions that are political in nature guarantee the rule of law, decentralize authority in political things, and where internal balances are set in motion automatically, inclusive economic institutions provide for secure property rights and maintain law and order for economic matters. Public facilities and education services are facilitated by the two sets of institutions assisting one another in ensuring that everyone has equal chances. Other crucial aspects that can either enhance or hinder a nation's success include availability of natural resources, adequacy of infrastructural and human facilities and assets, education and skills of the populace, and the ability to manage change and its related circumstances (Huang 2010).

Practical political and economic advantages are produced by inclusive institutions, which promote consumption, effective resource management, and the development of novel concepts and technologies. The need for a political and economic institutional framework is emphasized by William Easterly (2001) to give all economic players incentives for better output levels, technological innovation, and adaptation.

Open access orders have features with inclusive institutions, as Acemoglu and Robinson (2012) described, whereas restricted access orders share restrictions with extractive institutions. Extractive institutions are autocratic, aggregating power and influence in the control of a select group of people with no accountability, no adherence to the rule of law, and no real restraints on their authority. Excessive economic institutions are defined by an absence of the rule of law, fragile property rights, impediments to access for new enterprises, and laws that interfere with operating markets. Power brokers have a tremendous motivation to defend the institutions they control, such as monopolies, which function at the cost of the citizens. Institutions that are both exclusive and inclusive cannot coexist over time.

Like the Soviet Union did up to the 1970s, extractive institutions might direct assets from low-productivity enterprises to high-productivity ones via the state power and political elite. Economic development might result from such wealth transfer. The autocratic power class will permit inclusive economic institutions under their supervision since they are relatively safe in existing roles. China's implementation of inclusive economic institutions is anticipated to further promote economic growth. As inclusive economic institutions produce uncontrollable political pressures, the growth paradigm predicts that extractive political institutions will eventually give rise to inclusive ones. Instead, extractive economic institutions will revert to being inclusive (Mizuno et al. 2017).

6.3 Economic Freedom and Institutions in the KRI

Economic freedom denotes the capacity of individuals and businesses to autonomously make economic choices without government or external interference. It includes principles such as free markets, property rights, and the rule of law. Moreover, in an economically free society, individuals can buy and sell goods and services without restrictions, and businesses can operate without excessive government regulation. It means that economic freedom will make people to make their own decisions instead of having those made for them by others through coercion, assault, stealing, or fraud. The concept of economic freedom asserts that it fosters prosperity and innovation because individuals and businesses can freely pursue their interests and generate wealth. Central to this idea is the principle of self-ownership, which underpins economic independence. Importantly, economic freedom does not entail a right to claim other people's time, abilities, or assets. Hence, they lack the authority to grab from others or request items be provided to them (Hall and Lawson 2014).

Several indicators, like the Index of Economic Freedom issued by the Cato Institutions and the Fraser Institutions, are usually used to quantify economic freedom. These indexes consider various characteristics, including governmental expenditure, rates of taxes, intellectual property rights, trade regulations, and the ease with which businesses may operate in a particular country. Globally, nations considered to have free economies are always regarded to be at higher standards of living as opposed to the closed economy nations (Hall and Lawson 2014).

The Economic Freedom Index of the World (EFW) is an evaluation of how effectively its institutions and policies advance economic liberty. For better EFW ratings, four pillars exist that include free trade, the ability to protect persons and property against violence, property rights, and the rule of law to having access to sound money. Further, they have to avoid actions that reduce free will, reduce and restrict commerce, and ban access to markets. It can assist researchers in evaluating better the part played by economic institutions in development and growth since it helps isolate economic institutions from other development and growth determinants such as politics, environment, geography, culture, and history (Gwartney et al. 2015).

If one wants to attain economic freedom, it is crucial to have not only a small government but an effective one as well. There is then the need to also ensure the protection of freedoms and property rights and the enforcement of contracts as well. Also, sound money in the form of a stable currency is an essential factor and autonomy in trade, investment, business operations, and labor (Gwartney and Lawson 2003). In addition, principles including integrity, inclusion, honesty, and human dignity are also social requirements that can be considered mandatory for the creation of economic liberty.

Analyzing the economic independence of the Kurdistan Region of Iraq (KRI) might give rise to certain issues of the political, administrative, and financial status of KRI with Iraq. The style of the research carried out in the KRI and Iraq inclines more toward the elements of measurement and quality of production rather than institutions that support economic freedom as agents of economic growth and development. After the US-led invasion of Iraq and the formulation of the Iraqi constitution in 2005, Kurdistan was awarded a formal semi-autonomous status (Anaid 2018). While the KRI can be recognized as having more political stability than the rest of Iraq, there are still significant economic and social differences between the two areas. These disparities contain laws and policies affecting the private sector, commerce, investment, taxation, employment, natural resources, business management, and women. Modifications in the customs system and legal frameworks, as well as the reforms in public finance, have been initiated and applied at the same time (Auzer 2017).

According to the study conducted by Khalid (2021), the level of economic autonomy of KRI was assessed to provide truthful and impartial analysis on the matter of economic policy. Its appearance helps to distinguish the real reform that provides access to business and employment for everyone regardless of their relations with officials from self-entitled reform that allows oligarchs to strengthen their positions both economically and politically. Moreover, it is crucial to assess economic freedom to give the policymakers some useful ideas on the current status of economic liberties in the KRI on how progress can be made and where strategies have been effective.

Moreover, Khalid showed that, therefore, before one thinks about economic independence in the KRI, one must consider its history and roots. Economic independence structures are also new and weak in the case of the KRI. They are influenced by long-standing social and cultural norms and the economic, political, and security precedents set by previous Iraqi administrations. Despite the continuity of institutions in the Kurdistan Region of Iraq under the Iraqi institutional framework, authorities in the KRI have endeavored to reform the structure and operation of political and economic institutions since 1991. This has involved the enactment of new legislation and regulations aimed at promoting free markets and democracy.

Modern institutions in Iraq have their roots in the British colonial era. The Kingdom of Iraq was formed by the British in 1921. They imposed a constitution and rules on the people of Mesopotamia and imported a monarch from elsewhere. Predatory (extractive and coercive) institutions were created to influence people and use them to the advantage of the new monarchy and British colonization. Even throughout the nation-state, Iraqi regimes in power implemented harsh economic and social regulations designed to enact state control over the country and its residents (Kirmanc 2013).

Three military governments ejected Iraq's core institutions from 1958 to 2003. The political authorities, judiciary, vital economic sectors, and monarchy-era civil society organizations were disbanded. Successive Iraqi administrations implemented socialist economic policies that centralized state authority and aimed to achieve social and economic justice. This was primarily done through agricultural reform legislation enacted in 1958, 1969, 1970, and 1971. These laws enabled the government to expropriate large agricultural estates and distribute them to peasants who supported the revolution and ruling parties. This resulted in a reduction in the concentration of land ownership and aimed to increase agricultural production.

They nationalized important sectors, including oil and gas, and state-owned businesses predominated. The Iraqi governments abolished the Parliament between 1958 and 1980, military courts were established, the Constitutional Court was abolished, and civil society groups were subject to government control (Abdul Jabbar 2006).

As a result, Iraqi government strategies led to the consolidation of political and economic power, creating significant obstacles such as bureaucratic hurdles for business operations, weakening judicial institutions, and instability in political and social spheres. This environment fostered dominance by political affiliations, patronage systems, nepotism, and adherence to traditional tribal customs, severely restricting the advancement of economic freedoms, including freedom of investment. Consequently, institutions that support economic freedom were vulnerable, neglected, unprotected, and subjected to heavy regulation.

However, the political transformations following the 1991 Gulf War and the 2003 Anglo-American invasion of Iraq spurred the Kurdistan Region of Iraq (KRI) to pursue economic independence more vigorously. Its government formulated economic freedom-friendly policies to foster the private sector, free markets, and investment. However, KRI leaders said free-market procedures would support its economy (Sümer and Joseph 2017).

6.4 Political Challenges to Economic Freedom Indicators in KRG

The EFW index is the definitive measure of a government's support for economic activity and growth. On the other hand, social and cultural norms impact economic freedom and people's capacity to benefit from it. Economic freedom is built on well-established values and standards frameworks, including acceptance of a fair judicial framework that is not influenced by personal, tribe, or other clientelism. The conservative, tribal nature of Kurdish culture is typified by the importance placed on family, societal, and religious ties in constructing the nation's social, economic, and political structures. These beliefs and conventions tend to be conventional, centralist, and conservative, which might fall at variance with the principles of economic liberty and representative government (Khalid 2021).

The existence of an individual is subordinate to the prosperity of the collective under traditional, collectivist beliefs and standards. The group has a central place in each person's life; they work inside the group and engage with other group members. These principles and familial connections are crucial to Kurdish political organizations' leadership, business dealings, and organizational structure, like KDP and PUK. As a result, traditional and conservative sociocultural ethics and family and political relationships govern economic, business, and financing operations. In the KRI, the political, financial, social, and welfare structures are all under the authority of the two governing parties. A particular class of tribe chiefs and retired military and security agency commanders hold excessive political, economic, and social influence. This political and social elite often disregards the rules and laws in place because they believe they are superior to these formal institutions. To dominate society and get their support during elections, they have established a network of contacts with most tribal chiefs (Hadad and Brandon 2017).

It was also noted by Hadad and Brandon (2017) that economic development faced setbacks due to the deteriorating security situation exacerbated by the emergence of ISIS in 2014. This led to the departure of numerous foreign companies and a decline in private investment in the region. With ISIS now defeated, the Iraqi central government and Kurdistan Regional Government (KRG) are tasked with reintegrating and reconstructing areas previously under ISIS control from 2014 to 2017. Addressing internal border disputes in disputed territories is also crucial. Presently, the Kurdistan Region of Iraq (KRI) is administratively divided between two governorates, and efforts by the KRG to unify Peshmerga forces under the Ministry of Peshmerga Affairs have been unsuccessful. Furthermore, security forces (*Asayish*) in the KRI remain under the control of the Kurdistan Democratic Party (KDP) and Patriotic Union of Kurdistan (PUK), resulting in factional divisions and Peshmerga loyalty to political parties rather than elected governments. This situation continues to pose challenges to internal security and impedes the government's ability to uphold the rule of law.

Since 2005, the KRI has operated as a federal entity within Iraq, with its economic potential closely tied to regional cooperation. The region has engaged in para-diplomacy to garner international support for its aspirations of independence, despite opposition from Baghdad, Turkey, and Iran. Measures such as the blockade of the Iranian border, closure of Kurdish airports, suspension of trade with Iran, and the central government's seizure of substantial oil and gas reserves in Kirkuk and other disputed areas have precipitated an economic downturn in the region (Sumer and Joseph 2018).

Irwani (2015) demonstrated that most business deals are completed lacking fair competition and accountability. Along with dominating numerous cabinet positions, the principal investment and business projects, including those in the construction, oil and gas, telecommunications, medical, and tobacco industries, among other sectors, have been shared to the benefit of particular people within remarkable who are committed to the governing parties. As a result, a vast network of clientelism, nepotism, and patronage has been developed and now dominates the primary economic activity. Thus, traditional cultural beliefs and practices have undermined citizens' trust in the marketplace, damaged corporate ethics, hampered trade, and investment freedom, and prevented the KRI from developing institutions that promote economic freedom. Individual independence, workplace freedom, and gender equality are also severely impacted by conventional societal norms. Due to the perception that some jobs are generally undesirable, many individuals are prevented from joining them.

This section assesses the level of economic freedom in the KRI using the index from the Fraser Institute's Economic Freedom of the World report (Heckelman 2000). Key elements of this index include various critical subcategories: the size of government intervention in the economy, the effectiveness of legal frameworks safeguarding property rights, the stability of monetary policies, the freedom to participate in global trade, and the regulatory framework governing economic activities.

6.4.1 Government Size

The primary source of public funding for the KRI comes from its share of the Iraqi federal budget. From 2006 to 2013, the KRG received 17 percent of the federal budget, excluding sovereign expenditures, amounting to nearly $12 billion in 2013. This allocation, constituting 80 percent of the KRI's total income, financed regional expenditures crucial to the KRI's economic development. However, political disputes led the central government to cease allocating the KRI's share of the national budget from 2014 onwards (World Bank Group 2015). Since then, the KRI has not passed a public budget bill, and its funding allocation remains unresolved.

According to Gürbey and Yildirim (2019), a significant issue in fiscal and economic policy in Iraq and the KRI is excessive dependence on oil revenue. This reliance has led to a rentier state economy characterized by boom-and-bust cycles and an uncertain economic outlook. In response, Erbil attempted to sell its oil independently of Baghdad and rely on local revenues to fund public services, but these efforts were unsuccessful. Instead, the KRI declared financial autonomy. The KRI was financially dependent on oil and non-oil industry. In 2011, 50 percent of the non-tradable sectors were generated by public administration and other services, including taxes. Mining and manufacturing contributed 9.4 percent, while agriculture contributed 17.5 percent. The banking and insurance industries only contributed 1.3 percent. However, these sources of income were insufficient to pay for the enormous amount of government spending caused by wasteful spending of resources and a lack of transparency. There is currently no reliable information on the entire amount of public income in the KRI, but while oil prices were high, the KRI's income rose, and its public spending grew (see Table 6.1).

The dependence on oil exports, the restrictions on exports, and the absence of a customs code make it challenging for the Kurdish territory in Iraq to flourish. A struggling economy results from the government's heavy reliance on oil income. Accordingly, financial security demands significant improvements in budgetary and broader structural transformation. Because KRG's economy relies on the price of oil worldwide, market volatility would worsen the issue. Economic difficulties would result, as was the case in the Kurdistan region in late 2019 when the oil price dropped due to the Covid-19 epidemic (Dilshad et al. 2023).

During the period from 2007 to 2013, when oil prices surged from around $65 to nearly $110 per barrel, public spending, including operational and investment expenditures, increased significantly. This era of high oil prices facilitated rapid economic development in the Kurdistan Region of Iraq (KRI), with GDP per capita growing annually by approximately 12 percent, from $1,705 to $5,500. This

Table 6.1 Public expenditures (US$ million) of KRG between 2007 and 2020

Year	Public expenditures (US$ millions)	Rate of operating expenses (%)	Rate of government investment (%)
2007	7847.66	71.00	29.00
2008	7628.783	62.20	37.80
2009	8857.263	74.00	26.00
2010	11,432.176	69.00	31.00
2011	13,940	70.00	30.00
2012	15,245.797	75.90	24.10
2013	16,945.749	68.50	31.50
2014	7999.68	N/A	N/A
2015	N/A	N/A	N/A
2016	N/A	N/A	N/A
2017	N/A	N/A	N/A
2018	8,520,000	86.34	13.66
2019	8,520,000	86.34	13.66
2020	8,520,000	86.34	13.66

Source: Ministry of Planning (2012), World Bank Group (2016), Rudaw Media Network (2020)

prosperous period allowed for expansion in government size and helped buffer vulnerabilities in the KRG's economy.

However, between 2014 and 2017, a sharp decline in oil prices—from about $85 to $46 per barrel—and the Iraqi government's decision to halt the allocation of the national budget to the KRI led to austerity measures. Corruption, revenue diversion, and tax evasion further compounded the financial challenges, resulting in reduced government expenditures. The KRI faced a severe financial and economic crisis as local revenues proved insufficient to cover government expenses, nearly causing a breakdown in public sector salary payments and benefits.

Following negotiations and temporary agreements, the federal government began disbursing monthly payments ranging from $350 million to $450 million to the KRG between 2018 and 2020, aimed at covering public sector salaries (Joseph and Sümer 2019).

One criterion for a state or territory to be considered rentier, as Beblawi (1987) outlined, is that it relies upon little to no taxes. In KRG, residents either pay no taxes or just a tiny amount. Neither the reports nor the budget legislation indicates that the KRG receives tax revenue. It is also worth noting that the average salary in the area is relatively low (Budget Laws). People in KRG are not used to making such enormous monetary contributions to the state. The government is likewise lacking in the means to collect taxes and customs. Specifically, poor services and a failure of collective taxation from the population resulted in the government failing to collect water and electrical usage taxes, ultimately leading the government to transfer energy and water administration to the private sector. Other revenue sources, such as internal government taxes and border customs, are not under centralization. Another problem with local earnings is that tax revenue collected by tax collectors is not returned to the government. Political parties do control major revenue generators in the cities, and the central administration in Erbil alleges that certain municipalities are not transferring their fair share of revenue back to the capital (Dixit and Sharif 2020).

The handling of taxes and the repatriation of local revenue, according to certain KRG Parliament members, are problematic. Instead of low tax rates being the problem, corruption has destabilized the KRG taxation system. For instance, taxes and customs duties at the border by individuals and businesses do not return to the government. According to the KRG's 2021 budget, local revenue, including taxes and other local payments, is approximately 200 million Iraqi dinars per month. This amount is relatively small compared to the total taxes collected from individuals and businesses (Muhamad 2022).

Additionally, technical and administrative problems, such as the inefficiency of the taxation system and its personnel and the growth of the illegal economy, hurt KRG's tax framework. Inappropriate written laws and regulations caused tax avoidance and an absence of openness in collecting taxes. Taxes comprise a small portion of governmental income; for example, they contributed only 0.4 percent in 2013, 1.2 percent in 2014, 0.9 percent in 2015, and 0.9 percent in 2016. Besides this, the COVID-19 outbreak resulted in the KRG exempting the private sector from paying taxes for two months in 2020. Afterward, a gradual income tax of 5–15 percent was enacted, and the general rate for real estate taxes was established at 9 percent (Muhamad 2022; KRG-General Directorate of Income Tax and Real Estate Tax 2020).

The KRG offers foreign businesses a 10-year tax and fee exemption to incentivize international investment. According to the General Directorate of Taxation of the KRG, numerous domestic and well-established international businesses avoid paying taxes. As of 2020, there were 31,921 registered firms in the Kurdistan Region, with 28,579 local businesses and 3342 foreign subsidiaries. Some individuals evade paying taxes by making up legal or financial problems. In reality, since it depends on oil income and does so for political reasons, that is, to shield itself from public responsibility and democratic demands, the KRG does not see taxes as a critical income stream for the national budget. According to local officials, the KRI's low taxes are required to attract domestic and international investment (Sabir 2022).

6.4.2 Public Sector Employment

The Kurdistan Regional Government (KRI) and Iraq have sizable public sectors that draw *rent-seeking* operations, namely, a significant proportion of public workers in the governmental sector like in rentier states. Approximately 70 percent of the workforce in the KRI is employed in the public sector, compared to 50 percent in the federal state of Iraq, 26 percent in Azerbaijan, 26 percent in Jordan, and 12 percent in Turkey. The KRG allocates nearly 70 percent of its revenue to paying public sector employees (World Bank 2015).

Besides, the KRG's public sector roles have not been filled via a skill-based hiring procedure. The hiring process was more dependent on loyalty, which has led to the KRG's bureaucracy's inefficiencies (Joseph and Sümer 2019). The exact workforce was unclear until the biometric platform recorded that almost all employment ended in 2017. During the biometric registration, 1,244,000 persons were counted as pay-rollers, compared to the earlier estimate of 1,395,000 persons. The number of active government workers in Iraq is estimated to be approximately 682,000; however, KRG authorities claim that the overall number of employed civil servants (including military and civilian personnel) among those who get salaries is closer to 751,000 (Rawf 2018).

The dominant parties over-regulate administration, business, and society. Moreover, most public institutions, including fiscal allocations, have become politicized. The KDP and PUK strive to dominate government offices by filling the administration with devoted fans and eliminating opponents and politically independent individuals from official positions. These initiatives overstaffed the public sector and (over 100,000 fake public sector employment) distorted professionalism, which led to a public-sector-employment-dominated economy. Politically linked enterprises in Iraq receive public contracts for purchasing goods and services managed by the significant ruling parties. Then they transfer them at lower prices to other enterprises. Given the public sector's significance in KRI employment, it employs 70 percent of the workers, which made the governmental sector employ the second-most people worldwide (Table 6.2) (Bartnick 2017). Furthermore, over 70 percent of the public budget is allocated to wages, subsidies, pensions, and social assistance.

Once the federal government removed its portion of the federal budget, oil prices collapsed, and ISIS overtook the KRI's neighboring provinces, the KRG suffered

Table 6.2 The percentage of public sector employment in several countries, 2017

Share of work force employed by public sector (%)	Countries
85.2	Cuba
70	Kurdistan Region of Iraq
44.6	Kuwait
40.6	Belarus
40.0	Iraq
36.8	Seychelles
33.7	Bahamas
33.1	Jordan
32.8	Norway
31.7	Croatia
31.2	Latvia, Denmark
31.0	Serbia
21.3	Average of the OECD Countries (35 Countries)
Below 20	All Other Countries

Source: Adapted by the author from Bartnick (2017), ILO (2023)

economic and social instability. The KRG could not reimburse public-sector salaries and its commitments to private-sector firms. Several enterprises failed, and state debt was 27 billion USD in 2020 (Mills 2023). The KRI's economic and health organizations were increasingly distorted and fragile during the epidemic, shrinking the private sector and causing poverty, unemployment, and diseases. KRI ranks lower than Iraq for Size of Government because 70 percent of the employment is in the public sector, compared to 40 percent in Iraq. Due to a shortage of statistics, notably on Popular Mobilization Force finance, Iraqi spending may be more lavish than reported.

The labor force in the KRI faces numerous challenges, including deadlock, outdated legal requirements, a lack of technical and language skills, and insufficient managerial competence. The large size of the government significantly disrupts the labor market and restricts labor freedom. The public sector's dominance over the labor market is a major obstacle to the KRI workforce's development of knowledge and skills (Hansen et al. 2014a, b). Many individuals opt for government jobs due to benefits like pension payments, paid vacations, flexible working hours, and low skill and capability requirements. These benefits are scarce or nonexistent in the private sector. Most private-sector businesses neglect hiring and firing regulations and do not protect employees' rights, discouraging people from seeking private sector employment (Muhamad 2022).

6.4.3 Legal System and Protection of Property Rights

The judiciary and legal framework of Iraq and the KRI are influenced by a long history of conflict and ethnic diversity. The system incorporates elements from Arab law (primarily Egyptian), Western law, Islamic law (*Shari'a*), and justice values. It faces challenges such as mismanagement, institutional and regulatory issues, and political and religious interference (Toone 2012). The 2005 Iraqi Constitution's Article 23 and the KRI draft constitution's Article 19, Paragraph 20, protect private land and free enterprise. Additionally, the KRI's legislative and executive branches have enacted and amended laws to promote economic freedom. Specifically, they have passed legislation to enhance judicial independence, support free trade and investment, foster competitive markets, and implement anti-trust regulations. The KRI also allows individuals to own, sell, exchange, gift, and utilize their private property (World Bank 2018).

In 2013, the KRG launched an ambitious reform initiative titled *"The Kurdish Region of Iraq 2020: A Vision for the Future,"* targeting economic, civic, and security sectors across both government and private entities. The goals included reducing bureaucracy and corruption and fostering start-ups and innovation by easing regulations. Free economic zones were also established. These reforms liberalized the economy and attracted international investment more rapidly in the KRI compared to the rest of Iraq (KRG-Ministry of Planning 2013). The KRI's economic freedom institutions nevertheless confront obstacles. However, regulations, rules, and reform initiatives are mostly dead letters. Property rights, conducting business, investment, commerce, and labor laws are not adequately applied. According to Jameel (2017), this has created an extensive patronage network, as well as nepotism and rent-seeking, by supporting the ruling parties and enriching the traditional rulers and elites.

The judiciary faces institutional issues and government, tribal, and ruling party influence. Like other institutions, the KDP and PUK have politicized the judiciary. Judges, judicial officials, and staff are selected based on political allegiance rather than ability and competency. According to Human Rights Watch, the KRI's courts are politicized and restrict criticism. The UNHCR noted that KRI courts are inefficient and that local inhabitants are unwilling to utilize courts and police, although numerous legislations are valid and match global norms. Throughout Iraq, it is hard for those without ethnic, religious, or tribal ties to defend themselves in court (Smith and Shadarevian 2016).

In the KRI, courts use outmoded methods. This means the KRI's judicial system, and courts cannot act independently or with objectivity to enforce the law and safeguard the liberties of its citizens. Due to governing parties, politicians, and tribal leaders, courts have failed to unbiasedly judge legal, economic, and property disputes and prevent embezzlement. The disagreement over stakes in the Chavi Land project in Slemani and the Dasht Behesht housing complex in Erbil and Dohuk, among others, is still ongoing. Moreover, the KRI's insufficient legal, organizational, and security agencies have harmed private property and the rule of law. In addition, planning, charting, and observing land is considered ineffective in property registration. All bureaucratic operations need papers and handwriting. Due to infrastructural and judicial inefficiencies, KRI courts cannot address business conflicts for international enterprises and entrepreneurs. The registration process for purchasing or selling a property takes six steps, seven days, and 3 percent of the real estate's worth. Contract enforcement takes 183 days and 24 percent of the insurance. The populace distrusts the police and security agencies because they are loyal to the governing parties rather than the law (Abdullah 2018).

Nonetheless, the KRG has a legislative framework and organizations to promote the rights and freedoms of women. Therefore, their legal situation is better than it is in Iraq. Women's rights and liberties are not protected by such regulations and organizations in Iraq (Mojab and Hassanpour 2021). Notably, compared to Iraq, the KRI's laws and standards are more in harmony with the Convention on the Elimination of All Forms of Discrimination against Women's (CEDAW) guiding principles. The KRG also established the Special Directory to monitor domestic abuse incidents and the High Council of Women's Affairs in parliament to guide agencies on gender mainstreaming. Additionally, there is a considerable disparity in private ownership between men and women in the KRI and Iraq: males hold 73.8 percent of the property, compared to women's 26.2 percent ownership. Since society devalues women who work in the private sector, there are extremely few female entrepreneurs in trade and investment in the KRI. Women only comprise about 15 percent of the workforce (KRG-Statistics Office 2018).

Compared to Iraq, the KRI now has lower levels of gender discrimination, violence against women, polygamy, and child marriages because of these policies, rules, and KRG initiatives. Women in Kurdistan see their situations and circumstances more favorably than women in Iraq. For instance, just 40 percent of women in the KRI and 76 percent in Iraq say there is no equality between men and women, respectively (Kaya 2018).

The position of women in Kurdish society is significant. Kaya also added that, in essence, societal and cultural origins contribute to the advancement of women's standing in the KRI in comparison to Iraq. Regarding women's freedom and rights, sociological research shows that the Kurds are among the most accepting of Islam. There are still female-led Kurdish tribes and households. In Kurdish society, women sometimes hold positions that are higher than those of males. As a result, women have more economic independence in the KRI than in Iraq.

6.4.4 Sound Money

The region's history of political instability consistently affects the currency's value, causing fluctuations in the exchange rate. This uncertainty makes investors hesitant to invest. Furthermore, the lack of transparency in the financial sector fosters corruption and diminishes trust in the banking system. This uncertainty makes it challenging to establish sound monetary policies and implement them effectively in Iraq. Besides, many people in the country lack financial literacy and may not fully understand the importance of sound money policies, which makes it challenging to implement and enforce such policies effectively (Anaid 2018).

The Central Bank of Iraq (CBI) is responsible for overseeing monetary policy in the KRI. The KRG adheres to Iraqi financial regulations in terms of laws, rules, administrative procedures, and technological frameworks. Following the 1991 uprising, Iraqi public entities were removed from the KRI, rendering the financial and banking sectors there essentially nonfunctional. Additionally, banks in the KRI relocated funds and assets to CBI offices outside the region, resulting in a failure to provide financial services and a decline in public trust. In the early 1990s, the CBI introduced a new currency after an international economic blockade in Iraq. However, the KRI continued to use the old currency, known locally as the "Switzerland Dinar," and utilized foreign currencies, mainly the US dollar, for trade (Karem et al. 2022).

Due to constitutional constraints, KRI authorities lack the jurisdiction to manage monetary policy. Consequently, residents and businesses in the KRI are required to conduct transactions in Iraqi currency under the CBI's financial system. In 2003, the Coalition Provisional Authority (CPA) introduced a new Iraqi dinar, which unified the monetary system across Iraq, including the KRI. According to the 2005 Iraqi constitution, the CBI is safeguarded from interference by the executive and legislative branches of government. This legal safeguard kept the CBI independent up until recently, which has helped its contribution to economic behavior, which resulted in the stability of monetary policy (Haji and Mohamed 2022). However, inflation was 0.117 percent each year from 2017 to 2019, while interest rates ranged from 4 to 8 percent during the same period. Additionally, the pace of money growth grew by 6.7 percent during this time (Iraq, Ministry of Planning 2020).

Meanwhile, in 2021, the KRI's Consumer Price Index (CPI) rose to 7.5 percent compared to 2020 (KRG-Ministry of Planning 2021). In subsequent years, it is expected that both Iraq and the KRI's sound money ratings will drop. Under pressure from the federal government, the CBI depreciated the Iraqi dinar by nearly 23 percent against the dollar at the end of 2020. This was done to close the trade imbalance and boost the economy, but the primary objective was to close the national budget surplus. Due to this approach, prices for products and services have increased by around 30 percent in 2021, which caused societal instability (Oxford Analytica 2023).

6.4.5 Freedom to Trade Internationally

In the KRI, trade is one of the most significant industries. Between 2010 and 2017, the Ministry of Commerce and Industry of the KRG estimated total imports at approximately $11 billion, while non-oil exports were around $90 million. The KRG imposes customs duties ranging from 5 to 80 percent on all imported and exported goods and services. The licensing process for trade is bureaucratic, involving 16 steps, taking about 60 days, and costing roughly $3,000. Control over border crossings and the commerce sector remains a major point of contention between the KRI and the federal government of Iraq (KRG-General Directorate of Customs 2020). Since 1991, the governing parties have dominated and politicized the KRI's trade industry and border crossings, leading to issues of political duopoly, smuggling, and widespread corruption.

Due to the heavy reliance of the KRG on imported commodities and export of natural resources, budget projections have proven challenging, and natural resources have been used excessively. By promoting the existing marketplace and trade agreements in the region, the authorities hardly ever attempt to transfer the technology and industrial facilities required for manufacturing the imported products. The primary cause of the development issue in the KRG may be the absence of learning attempts and the absence of technology to support improvement. It is additionally a vital sign of a country's lack of technological advancement, self-sufficiency, and low performance targets (Heshmati 2007).

The KRG grants significant licenses to oil and gas companies in the region, but the process is secretive and key details are kept confidential. Since the 1990s, oil smuggling has posed challenges in the KRI. Therefore, it's crucial to ensure that revenue from oil and gas is used to benefit the public, providing essential government services and goods. Evaluating the KRG's export earnings is complex due to the lack of reliable data on the quantities of goods sold directly by the KRG or through Iraq's national channels. Notably, a large portion of the KRG's exports consists of oil (World Bank 2015).

In 2007, despite the KRI having a vast amount of rich arable land, 35 percent of the KRG's food was locally produced; more than 65 percent (out of 65 percent: Turkey 35 percent, Iran 25 percent, and China 30 percent) was imported; this was primarily due to the economic crisis in the region (Salim et al. 2019). The actions of the past Iraqi regimes decimated this industry for a very long time. However, the Kurdish administrations have not done much to rehabilitate the agricultural sector (Ramazan 2015: 4). The Ministry of Commerce and Industry's figures indicated that the KRG's total imports were projected to have been about $20.8 billion in 2013 (World Bank 2015). In 2021, commerce between the KRG, Iran, and Turkey was roughly $7 billion and $9 billion, respectively. Even though exports were relatively low compared to imports in 2021, trade activity rose by 45 percent, which was positive since some local goods were shipped to foreign nations and marketed abroad (Omar 2022).

Although the agriculture sector is considered one of the driving sectors in other nations, the KRG's yearly budget for the agricultural sector was just 2 percent (Hadfield 2020). Due to the reduced prices of goods from Turkey, Iran, China, certain EU nations, and others, local farmers and businesses find it challenging to sell their goods in the local marketplaces. Traders connected to the governing elites in the KRG oversee the import industry. The ideology of a rentier state from Iraq was developed by locating all of Kurdistan's interests in its environmental assets, oil and gas export potential and disregarding the agriculture industry (Romano 2018).

Kurdish farmers see imported commodities as a danger to local industry. Both agricultural and economic specialists criticize the administration for lacking a solid strategy to encourage local output. The producers requested that the government establish tariffs on imported goods and develop a market for local goods. The local goods were eliminated by cheaper goods from nearby nations (Jongerden 2019). The "Oil for Food" initiative in 1997 marked the beginning of the criticism of the nation's reliance on imports. As mentioned by the specialists, the main tasks of the humanitarian aid bestowed to the KRI were to reconstruct the communities and restore agriculture. However, the "Oil for Food" program brought an end to this campaign and set up the procedure for delivering food aid (Nuri and Karakir 2022).

6.4.6 Regulation

Foreign companies are also encouraged to invest in the KRG by formulating several changes as follows: for example, the Kurdistan Investment Law passed in 2006, under which the government offers important tax exemptions and similar facilities for international investors. Moreover, free economic zones have been established in the region, and these additional incentives, such as customs and access to supportive structures, The KRG has been rather busy with numerous projects and actions; among them, there have been attempts to improve transport, aviation, and communication facilities in the area. Thus, the volume of investments in the area business environment has become more favorable because of these measures. They have relatively more infrastructure than the rest of Iraq and are more politically and security safe.

The KRI during 2006–2014 received a more favorable and stable business environment compared to its competitors. Data from the economist intelligence unit revealed that the KRI's Business Environment Index total score was close to 5.7, putting the country at position 57 of 83 in the composite rankings. Interestingly, the KRI fared better in this indicator compared to the Middle East's and Iraq's averages at 5.66 and 5.04, respectively, as has been highlighted by the EIU in 2014. In the meantime, the KRI has been viewed as an attractive hub for international commerce and investment markets until ISIS invaded some areas of Iraq in 2014. However, the government's setback did not overall hinder the KRI's economy.

The monetary system of the KRI remains vulnerable, which is based on cash, and has poor facilities. Small and medium enterprises (SMEs) experience challenges in entering and eventually obtaining finance. The financial crisis in 2014 highlighted the lack of institutional support for attracting significant private investment and limited funding opportunities for start-up entrepreneurs. According to World Bank research, just 3 percent of businesses in KRI depend on the banking industry for cash flow and investments, demonstrating the region's regular financial distress and turbulence and customers' desire for cash in financial activities (Bartnick 2017).

Out of the 49 financial institutions and banks in the KRI, only six are owned by the state and are primarily responsible for distributing salaries and benefits to public sector employees. The remaining 43 banks and financial firms are privately owned. It is rare for state-owned and private banks to offer their services to each other. There are complicated financial transactions both inside the KRI and between the KRI and the rest of Iraq. According to KRG legislation, private banks cannot pay public sector workers' salaries and wages, nor may government entities have savings or current accounts. This condition hurts the banking system in the KRI and restricts competitiveness in the banking industry. The role of private banks in funding private-sector initiatives is hampered since they rely on complicated, old mechanisms and lack access to significant supplies of capital (World Bank 2016).

Due to the ongoing financial unrest and economic instability in the KRI and Iraq, the banking and financial sector attracts poor public trust, which hinders its capacity to draw deposits and investments. This makes getting credit extremely difficult for SMEs in KRI. Nevertheless, some private banks can finance SMEs. They provide SMEs with loans between $2000 and $10,000 with interest rates between 7 and 12 percent. However, the share of GDP these banks provide to the private sector by lending is less than 2 percent (World Bank Group 2016).

Although the KRI law of investment provides incentives for investments, considering the condition for finance, labor, and business rules in KRI altogether shows that there is little flexibility to operate a company or make an investment there. As a result, the KRI continues to have a short, fragile, and unsteady position for investment in long-term macroeconomic stability. However, despite various laws and regulations promoting the freedom of business and investment, the KRI's business climate keeps hampered by corruption, patronage, complicated bureaucratic hurdles, and a lack of transparency. In addition, Ghaffoori (2021) observed that the region's business environment is fragile due to inadequate and inaccurate statistics on significant sectors, partly due to the KRG Statistical Office's failings and the presence of a substantial informal economy.

6.5 Economic Freedom of KRI Compared to Iraq and the World

Various factors evaluate the economic freedom of a country. These factors include a government that is accountable and has limited power, a legal system that can protect private property rights and enforce contracts, and access to stable and reliable currency. Other parameters include freely exchanging goods and services, investing in businesses, engaging in commerce, and working without unnecessary restrictions. In addition, principles such as trust, tolerance, honesty, and dignity are also important in determining a country's economic freedom (Gwartney and Lawson 2003).

Understanding the history and foundation of economic independence in the KRI is essential before delving on the topic. The economic independence frameworks of the KRI are novel and unproven. They are influenced by ingrained social and cultural norms as well as the political, security, and economic legacies of past Iraqi administrations. After the Iraqi institutional structure, KRG organizations kept running. Since 1991, the KRI leadership has worked to alter the KRI's direction and structure by enacting new laws and regulations that support democracy and free markets. Evaluating economic freedom also provides decision-makers with important data on economic liberty in the KRI, potential areas for development, and areas where appropriate measures have been put into place.

According to the Fraser Institute's EFW methodology, Khalid (2021) estimated the economic freedom index for KRI. Khalid gathered the information using primary and secondary sources and approximated the KRI score. The estimated scores for the KRI compared to Iraqi scores are presented in Table 6.3. The estimated score of the KRI is in line with the literature and data presentation of this chapter. The low

Table 6.3 Estimated EFW index for KRI in 2020 and Iraq in 2021

No.	Indicators	KRG, 2020	Iraq, 2021
1	Size of Government	3.4	5.05
2	Legal System and Property Rights	3.65	3.2
3	Sound Money	7.55	7.8
4	Free Trade Internationally	6.23	4.8
5	Regulations	4.94	6.9
Mean EFW Index		5.15	5.55

score is approved that KRI has been going through various crises and problems in conducting a better environment for economic freedom due to the low quality of political and economic institutions.

Moreover, to better understand KRI's economic liberty, it is a privilege to compare the score of KRI with all other listed countries (Table 6.4) and rentier states studied in the previous chapter. The data demonstrated that the KRI is among the weakest countries in the world in the case of the EFW index with a score of 5.15,

Table 6.4 Comparison of business indicators and economic freedom in KRG, 2020

Indicators	Business indicators (KRG, 2020)	Economic freedom (EFW index, KRG, 2020)	Interpretation
Starting a Business	– 12–17 procedures – 60 days – 45% of per capita income as cost	Regulations: 4.94	The high barriers to entry, extensive regulatory periods, and substantial start-ups costs are evidence of the poor business starting index. Whereas, since 2023, the registration becomes online and it only takes 3–10 days to register a company with about 30% of per capita income as cost.
Property Registration	– 10+ procedures – 60 days (citizens) – 365 days (foreigners) – 3% of property value	Legal System and Property Rights: 3.65	The poor result of rights to property is consistent with demanding processes and extended registration delays, which point to inadequate legal safeguards and inefficient methods.
Enforcing Contracts	– 183 days – 24% of lawsuit value as cost	Legal System and Property Rights: 3.65	The poor property rights value is compatible with considerable legal inconsistencies, as indicated by the lengthy settlement periods and high expenses associated with enforced agreements.
Getting Electricity	– 28 procedures – 30 days – 80% of per capita income as cost	Size of Government: 3.4	Inefficient service delivery and limited financial independence in the region are reflected in the high prices and difficult application processes for obtaining electricity.
Trading Across Borders	– 16 procedures for imports – 38 days – 13 types of fees[a]	Free Trade Internationally: 6.23	Despite the fairly good EFW score for free trade, enterprises involved in international commerce may face difficulties due to the high expenses and lengthy procedures at frontier crossings.

[a]The data of Kurdistan Business Indicators are received from various KRG departments; Companies Registration Department, General Directorate of Customs, and General Director of Income Tax and Real Estate Tax

which means KRI, with various political and economic difficulties, needs to work toward overcoming challenges to improve its EWF score and touch a flourishing economy.

To grasp a broader picture of economic and business indicators of the KRI, it is necessary to compare the indicators of economic freedom and business indicators for 2020; it will thus provide a better understanding of the place the KRI stands in the case of business and economic development (see Table 6.4).

Through the comparison among these metrics, the findings highlight the interdependence of legislative protections, administrative productivity, and quality of service, demonstrating how shortcomings in one domain can have a detrimental impact on other spheres. This comparison method is important because it highlights structural flaws that impede the expansion of the economy and the entrepreneurship sector. Comprehending these interconnections is crucial for providing guidance for policy modifications that seek to optimize corporate procedures, strengthen legal protections, and eventually establish a more conducive atmosphere for capital inflows and inventive endeavors.

6.6 The KRI Transformation from Independent to Dependent Region After 2020

Kurdish political aspirations progressed between 2005 and 2008 due to the American invasion of Iraq. The leaders of the KDP and PUK took advantage of this situation and established a coalition government in 2006. Jalal Talabani of the PUK was elected President of Iraq, and Massoud Barzani of the KDP was chosen President of the Kurdistan Region. Erbil and Baghdad have been involved in persistent disputes over governance and the allocation of oil wealth, stemming from legal uncertainty inherited in the 2005 Iraqi Constitution. Tensions between the federal government and the KRG have increased due to the absence of conclusive legislation. This is especially true concerning the distribution of income, which was intended to be based on estimated Kurds population share accounting for 17 percent of the national budget but is still up for question (Gunter 2017).

The fiscal disagreements between both parties intensified in 2008 and 2012, which led the KRI to establish diplomatic and economic links to strengthen its independence. The main point of contention in the disagreement was the distribution of the federal budget: Erbil maintained that it ought to get 17 percent of the original national budget, whereas Baghdad maintained that this proportion ought to be determined after excluding national costs attributed to public debt, extraction and various investments costs. Because of this, the KRG only got 11–12 percent of the federal budget, which motivated it to concentrate on handling and utilizing its energy supplies to achieve financial autonomy. The KRG started negotiating contracts with big foreign oil corporations and greatly expanded its oil output (Hama 2018).

In reaction to Iran's expanding impact in Iraq and the Kurdistan region through the PUK, the KRI, developed its diplomatic and economic ties, especially with Turkey, to mitigate Baghdad's dominance. Throughout this time, Turkey's investments in KRI increased dramatically, making Iraq its second-largest export market. With the establishment of consulates in Erbil by numerous nations between 2010 and 2012, notably France, Turkey, and the United States, the KRI became recognized internationally as a geopolitical player (Hasan and Perot 2021).

Relationships were further strained after Nouri al-Maliki was reappointed as prime minister of Iraq and harsh actions were taken against Kurdistan, such as the deployment of Iraqi Security Forces to Kirkuk in 2012. Additionally, economic tensions grew as Baghdad gave the KRG far less cash than asked for. In retaliation, the KRI increased its economic independence and circumvented Baghdad's authority by building an oil pipeline to Turkey in 2013. After effectively expelling the IS from Kirkuk in 2014, the KRI also took control of the oil-rich territory. A deal on oil production and profit distribution was reached initially during discussions headed by Prime Minister Haider al-Abadi in late 2014; however, the accord swiftly collapsed as both parties accused one another with monetary fraud, obstructing a final settlement (Gürbey and Yildirim 2019).

Kurdish oil extraction increased to account for a sizable portion of Iraq's total manufacturing between 2013 and 2017, more than doubling in the country. The KRI became a more autonomous player throughout the conflict with IS (2014–2017), growing its territory, fortifying its armed forces, and receiving global support. The KRI's position in the international arena was enhanced by its strong collaboration with the international coalition against the IS, especially with the United States, UK, France, and Germany. The 2016 Memorandum of Understanding between the US Department of Defense and the KRG's Ministry of Peshmerga served as an example of this (Knights 2020).

Kurdish authorities spotted the post-IS era as a crucial chance to advance statehood as their country cemented its position as an independent political actor. They used their military victories and sacrifices—including the deaths of 1,800 Peshmerga fighters and 9,000 injuries—to win support for a possible autonomy referendum.

Following that, the situation between Erbil and Baghdad worsened even further when the KDP abstained from the budget vote and both parties accused one another of not living up to their agreements (Mills 2023). This impasse highlighted Kurdistan's precarious financial situation and caused concern on the sustainability of an autonomous Kurdistan reliant on outside financial assistance. Kurdistan made progress toward de facto statehood, but there were serious concerns about its capacity to maintain complete independence due to its restricted power over crude exports and financial dependency on Iraq.

The KDP returned to Baghdad after former Prime Minister Haider al-Abadi lost the 2018 election. The division of the Shiite community bolstered the Kurds' position in Baghdad. Political forces conferred with leaders of the Kurdish community to establish a solid governing bloc (Palani and Fazil 2023). By taking a proactive stance in settling disagreements with Erbil, Prime Ministers Adel Abdel-Mehdi and

Mustafa al-Kadhimi have enabled Kurdistan to maintain de facto authority and win back international support without upsetting the Iraqi government.

Salary increases in the KRG's public sector in 2019 were substantial, indicating an effort to defuse tensions. Additionally, the KRG was required by the budget to export 250,000 barrels/day (b/d) through State Organization for Marketing of Oil (SOMO) and transfer the profits into central accounts. This trend persisted in 2020 when an arrangement was made wherein Baghdad funded $900 million for wages in exchange for the KRG providing SOMO with 250,000 b/d. Notwithstanding plans to raise the KRG's budget allocation to 14 percent in 2021, the KRI was only given 12.67 percent and was required to produce 460,000 barrels of oil per day, of which 250,000 were to be sent to Baghdad (Salam 2024). Subsequently, the federal budget's passage is a positive step toward improving ties with the federal government and reviving productive collaboration.

For some factors, 2022 was a new turning point in relations between Kurds and Iraqis. The KDP was a major player in the new administration that Mohammed Chia al-Sudani created. The KRI's 2007 Oil and Gas Law, which had permitted the KRI to ship out its crude oil on its own for earlier years, was ruled unlawful by the Federal Supreme Court. The judicial legitimacy of the prior order was reinforced in March 2023 when the International Chamber of Commerce in Paris rendered a fresh verdict that affirmed the earlier decision. The KRG was thus compelled to reach a deal with the federal government after losing its oil earnings. In 2023, two tentative agreements were made that centered on a new system for allocating oil earnings and the federal budget (Karim and Aziz 2024).

In addition to paying foreign oil corporations, commercializing exports, and depositing gross income into a bank account under the KRG Prime Minister's supervision, the Iraqi government also instituted a new system for sharing oil earnings. This guaranteed that the KRI got its fair portion of the federal budget from petroleum revenues plainly, rather than through the Ministry of Finance allocating funds indirectly. The prospective deal on Iraq's oil and gas earnings was reflected in the planned 12.7 percent share of the KRG in the federal budget.

There has been a history of failure with deals between Baghdad and Erbil in recent history, which contributes to the ongoing lack of confidence. The fundamental volatility of Iraqi politics, which is typified by interest groups' short-termism and pervasive unpredictability about their futures, is one of the main barriers to the longevity of this accord. The challenge of attaining a long-term, rather than a short-term, relaxation of tensions between the KDP and the PUK is another barrier. This required uniting the KRG's institutions and implementing fair and transparent resource-sharing procedures (Krasna 2023).

Following the ruling by the Paris Court, the KRI has been dealing with a serious problem for the past months as a result of the shutdown of a vital oil pipeline. Since March 25, the pipeline that exported over 400,000 b/d of oil has been closed, endangering the KRG's budget, which is highly dependent on oil income, and the country losing nearly $30 million every day. The shutdown came about as a result of an arbitration decision that benefited the Iraqi government and mandated that Turkey cease loading Kurdish oil and reimburse Baghdad with fines totaling $1.5 billion.

Baghdad alleged that Turkey's autonomous management of Kurdish oil exports contravened a 1973 agreement requiring oil sales to only go via Iraq's government-run operator.

The KRG's oil exports depended heavily on the pipeline, which was constructed in 2013, and its shutdown has made matters worse for the Kurdish economy. The pipeline blockage has also disrupted the illegal transportation of oil from Iraq to neighboring nations through the KRI. A temporary agreement between Erbil and Baghdad and continuing discussions with Turkey are two attempts to fix the crisis. Yet, political complexity and recent turmoil in Turkey, such as earthquakes and elections, make the revival of oil exports questionable. Iraq's overall oil exports have decreased as a result, which has hampered economic expansion and complicated recovery efforts (Steketee 2023).

The authority of the KRI's oil has become more of a point of contention between Erbil and Baghdad. Originally, the KRG was to get a portion of the national budget in return for exporting oil via SOMO. The KRI's 2007 oil law was declared unlawful by the Iraqi Supreme Court in February 2022, and Baghdad was mandated to regulate the export of KRI's petroleum. Major oil service providers limited their activities in Kurdistan as a result of this move, which also sparked legal challenges against Kurdish oil contracts. The KRI denounced the decision as politically driven, seeing it as an effort to weaken Kurdish autonomy by Shiite groups affiliated with Iran.

A provisional deal signed in April 2024 gave SOMO the authority to sell KRG oil, but the KRG maintained authority over the administration of revenues and generation, although with more monitoring. In June 2024, a new budget legislation was passed, formalizing these agreements. The KRG will supply the Iraqi government with 400,000 b/d of oil per the new legislation; the income will be overseen by an international auditor and Iraqi authorities who have access to a Central Bank account. It has been stipulated that 12.7 losing of the national budget will go to the KRG, but the bill has clauses that might reduce the KDP's clout and strengthen the PUK's control of Sulaymaniyah. Although there is an agreement, these fresh mechanisms emphasize how complicated Kurdish autonomy and federal authority are in Iraq (Rudaw 2024).

The court's ruling and the oil shipment halt by Turkey have facilitated Baghdad's attempts to undermine the KRI's standing internationally and restrict its autonomy in foreign and economic matters. Erbil had earlier opposed the terms under the latest budget legislation, but the new political and economic realities force it to embrace them. Losing control over its main revenue stream will result in a substantial loss of freedom, but it may also partially address the economic issues that have troubled the Kurdish territory over the past ten years, such as corruption and unpaid salaries and pensions. As a result of the fresh circumstances, Baghdad will be better able to oversee national energy development and regulations, ensuring that the KRI carries out its part of any future OPEC cutbacks that Iraq commits to and that Kurdish energy and trade strategy does not conflict with or undermine national objectives.

6.7 Summary

Political and economic entities play a crucial role in ensuring stable and sustained growth of the economy. These entities promote sustainability, attract investments, facilitate trade, and encourage competitiveness. It is unlikely to achieve sustainable economic growth without strong political and economic structures. This chapter checked the compatibility of the KRI's economic and political variables contributing to the economic development, including the category of democratic political systems and market-oriented financial systems.

The KRI is confronted with system-wide problems in the domains of democratic governance, recognition of the rule of law, delivering basic utilities and public services, and guaranteeing law and order for the protection of property rights and trading. This is due to defects in the institutional setting causing damage to the public sector, political manipulation, and rent-seeking mechanisms being deep-seated. The chapter notes that better constitutional principles and adherence to the rule of law are needed to address these deficiencies. However, the region has other problems, such as the special interest groups engaging in rent-seeking, political rent-seeking, rent extraction, and a large and ineffective bureaucracy. While the current KRI economic environment is considered profitable, it is also plagued by endemic rules, or those that can be modified only through the alteration of the constitution and the following laws. From the above analysis, it can be concluded that the various departments need to be differentiated strictly and the checks and balances arranged using the authority provided to the said departments. There is a need to introduce superior political conditions and essential limitation of general power of the government by the constitutional norms.

The KRI's economic administration is hampered by the division of budget administration among many ministries, including the Ministry of Natural Resources, the Ministry of Planning, and the Ministry of Finance and the Economy. Likewise, the KRI's capacity to successfully develop economic policies is hampered by the absence of a solid balance sheet. Besides, the administration of the economy is significantly impacted by variations in budgeting procedures throughout the KRI's provinces.

The KRG is trying for a reorganization that will lessen its dependency on oil and shrink the public services while simultaneously supporting the expansion of the private sector and economic diversification. To encourage the expansion of the private sector, the KRI's financial sector has to be modernized. Giving up the cash-based system would assist with public accounting and visibility. To sustain a market-based economy, the legal structure governing firms must be strengthened to encourage and safeguard local SMEs and foreign direct investment.

The public sector's accountability and openness must be enhanced to promote such actions. Integrating public sector financial statements and improving economic data collecting and policymaking is also necessary. To stop the fruitless actions in the industry, corrupt authorities must be found and penalized. More administrative intervention is expected to uphold the rule of law generally, secure property rights, and respect agreements. Without such changes, the KRG's economy would keep suffering from exploiting the government sector for rent-seeking and political theater.

Most of the KRI's political and financial structures remain dysfunctional but weakly formative. Moreover, these entities have weak foundations due to the legacy of the previous Iraqi governments' economic, political, and security policies and the persistence of classic social standards and values that oppose market economics, effective governance, and democracy. The majority of the region's reform provisions and initiatives still remain only on paper.

The region's economic freedom faces significant obstacles due to a cash-based economy, political biases, excessive centralization in managing financial and economic resources, heavy dependence on energy exports, and transparency issues.

Moreover, a saggy and fragile judicial framework, a complicated bureaucracy, and inadequate and imprecise statistics over most industries impact the fragility of the economic growth in the region. In addition, corruption, clientelism, nepotism, corporate irresponsibility, and inequity in KRI all hinder economic freedom. As a result, heavily biased financial and political structures have arisen, with their main goal being to dominate the population and its capital means according to the principles and norms of the dominant political parties. The organizations of economic freedom, particularly the positive principles and standards of the free market, have been severely damaged by the above-mentioned forces.

Despite property rights being protected by Iraqi and KRI laws, the current legal infrastructure is inadequate to facilitate significant private investment. Strengthening intellectual property's legal safeguards would also encourage business and innovation since it now lacks it. Strong governmental institutions that can maintain law and order are essential for the effective execution of contracts along with the safeguarding of property rights. As previously stated, the capacity of the Kurdish and Iraqi governments to defend property rights may be adversely affected by deficiencies in the region's broader security and legal system. In addition, because several people can claim possession of the same piece of property, the KRG must improve its ability to register assets, especially land. Consequently, the land titling and selling procedures must be done correctly by the government.

The KRI is still undergoing a political transition, and its economy demonstrates rentier state features. According to the rentier state theory, the government is the primary beneficiary of the government, while just a tiny portion of the population participates in renting generation. The KRI derives its primary source of income, the hydrocarbon rents, from oil contracts with multinational corporations. The KRI's population relies on this rental in the form of employment in the public sector. Moreover, the importance of the private sector is undervalued, and economic diversity is rarely noticeable in KRI. All other products are imported into the KRI from domestic and foreign markets, and the country's economy is growing slowly.

To strengthen the institutional environment, however, some flaws must be addressed. To ensure the long-term sustainability of its diverse economic and political structures and to promote transparency, accountability, and productivity in its government sector, the KRI structure needs to proceed with structural reform. Open organizations backed by a more robust legal framework will ensure fair chances for all firms and develop a growth-friendly ecosystem. Improved delivery of essential public services, including healthcare, education, and infrastructure, might help the Kurdistan Region of Iraq create the conditions for more significant social and economic development.

Moreover, this chapter finds out that the KRI is facing a significant issue due to the closure of its vital oil pipeline, which has caused a daily loss of nearly $30 million. The pipeline, which exported over 400,000 b/d of oil, disrupted illegal oil transportation from Iraq to neighboring nations. The authority of the KRI's oil has become a point of contention between Erbil and Baghdad. In June 2024, a new budget legislation was passed, formalizing agreements between the KRG and Iraq. The court's ruling and the oil shipment halt have facilitated Baghdad's attempts to undermine the KRI's international standing and restrict its autonomy in foreign and economic matters.

References

Abdul Jabbar F (2006) Civil Society in Iraq: post-war (Arabic). Institute for Strategic Studies, Baghdad-Beirut

Abdullah FH (2018) The political system in Iraqi Kurdistan: party rivalries and future perspectives. Asian Affairs 49(4):606–624

Acemoglu D, Robinson JA (2012) Why nations fail: the origins of power, prosperity, and poverty. https://ds.amu.edu.et/xmlui/bitstream/handle/123456789/8822/Why-Nations-Fail-Daron-Acemoglu.pdf?sequence=1&isAllowed=y. Last Access on 4 May, 2022

Anaid A (2018) The nature of political economy challenges of the Kurdistan region of Iraq. In: Iraqi Kurdistan's statehood aspirations: a political economy approach. Springer, Cham, pp 9–26

Auzer KA (2017) Institutional design and capacity to enhance effective governance of oil and gas wealth: the case of Kurdistan region. Springer. https://doi.org/10.1007/978-981-10-4518-9. Last Access: April 22nd 2022

Bartnick A (2017) Obstacles and opportunities for entrepreneurship in Iraq & the Kurdistan Region. The Institute of Regional and International Studies (IRIS), the American University of Iraq-ulaimani, Kurdistan Region of Iraq

Beblawi H (1987) The rentier state in the Arab world. Arab Stud Q:383–398

Dilshad ZZ, Ahmed SO, Rahman B (2023) The effect of COVID-19 on the Kurdistan region government (KRG) economy. J Knowl Econ, pp 1–16. https://doi.org/10.1007/s13132-023-01130-1. Last Access June 12th 2023

Dixit P, Sharif RJM (2020) Standard Taxation Gaps & Reforms: a critical review of revenue policies of Kurdistan region of Iraq. Sriwijaya Int J Dynamic Econ Bus 3(4):341–354

Easterly W (2001) The lost decades: developing countries' stagnation in spite of policy reform 1980–1998. J Econ Growth 6(2):135–157

Ghaffoori A (2021) Understanding the institutionalization of corruption and the role of accounting in rentier states: a case study of Kurdistan Region of Iraq (KRI). (Doctoral dissertation, University of Essex)

Gunter M (2017) The Kurds; a modern history, 2nd edn. Markus Wiener, Princeton, pp 60–75

Gürbey G, Yildirim C (2019) Perspectives of an independent energy export policy of Iraqi Kurdistan. Iraqi Kurdistan's statehood aspirations: a political economy approach, pp 57–85

Gwartney J, Lawson R (2003) The concept and measurement of economic freedom. Eur J Polit Econ 19(3):405–430

Gwartney J, Lawson R, Hall J (2015) Economic freedom of the world, 2015. Annual Report
Gwartney J, Lawson R, Hall J, Murphy R (2020) Economic freedom of the world: 2020 annual report. Fraser Institute
Hadad H, Brandon LW (2017) The Iraqi Kurdish security apparatus: vulnerability and structure. Small Wars J, 2017. http://smallwarsjournal.com/jrnl/art/the-iraqi-kurdish-security-apparatus-vulnerability-and-structure. Last Access on April 2nd 2023
Hadfield C (2020) Research economic development of Kurdistan region through the telescope of diversification oil. Tennessee Res Int Social Sci 2(2):16–26
Haji IR, Mohamed MS (2022) The role of monetary policy indicators in achieving monetary stability in Iraq and The Kurdistan Region-Iraq for the period (1988–2019). TANMIYAT AL
Hall JC, Lawson RA (2014) Economic freedom of the world: an accounting of the literature. Contemp Econ Policy 32(1):1–19
Hama HH (2018) Partisan armed forces of Kurdistan regional government. J South Asian Middle Eastern Stud 41(2):38–51
Hansen ML, Howard JS, Louay C (2014a) Strategies for private-sector development and civil-service reform in the Kurdistan Region-Iraq. Rand Corporation
Hansen ML, Shatz HJ, Constant L, Smith AC, Kumar KB, Krull H, Usanov A, Dogo H, Martini J (2014b) Fostering private-sector development: taking advantage of private investment and reforming the enabling environment. In: Strategies for private-sector development and civil-service reform in the Kurdistan region—Iraq. Rand Corporation, pp 17–38. http://www.jstor.org/stable/10.7249/j.ctt6wq8hc.12. Last Access on December 23rd 2021
Hasan Q, Perot K (2021) Production sharing contracts and rentierism: reforming transparency gaps in Kurdistan's oil and gas contracts. Extract Indust Soc 8(2):1–7. https://doi.org/10.1016/j.exis.2021.100899. Last Access on November 27th 2022
Heckelman JC (2000) Economic freedom and economic growth: a short-run causal investigation. J Appl Econ 3(1):71–91
Heshmati A (2007) A model for industrial development of the federal region of Kurdistan: science and technology policy, instruments and institutions. IZA Discussion Papers, No. 3213, Institute for the Study of Labor (IZA), Bonn
Holmes RM Jr, Miller T, Hitt MA, Salmador MP (2013) The interrelationships among informal institutions, formal institutions, and inward foreign direct investment. J Manag 39(2):531–566
Huang Y (2010) Political institutions and financial development: an empirical study. World Dev 38(12):1667–1677
International Labor Organization (ILO) (2023) Data on employment. International Labor Organization. https://ilostat.ilo.org/topics/employment/. Last Access on April 6th 2023
Iraq, Ministry of Planning (2020) A Report on the Iraqi Economy (Arabic)
Irwani M (2015) Clientelism and implementing social security programmes in post-conflict Iraqi Kurdistan region. Cambridge Scholars Publishing
Jakšić M (2018) Inclusive institutions for sustainable economic development. J Central Bank Theory Practice 7(1):5–16
Jameel HN (2017) A case study of political corruption in conflict-affected societies (The Kurdistan Region of Iraq 2003–13). The University of Leicester. Thesis. https://hdl.handle.net/2381/39926. pp 13–54. Last Access on April 6th 2022
Jongerden J (2019) Governing Kurdistan: self-administration in the Kurdistan regional government in Iraq and the democratic federation of Northern Syria. Ethnopolitics 18(1):61–75
Joseph J, Sümer F (2019) Public sector reforms in the Kurdistan Region of Iraq: tackling the socially constructed barriers to change. Iraqi Kurdistan's statehood aspirations: a political economy approach, pp 125–153
Karem LE, Bayz HA, Darwesh MG, Ali DJ (2022) Impact of monetary and financial policies on the performance of commercial banks in Iraq-BBAC banks and Kurdistan international bank. Sci J Cihan Univ–Sulaimaniya 6(1):157–172

Karim BM, Aziz PH (2024) Legal disputes between Iraq and Turkey over the KRG's oil fields and the implications of the ICC Court's ruling on them. J Islam Asia 21(1):166–190. E-ISSN 2289-8077
Kaya Z (2018) Gender equality in Iraq and Iraqi Kurdistan. LSE Middle East Centre Blog (January 5). https://blogs.lse.ac.uk/mec/2018/01/05/gender-equality-in-iraq-and-iraqi-kurdistan/. Last Access on April 7th 2023
Khalid NS (2021) The state of the institutions of economic freedom in the Kurdistan region of Iraq. Economic Freedom of the World, 211
Kirmanc Ş (2013) Identity and nation in Iraq. Lynne Rienner Publishers, Incorporated
Knights M (2020) Iraqi Kurdistan: priority issues for international mediation. Middle East Research Institute. http://www.jstor.org/stable/resrep25306
Krasna J (2023) Autonomy curbed? Kurdish oil exports hit snags from Turkey and Baghdad. The Moshe Dayan Center for Middle Eastern and African Studies. https://www.fpri.org/article/2023/07/autonomy-curbed-kurdish-oil-exports-hit-snags-from-turkey-and-baghdad/. Last Access on 5th September 2024
Kurdistan Region's Statistics Office (2018) The demographic survey of the Kurdistan Region of Iraq. Kurdistan Regional Government. https://krso.gov.krd/content/upload/1/root/kurdistan-population-analysis-report-6-english-final-corrected-29052022.pdf. Last Access on April 4th 2023
Kurdistan Regional Government [KRG], General Directorate of Customs (2020) [Various information and data]. https://services.gov.krd/en/service/mof-14-en-0. Last Access on July 29th 2023
Kurdistan Regional Government [KRG], General Directorate of Taxes (2020) [Various information and data]. https://services.gov.krd/en/taxonomy/term/281. Last Access on July 18th 2023
Kurdistan Regional Government [KRG], Ministry of Planning (2013) Kurdistan region of Iraq 2020: a vision for the future. KRG
Marr P (2018) The modern history of Iraq. Routledge
Mills R (2023) Kurdistan gas and diversification. MEI.edu. https://www.mei.edu/publications/kurdistan-gas-and-diversification. Last Access on April 7th 2023
Mizuno N, Naito K, Okazawa R (2017) Inequality, extractive institutions, and growth in nondemocratic regimes. Public Choice 170:115–142
Mojab S, Hassanpour A (2021) Women of Kurdistan: a historical and bibliographic study, vol 4. Transnational Press London
Muhamad GM (2022) Private sector development analysis in post-conflict Kurdistan region of Iraq. UKH J Social Sci 6(2):19–32
Nuri ZM, Karakır İ (2022) The impact of 'rentier state' on economic development: the case of Kurdish regional government (KRG) of Iraq. Türkiye Politik Çalışmalar Dergisi 2(1):1–17
Omar H (2022) Kurdistan Regional Government (KRG) Importers and Exporters Union announced the trade volume of 2021, (Kurdish). Kurdiu.org. Available at https://www.kurdiu.org/ku/b/505414. Last Access on April 4th 2023
Oxford Analytica (2023) Imposing Iraqi fiscal discipline will face challenges. Emerald Expert Briefings, (oxan-db).
Palani K, Fazil S (2023) Fluid state-building in the Kurdistan region of Iraq: taking advantage of the 2003 US-led invasion. Int Peacekeeping 30(5):642–667
Prasetyo PE, Kistanti NR (2020) Human capital, institutional economics and entrepreneurship as a driver for quality & sustainable economic growth. Entrepr Sustain Issues 7(4):2575
Ramazan AP (2015) Economic hub Kurdistan Region's during the 2014 economic crisis. Polgari Szemle 11(1–3):1–8
Rawf M (2018) The salaries of KRG's employees. Draw Media. (Kurdish) https://drawmedia.net/page_detail?smart-id=130. Last Access on April 5th 2023
Romano D (2018) The oil imperative in the KRG. In: Routledge handbook on the Kurds. Routledge, pp 125–138
Rudaw (2024). *Rudaw.net*. Available at https://www.rudaw.net/english/kurdistan/140720241. Last Accessed on 07 September 2024

Rudaw Media Network (2020) [Various information and data]. https://www.rudaw.net. Last Access on April 4th 2023
Sabir RA (2022) The role of international financial reporting standards (IFRS) to encourage International Investments in the Kurdistan Region-Iraq: an applied study on a sample of banks listed in the Iraqi stock exchange. Acad J Nawroz Univ 11(1):30–46
Salam D (2024) The interrelationship between sovereignty, state building, and good governance: the case of the Kurdistan region. Democratization, 1–21
Salim BT, Abubakir DM, Yuryevna MS (2019) The economic relations of Kurdistan region (KRG) with Turkey and Russia. Vestnik MIRBIS 20(4):40–53
Sanandaji N (2018) The birthplace of capitalism: the Middle East. Timbro
Sherwani KH, Ahmad W (2023) An exploratory study of economic factors that hinder economic development of Kurdistan region. Int J Social Sci Educ Stud 10(1):82
Smith C, Shadarevian V (2016) Wilting in the Kurdish Sun: the hopes and fears of religious minorities in northern Iraq. This report was prepared for the United States Commission on International Religious Freedom between May and August.
Steketee O (2023) A macroeconomic analysis of Kurdish-iraqi relations, cfri. Available at https://cfri-irak.com/en/article/a-macroeconomic-analysis-of-kurdish-iraqi-relations-2023-12-27. Last Accessed on 07 September 2024
Sümer F, Joseph J (2017) Compatibility of the Kurdistan region of Iraq's institutions and economic development within Iraq. In: Anaid A, Tugdar EE (eds) Iraqi Kurdistan's statehood aspirations: a political economy approach. Palgrave Macmillan, pp 27–54
Sumer F, Joseph J (2018) The paradox of the Iraqi Kurdish referendum on independence: contradictions and hopes for economic prosperity. Br J Middle Eastern Stud 45(4):574–588
Toone JE (2012) Foreign direct Investment in Post-war Iraq: an Investor's introductory guide to the legal framework. Int Law Manag Rev 9:141
Transparency International (2020) Corruption perceptions index 2020. https://www.transparency.org/en/cpi/2020. Last Access on April 5th 2023
Wahab B (2014) Iraq and KRG energy policies: actors, challenges and opportunities. The Institute of Regional and International Studies, 14
World Bank (2015) The Kurdistan region of Iraq: assessing the economic and social impact of the Syrian conflict and ISIS. The World Bank
World Bank (2016) The Kurdistan region of Iraq – reforming the economy for shared prosperity and protecting the vulnerable: executive summary (English). X. Washington, DC: World Bank Group. http://documents.worldbank.org/curated/en/708441468196727918/Executive-summary. Last Access on May 18th 2022
World Bank (2018) Iraq – Kurdistan Regional Government (KRG): comprehensive review of legislation (transition phase report). World Bank (June 12). https://documents1.worldbank.org/curated/en/760851537392719616/pdf/KRG-Compreshensive-Review-of-Legislation-Transition-Phase-FINAL-14-June-2018.pdf. Last Access on April 4th 2023

Chapter 7
Political Challenges and Economic Development in the KRI

Political decisions have a significant role in quashing both social and economic inequalities. Policies that immediately affect the nature of income distribution, social welfare programs, and educational opportunities make independent contributions toward constructing the socioeconomic order of any nation. Governments that pay attention to inclusive development with well-designed social policies are, therefore, more likely to ensure a redistribution of resources and opportunities. In contrast, policies that ignore social welfare or go on to promote the income gap between members of society can lead to disgruntled societies and hamper the overall economic development. The intricate interplay of politics with economics thus demands informed governance elucidates (Acemoglu et al. 2005). Aware and responsive politicking decisions should be made to ensure a thriving and feasible economic environment.

The interaction between politics and economics in Kurdistan has unique characteristics, including the geopolitical situation and the historical features in this region. Anaid (2018) shows that the Kurdistan Region is concerned with the direct implications of crises on its economic development, trying to extricate itself from political crises. Political decisions at the regional level influence relations with the central government of Iraq, deeply impinging on financial stability and growth prospects.

Further, he argues that due to overdependence on oil revenue, the KRI economy has been exposed to fluctuations in world oil markets. That means fiscal health is susceptible to the region due to economic shock from fluctuations in oil prices. Further complications in planning and development initiatives arise from disruptions in streams related to the rival ambitions of Erbil and Baghdad to handle and take a share in oil revenues. These political instability and tensions, then, are the principal deterrent to foreign investment and hence affect the economic outlook for the region. It offers a broad perspective on subtle multifaceted political dynamics that go deep to influence the trajectory of economic development in this region from 2003 to 2020.

R. C. Biro, *Political Challenges of Economic Development in Rentier States*, Perspectives on Development in the Middle East and North Africa (MENA) Region, https://doi.org/10.1007/978-981-96-0563-7_7

7.1 Political Instability

This means that political instability is incoherent, unpredictable, or variable. It may well include frequent changes to the ruling, legislation, or institutional framework, together with internal disputes or power struggles. Instability affects not only how the government goes along but also erodes economic confidence, discourages investment efforts, and creates an unpredictable environment for companies or individuals to operate. In this respect, Abdullah (2018) notes that the perpetuation of conflicts and political instability in KRI, including those tensions with the central government of Iraq, has had an impact on the economic stability of that region. Indeed, such instability acts to deter foreign investment and generates ambiguity among businesses operating in this region. According to Bali (2016), it is a truism that political instability casts an extended inclusive shadow over economic development and creates impacts that resound within many societies, regions, and nations of the world. The several dimensions via which political instability has multifaceted and far-reaching influences on economic growth are those factors that shape, as it were, the trolley of a nation's prosperity and progress. Political instability hurts investment: domestic or foreign.

The risk and uncertainty that characterize political conditions discourage investors from risking their resources in such settings. To this end, political instability predominantly affects FDI since these investors fear the possibilities associated with a change in policy, expropriation, or civil upheavals that cause them to shift their investment to stable regions. Such reduced investment restricts capital formation, job creation, and expansion of businesses, hence retarding the overall economic growth of Iraqi Kurdistan (Nazeer and Masih 2017). The reduced investment in KRI restrains capital formation and constrains job creation and business expansion, thus hindering overall economic growth. There is a potential that this could affect a wide range as it reduces the chances of attracting FDI within the area under study would also be reduced.

For example, turmoil in the KRI has resulted in a sharp decrease in FDI from $5.2 billion in 2013 to $896.7 million in 2018, thus indicating both the pre-ISIS war and the post-ISIS war period. Declining FDI already suggests something significant: it reduces access to crucial capital, technology, and skills relevant to long-term economic growth and development. It is such a destructive cycle of decreased investment and restricted access to primary resources, which only gives weight to these economic challenges, making them objective obstacles for the development processes within the region. These are interlocked issues, underlining the importance of coming up with solutions that will work at the root causes of political uncertainty in the KRI, giving increased stability and predictability to the region so it allows intruding investments to be essential for creating jobs and expanding businesses. FDI initiates the trend, which can only transform into an ascending one by strategic refocus on the rebuilding of investor confidence through the adoption of economic developmental-friendly policies (Heshmati 2010).

Political instability in the KRI is a sure way of killing local and international trade. This is because it negatively influences supply chains, just like it does to the diplomatic ties between the KRI government and those of other nations across the globe. Such a situation creates barriers to trade by hindering the free flow of goods and services, diminishing exports and imports. Fluctuation in currency values makes international trade dynamics even more complicated and less attractive to businesses, introduces additional volatility.

Despite the rivalry these two countries share regarding oil, there is considerable economic participation in Kurdistan. For example, in 2012, Turkish companies invested an estimated $4.3 billion in the housing sector. The bilateral trade between Kurdistan and Turkey also increased manifolds from $4 billion in 2009 to $8.4 billion in 2012. The outcome of political unknowns in the KRI after 2013 reduced the bilateral trade to $8 billion in 2016 (Fidan 2016). That issue epitomizes how an unstable political structure has conducive and been destructive to the sustainable growth of the KRI. The several consequences and manifestations associated with political instability in the KRI have puffed up weak governance structures, corruption cases, and a compromised rule of law. These challenges slowed down investment in critical public infrastructure and essential services—consequently slowing down development while at the same time causing an erosion of public trust. The result of inefficient and unstable institutions was economic stagnation. This happened in the region after the financial crisis of 2014 as citizens of the KRI lost faith in the government and its governance in running financial affairs, resultant from the disposal of a 17 percent share of the national budget. Not only does political instability jeopardize economic development in the KRI, but it also influences human capital and, thus, social development.

It disrupts education systems, delivery of healthcare services, and social welfare programs that people of a nation need for better living. The diminished access to quality education and healthcare consequently leads to brain drain toward other countries that are socially stable, a less skilled and healthy workforce, and import of workers from other states like Bangladesh and the Philippines. In essence, the disrupted implication is felt in a reduced level of productivity and innovation needed for economic growth to be at its best in the region (Savasta 2019).

The complex interaction between political instability and socioeconomic problems in KRI becomes manifest with the impact of political unrest on the distribution of economic development. In such politically troubled areas of KRI, there is likely to be a marginalization of economic growth, hence worsening existing problems of poverty and inequality. In addition, the concentration of these opportunities in more stable regions themselves enhances social gaps, increases poverty, and provokes resentment within the population, further enhancing a self-sustaining cycle of instability in the area (Noori and Sidiq 2021).

Noori and Sidiq (2021) added that what strikes as a representation of the consequences of political instability on socioeconomic indicators in KRI is the poverty rate fluctuation. Indeed, in 2012, KRI attained its lowest historical poverty rate, only 3 percent. In contrast to the relatively high national poverty rate of 18 percent in Iraq, this represented a substantial difference. The trajectory of progress into action was set back by the economic crisis that occurred in 2014, and poverty resurfaced within the KRI. The poverty rate then rose once more to the high figure of 8.1 percent, underpinning the idea that good socioeconomic trends can be reversed in their tracks at very high speed by political and economic uncertainties. These are dynamic, linking political instability to the socioeconomic well-being of the Kurdistan Region. The political and economic problems of the Kurdistan region are highly complex and closely interlinked.

This means that governance and distribution of resources become scarce within a region, and the investing world fears to reach out to it, reducing access to external resources and expertise and making diversification from an oil-based economy quite challenging. Lack of local business growth retards job creation, further crippling economic diversity amidst continued political problems. Furthermore, the backlog in sufficient infrastructure development also reveals the necessity of efforts targeting the mitigation of the impact of political instability on central services that are at the core of creating an enabling environment favorable to economic growth. First, stability, and second, collaborative engagements represent strategies relevant to attracting foreign investment, diversifying the economy, and thus laying the ground for long-term growth and development in the KRI. The two giant political parties in Kurdistan—the KDP and the PUK—have a long history of rivalry, extending into the economic domain.

Both are trying to be in control of the economic resources, particularly the revenues from oil and natural gas, due to which there are always disputes between them for budget allocation and management of the resources. These differences have sadly delayed payments, led to financial hardship for KRG, and disrupted public services since the beginning of 2014 after 17 percent of their budget allocation by Baghdad was cut (Ala'Aldeen 2016). Ala'Aldeen learns that, in some capacity, this dual governance structure institutionalized by the KDP and PUK has induced administrative inefficiencies. This has brought about redundancies in government departments, causing distinct problems for effective service delivery. Furthermore, competition for control over the economic resources—the oil and gas revenues—translates into disputes over budget allocations, which hurts the ability of the KRG to invest in infrastructure and economic diversification. This has also made the KRI use 60 percent of its security budget to maintain separate Peshmerga forces affiliated with the KDP and PUK.

However, this has been at the cost of economic development due to these military expenditures.

Supplementing this, the differences between the KDP and PUK's Peshmerga forces have resulted in a lack of coordination in actions, particularly within the disputed areas. This creates security vacuums that negatively affect economic activities such as investment, farming, and trade (Paasche and Sidaway 2015). Political fragmentation has played at the heart of governance challenges, including corruption and inefficiency in public institutions. Corruption in government contracts portrays an evil institution where the procurement of services is compromised by political interests that never connect to public interests. In addition, most of the time, political rivalries and enmity retard the very implementation of infrastructure development for health and education, thus retarding economic growth and the welfare of individuals (Anaid 2018).

Furthermore, one of the strong legacies configuring current economic dynamics within Iraqi Kurdistan is internal political fragmentation. The power struggle and deep historical tension between the KDP and PUK energies have had severe impacts on the course of economic development in the KRI. These conflicts entrench a lack of cooperation on crucial matters about the economy, delay decision-making processes, and establish an atmosphere of political uncertainty. For instance, the 2006 Erbil Agreement was a historical power-sharing pact negotiated with support from the United States, and it was to combine the KDP and PUK into one government. This agreement has become very problematically effective in realization because of the disagreement about providing critical positions and powers. This political instability shifted focus from pressing economic development matters to such disputes (Asadi 2013).

7.1.1 Security Considerations

The main perpetrator, apart from in certain instances, has been ISIS, and such threats have continuously plagued the Kurdistan Region.

Though territorial holdings were lost, ISIS continued to launch intermittent attacks and partake in insurgent activities across the region against the security forces and civilians. These security threats have entailed continuous counterterrorism efforts and intelligence operations to prevent further assaults. The need, however, to maintain a robust security apparatus as a counter to the continuing ISIS insurgency has significantly siphoned off critical financial and human resources from the very economic development projects that are so sorely needed, thereby slowing down overall progress in the region. In addition to the security threats, insecurity along the borders of the KRI has also been exacerbated by cross-border military operations carried out by its neighboring countries, particularly Turkey and Iran. These activities have, in most cases, been associated with the disruption of economic activities and the displacement of local populations.

For example, Turkey has had military confrontations with the PKK in northern Iraq, where infrastructure has been destroyed and trade routes disrupted, not to mention that communities have also been displaced. Spillover effects to border areas have meant trading, and farming have proved to test, ultimately creating economic problems in these areas as well (Gunter 2017). It's a holistic balancing act required to address these intricate security issues. This means balancing the resource allocation to security with that of economic development in finding ways whereby security can be maintained while investing in infrastructure, education, and healthcare. Algebraic engagement for diplomatic methods with neighboring countries to discuss security concerns and seek peaceful resolutions on cross-border issues is essential for promoting regional stability.

Resilience offsets part of the economic impact of cross-border operations and security threats that border communities face, curbing trade. Biro added more weight in 2019: improving security and stability is one of the fundamentals needed to attract foreign direct investment and private sector participation, which will drive growth. This is a complex balancing to ensure safety and stability while meeting the financial needs of the population, which requires an equally comprehensive approach for the solution of various challenges that the Kurdistan Region of Iraq faces. Based on these abovementioned reasons, the KRI has failed in the practical application of the approaches.

7.2 Oil Dependency

Such countries that depend on oil to drive their economies and energy supply are susceptible to political and internal instability. The oil sector is of essence to the economies of several rentier countries, such as Russia and Iraq, and a contraction or fall in demand may have dim prospects for the future. In this regard, the extent of dependency on oil, with the combination of international debt, may also impact the rise of belief-based economic fluctuations. In the case of Iraq, changes in oil prices have had mixed effects on monetary stability, negatively impacting the exchange rate and contributing to inflation rates, which aligns with the theory of the resource curse. Similarly, Iraq's economic dependency on oil has distorted its economic structure and exposed it to geopolitical weaknesses. Therefore, reducing oil dependency and promoting diversification into non-oil sectors, such as agriculture, is imperative to achieve sustained economic growth and stability.

The finding of significant natural resources in the KRI has raised important questions about whether the country would thrive from this oil and gas discovery or whether it will instead become a burden, similar to what has happened to many other oil-rich nations (Ross 2001). It is widely believed that nations with more resources than needs have the capacity to build their economies more than those with less resources. This assertion has been validated in various parts of the world, with Norway, Canada, Australia, the Emirates, and Qatar. These countries have effectively leveraged their natural resources by investing in infrastructure upgrades and implementing comprehensive welfare systems. These systems encompass top-tier institutions along with provisions for free education and healthcare, contributing to their overall societal well-being and economic prosperity (Sachs and Warner 1997).

Nevertheless, a substantial number of resource-rich nations, such as Nigeria, Iraq, Libya, Sudan, Yemen, Venezuela, Angola, and the Democratic Republic of Congo have grappled with the adverse consequences of their natural resources, succumbing to the infamous "resource curse" (Gelb 2014). There are political and economic aspects to this curse. From an economic perspective, a nation that depends heavily on the export of gas and oil is vulnerable to shocks to its finances brought on by changes in the pricing of these resources on global markets. Due to this susceptibility, the government is forced to borrow heavily as a safeguard against price reductions, making it more difficult for it to undertake social programs without running large budget deficits.

The region has abundant oil reserves and has made significant efforts to increase oil production and attract investments. However, this reliance on oil revenues has put the region in an unstable position, where fluctuations in global oil prices have a disproportionate impact on its economic stability. The KRI's weakness to global oil price volatility was evident during the oil price crash in 2014. As global oil prices fell sharply, the region experienced a severe economic crisis. This meant they suffered a heavy decline in regional government revenues due to oil revenues. Salary cuts of between 50–70 percent, depending on the level of the employer and civil servants' delayed salaries are contributing to disruptions in public service delivery. The crisis has thrust open the region to external market forces and underlined the need for economic diversification (Mills 2023). The case of 2014 shows the risks associated with high dependence on oil revenues. At that time, the economy of the Kurdistan Region had never been so profoundly in turmoil, thus teaching them a lesson to have diversified economic strategies. This shall strengthen the region against shocks of global markets, reducing the effect on financial stability. Emphasizing economic diversification remains a critical aspect of long-term economic planning, which is necessary to ensure sustainable and stable growth.

7.3 Corruption

Political barriers have obstructed economic growth in Iraqi Kurdistan. Oil-dependent states often face corruption, exacerbated by poor management and strategies of dominant groups. Additionally, Kurdistan, being conflict-prone, has endured numerous clashes with successive Iraqi governments and internal strife among armed groups and political factions. This persistent turmoil has significantly impacted Kurdistan's political and economic development (Shareef and Kiani 2020).

Research on various post-conflict situations suggests that corruption can arise when wartime power structures persist in the post-conflict period. Rich natural resources often lead to wealth concentration within the state, creating a rentier economy. While not all resource-dependent states are corrupt, reliance on resource income can create conditions conducive to corruption, such as budget fraud in Iraq. The governmental and economic frameworks before and after civil wars in Kurdistan have created corruption opportunities. The KDP and PUK, two powerful parties, agreed to share power and wealth equally, disregarding corruption risks. This power-sharing model incentivized corruption, with both parties exploiting government positions and resources within their joint administrations (Bali 2018).

Though post-civil war governance brought some peace among parties, it also increased the tendency to politicize fragile public institutions, hindering the establishment of effective state institutions. This analysis explored three cases where the post-conflict environment in the KRI allowed ruling parties to misuse public positions and national wealth for political and personal gain, to the public's detriment. Corruption in the KRI has been a contentious issue for at least a decade, acknowledged by key KRG figures, leaders of ruling and opposition parties, journalists, and civil society activists.

Given Iraq's consistent ranking among the top ten most corrupt countries globally by organizations like the Transparency Index, this acknowledgment is unsurprising. Argues that powerful groups in post-conflict settings often control recovery processes to serve their interests. In the KRI, political parties were crucial in building public institutions post-1991 uprising but failed to empower these institutions during the transition to serve public interest and resist corruption. Instead, ruling parties turned public institutions into tools for their political agendas.

Prominent KRI leaders, mainly from the KDP and PUK, have used their powers to selectively provide public services to their party members, following a model of particularism (Abdullah and Gray 2022). KRG leaders, especially from the KDP and PUK, have exploited the *Tazkia* process to appoint numerous party loyalists, excluding non-political citizens and members of other parties from these benefits for years. Although the sixth KRG cabinet attempted to institutionalize a recruitment system in 2011, later cabinets reverted to partisan appointments by 2013, showing a lack of official recruitment processes for years (Jameel 2017).

The ruling parties have also monopolized key administrative positions, reserving significant ministries for themselves and assigning few to other parties. Even non-political roles like school heads, public university chancellors, deans, and department heads were influenced, with appointments favoring individuals supported by the KDP in the Yellow Zone and the PUK in the Green Zone. This absolute particularism made political affiliation the sole criterion for positions within KRG institutions (Paasche 2016).

The analysis concludes that ruling parties implemented these politicized measures to secure exclusive access to public institutions through their members, who protected party interests and sometimes engaged in illegal favoritism. Instances of officials granting favors, such as housing and academic opportunities, to party members highlight corrupt reciprocal relationships, bypassing laws for personal benefit. It also comments on the irregularities in offering extraordinary pensions and salaries to politicians, party dignitaries, and political institutions that are carried out by breaking laws. These practices—known to be used at elections to preserve majorities for ruling parties—violate the rules and regulations of public service.

7.3.1 Political Clientelism

It reveals how parties practice political patronage and clientelism by exchanging public jobs, positions, and financial perks for support. In so doing, it establishes a system of political corruption benefiting KDP and PUK members at the expense of non-members. It highlights factors that perpetuate political corruption within the weaknesses of public institutions, which permitted discretionary power to emerge without oversight by the KRG leaders. The central KRG authorities followed secretive processes to favor their co-partisans to attain continuous support. This furnished the grounds for them to use discriminatory standards by political affiliation, not principles of equal treatment and access to public services as universally mandated. This would have been difficult if government institutions did not play a crucial role in society.

Due to limited opportunities outside government institutions for jobs and salaries, especially in the absence of comprehensive plans for other sectors by KRG cabinets, the ruling parties attracted individuals by offering various privileges to their members. This reinforced KRG's role as the main provider of goods and services. The government's dominant position in service provision, along with the impartial functioning of government institutions, gave the ruling parties more opportunities to exploit public services for their political benefits (Irwani 2015).

However, the politicization of public services could have faced significant challenges with a functional system of checks and balances. The Kurdistan Parliament (KP) lacked effectiveness in holding KRG leaders accountable, as the KDP and PUK, along with their allies, consistently held a majority of seats to thwart any attempts challenging their governments. This indicated a deficiency in political accountability, allowing key officials to misuse their positions without fear of official scrutiny. These findings underscore the absence of official accountability and the ineffectiveness of monitoring institutions in the KRI, aligning with post-conflict studies highlighting issues like dysfunctional public institutions, a lack of political will for reform, and the dominance of political figures over fragile institutions, transforming them into tools to serve personal interests (Bali 2018).

The PDK and PUK dominate the public sector in the KRI. It has held a highly tight historical grip on key government positions and institutions. Through giants of government, this control provides the ability described in Chap. 3 to maintain authority over the distribution of jobs, contracts, and resources to their supporters. Furthermore, extending these power-sharing agreements to the regional government level has resulted in a sharing of government ministries and resources by party affiliation. This continues to entrench its influence within the public sector. The long-standing rivalry between KDP and PUK finds expression in government institutions, each trying to wrest control from the other. This can lead to inefficiency, as appointments and promotions are usually determined by political allegiance rather than qualification. Consequently, this led to mismanagement, resource wastage, and corruption, as people can use the position to their advantage (Irwani 2015). Furthermore, political parties dominate everything, allowing no space to accommodate effective accountability mechanisms, thus making it hard for the checks and balances to work effectively as anticipated.

Political decisions overwhelmingly influence the formation of the economic landscape in the Kurdistan Region regarding both the public and private sectors. The regional government had to rely heavily on some revenues collected from exports of oil and natural gas. This had portrayed an allegiant reliance on discouraging growth of a diversified private sector. As a result, the KRI has been exposed to economic weaknesses, mainly due to oscillations in the global oil price and market situation, such as the economic contraction in 2014 that took place and hampered any further economic development within the region (Joseph and Sümer 2019). Furthermore, Joseph and Sümer pointed out that in the KRI, adhering to the rentier state theory has led to some significant social and economic repercussions.

Furthermore, the negligence of the private sector has been a contributory factor to high unemployment rates, which is quite common in the youth. The wealth and opportunities continue getting concentrated on just a few well-politically connected individuals at the expense of regional social and economic inequalities. Therefore, against the KRI backdrop, sorting out these issues through enhanced development of the private sector will lead to more inclusive and stable economies.

7.3.2 *Media Corruption*

The literature on rentier states believes institutions, including the media, are partial to wrongdoings manipulated by ruling elites in these countries (Hafez 2009). Now, the KRI of influential individuals' acts, especially in formation concerning the specific case of media organizations, fits a broader pattern typical for rentier states. The susceptibility of the media to corruption is connected to economic conditions and deeper dynamics of the rentier state in the KRI.

The concept of economic development that describes rentier nations can often be defined by heavy dependence upon revenues involving natural resources, such as oil. The ownership of media channels by ruling elites can be seen as part of a larger scheme to hold on to the twin levers of economic and political power. Media institutions are longevity conduits for their energy, for they not only are financial beneficiaries of the ruling establishment in terms of direct government dole or political party funding but also serve as means for these elites to perpetuate their influence. Such media manipulation furthers the economic and political ends set by the ruling parties and forms part of a more outstanding design of corruption (Gillies 2020).

This was a clear manifestation of the economic aspect of narrative and control of information flow, as many media stations were opened for KRI. Media institutions hence become tools that the ruling elites use in shaping public opinions meant to protect the political status quo and further economic interests linked to resource windfalls. The symbiotic relationship that the economic and political elites have, owing to the dynamics of the rentier state in which rich resources are usually accrued, further enhances the vulnerability of media institutions to corruption.

The mixture of economic interests and media influence within rentier states, like the KRI, undermines the latter's capacity to behave as an independent auditor. The media's professionalism and independence are compromised when they align with political parties, as party allegiance precedes journalistic integrity (Gharib 2016). Consequently, the media's capacity to function as an effective activist or whistleblower against corruption is compromised, as its function becomes intricately linked with advancing the governing elite's interests.

This has resulted in a decline in media quality and introduced political bias into their coverage. Such a media outlet would be incapable of performing a practical monitoring function. Most press networks rely on financial support. They are either unregulated KRG funding sources (e.g., KDP and PUK media and shadow networks) or party funding sources (specific channels of the governing parties and other political parties). The KRG has intervened in establishing and operating incumbent and covert press media outlets. These outlets have primarily received funding from the government, which has not implemented formalized processes or regulations (Ismaeli 2015). Consequently, ruling parties have benefited from varying financial inequality among media organizations. Their channels have secured funding from the public treasury, whereas other organizations, most notably the private press, were dealing with financial difficulties.

The personal media significantly contributed to the exposure of corruption and controversies involving corrupt figures. Nevertheless, the absence of a functional monitoring system rendered their endeavors futile. While their consistent reporting on corruption may have increased public consciousness regarding the issue, it nevertheless inadvertently contributed to its expansion. Due to the near irrationality of the system of checks and balances, certain media outlets' coverage of corruption may inadvertently incentivize non-corrupt personnel within public institutions to engage in corrupt activities. The political control exerted by the KDP and PUK over the institutions of the KRI throughout the last two decades of transition has led to the absence of a functional monitoring process (Faris 2023). These political parties have actively intervened in nearly all public affairs and institutions, intending to establish and control them to advance their political dominance in the area and safeguard their political interests.

In summary, the preponderance of media networks in the KRI have ceased to serve as watchdogs of corruption and have instead integrated themselves into the corruption sphere, thereby creating a more conducive environment for the expansion of corruption in the region. They have continued to operate with funds obtained unlawfully and to the detriment of the public interest of KRG. These circumstances provided fertile ground for corruption as the fund, to divert public attention from corrupt cases, responded by ignoring corruption and even engaging in personal attacks against one another in the press. The government-funded press was heavily influenced by the ruling political parties, making KRG's attempt to reform the sector fruitless.

7.3.3 Political Party Funding and Politicization of Business

Despite implementing Law No. 17 by the KP to regulate political parties, for over twenty years, the lack of regulation in party funding persisted. This advancement was not made by the KP until 2014 because of intraparty conflict, civil conflict, and administrative polarization. Partisan financing has become an area where opportunities for corruption have been created during the Kurdistan transitional period. Since the enactment of Law No. 17 in 1993, when the KRG started offering public subsidies to political parties, regulatory frameworks failed to effectively prevent corruption. What's more, the distribution of these subsidies lacked proper supervision. Influential government officials used their position to direct public subsidies; this helped them ensure that their parties retained control over the KRI (Mustafa 2021). The possibility of misspending of public resources is hinted at by the fact that there is no law on financing parties, coupled with a lack of proper rules and supervision, and an expansive space is given to powerful government officials regarding allocating public subsidies to political parties. This could also have involved, to maintain hegemony, the diversion of public funds elsewhere that may have been allocated to critical public services or economic development initiatives otherwise by dominant parties.

Sabir and Hassan (2020) pointed out that in KRI, loose laws governing party affiliation to businesses facilitated the expansion of political corruption into the business realm. Dominant political parties and their most powerful leaders have primarily engaged in business commerce and used power to secure exclusive control over super-profitable projects. They would then acquire financial riches for themselves and their parties to consolidate their continued hold on political power. Public officials, influential members of the governing parties, and their relatives exploited their or their party's position to extract monetary compensation from other business investors in exchange for work permits and assistance in establishing their enterprises. Monopolies can lead to decreased efficiency, limited choices for consumers, and hinder the overall economic growth of the Kurdistan Region.

The politicization process in the KRI greatly obstructed the development of political opposition, preventing parties from establishing themselves as credible alternatives and opponents to the ruling party. The ruling parties exert significant influence over the government, national institutions, military, and finances, limiting the opportunities for opposition parties to attempt to alter the prevailing situation (Hama and Ali 2020). The significant influence of ruling parties over key institutions, including government, national institutions, military, and finances, raises concerns about checks and balances. Such influence can lead to policies prioritizing political interests over broader economic development goals, potentially hindering long-term sustainable growth.

7.4 Economic Diversification in the KRI

Excessive dependence on oil and gas resources may adversely affect the economy. It can lead people or organizations to prioritize controlling access to natural resources for their own advantage rather than participating in fair competition. Furthermore, in light of the urgent requirement to mitigate climate change-induced emissions and the depletion of oil and gas reserves, there is a possibility that worldwide demand for these resources will decrease (Matallah 2020).

Matallah (2020) also adds that economic diversification is necessary for oil-rich nations to ensure sustained economic growth. However, economic diversification may also challenge the political influence of oil and gas resource-controlling elites. Although there is widespread agreement that economic diversification is advantageous for resource-dependent nations, its potential to impede the impact of the privileged has not been adequately examined. Hence, it becomes extremely important to identify whether economic diversification can be an effective way to reduce overdependency on oil and gas and, therefore, to hamper the control of an elite.

The KRI has attempted to diversify its economy by lessening its dependence on the oil sector and promoting the development of non-oil sectors, revenues, and exports. In 2016, the Ministry of Planning set out a diversified package for structural economic reforms with the "Kurdistan Region of Iraq 2020: The Vision for the Future" to steer this economy away from an oil-dependent one. It focused on the development of just three major sectors, which were agriculture, manufacturing, and others like tourism (Hadfield 2020). At this point, with all the above efforts put in place, oil remains the region's primary export. It accounts for more than 80 percent of the country's income.

Hadfield (2020) pxuts it that KRI's political elites are cornered between the national economic gain from diversification and the associated political cost in terms of loss of power due to the growth of an independent private sector. Instead, the elites, in a bid to remain relevant, have had their influence expand to other enterprises in the broad economy, away from natural resources. This approach thus restrains economic diversification to avoid threatening their interests as well as protecting them against political competition from the private sector. There are immense restrictions on the independence of KRI, especially on the choices of economy, innovation, and diversification. The region's dependence on the central government on crucial aspects like budgetary allocations, hydrocarbon revenues, and formulations of economic policy is a significant challenge.

The overriding dependence described above significantly weakens the autonomous ability of the KRI to implement comprehensive development policies (Sherwani and Ahmad 2023).

The complexity of such interdependence underlines how compelling a reason the region needs to develop better control over its economic path. Increasing control over budget resources and hydrocarbon revenues is one of the critical challenges for the KRG in diversification and financial innovation. Furthermore, limited possibilities for contributing to the course of economic policies are a serious obstacle to further development and diversification of the KRG. Very often, central government policy frameworks guide the determination of financial incentives, regulatory environments, and policies.

The absence of autonomy imposed on the KRG diminishes its ability to tailor all economic strategies according to the unique needs and potentials of the Kurdistan Region (Aga and Hussein 2023). Besides having fiscal authority, it is challenging to have the power to influence economic policies relevant to the regional setup. Such strategic policy adjustments should be made together with promoting political stability, intergovernmental cooperation, and more inclusive decision-making processes. One serious challenge that the Kurdistan region is confronted with is a significant problem popularly known as the resource curse, from which it primarily suffers because of enormous oil and gas reserves that are present therein. Excessive dependence on oil and gas exports has made the economy vulnerable to unpredictable fluctuations in global oil prices, impeding the diversification of critical sectors necessary for sustainable development. In addition, since their becoming part of national heritage, their administration has been marked by continuous conflicts with the central government, principally over revenue distribution and the control of hydrocarbon fields. Concurrently, comprehensive economic reforms have been substantially hampered by political tensions in the region. Instability has resulted from power struggles, internal divisions, and a need for more agreement among various political factions, all of which have impeded the execution of sustainable and cohesive economic strategies (Nuri and Karakır 2022).

Dixit and Rzgar (2018) argued that the political complexities surrounding economic diversification in the KRI arise from the perceived challenge it presents to the prevailing power structure. A trade-off exists between the financial advantage of diversification and the potential loss of political influence due to the emergence of an autonomous private sector for the political elites in the KRI. A socioeconomic foundation independent of governing elites could be produced through economic diversification, threatening their patronage system. Consequently, the ruling class has expanded its dominion beyond natural resources to encompass businesses in the broader economy, limiting the scope and depth of economic diversification to protect their gains from numerous financial endeavors and eliminate any possibility of the private sector challenging their political authority. This strategy is regarded as counterproductive and runs the risk of inciting challenges to the political legitimacy of the governing parties. Addressing the political limitations that impede economic diversification would almost certainly necessitate completely restructuring the settled and resistant-to-change system of political favoritism.

For Kurdistan to achieve sustainable growth, economic diversification, which entails the expansion of sectors unrelated to hydrocarbon revenue, is vital. It is critical to establish a sustainable and substantial income level by focusing on the agriculture sector and developing a modern economy that is not dependent on energy. The volatility of oil prices and the inability of the energy sector to generate adequate employment opportunities in the Iraqi Kurdistan have underscored the importance of diversification. The dependence on hydrocarbon revenues impacts employment opportunities, external and economic positions, and overall development rates (Joseph and Sümer 2019).

Diversification assumes significance for multiple rationales, including mitigating risks linked to oil price volatility, facilitating economic progress, restricting the repercussions of oil-related uncertainties, and generating employment prospects for the swiftly expanding domestic labor force. As hydrocarbon revenues provide more than 90 percent of state revenue, the KRI and Iraq's finances are under significant threat. The costs associated with fighting the Islamic State, providing for internally displaced persons, and sustaining an expanded public sector have placed increased strain on the Iraqi economy. As a result, it is imperative to undertake immediate and comprehensive measures to implement structural changes to ensure long-term resilience and resolve the immediate revenue shortfall.

Economically, most of the populace of Kurdistan is reliant on the government, which is significantly reliant on hydrocarbon revenues. The region's economy is closely wired to the vagaries of the energy sector. With the financial situation so dire in the area, priority must be shifted to the development of a diversified economy—with an eye on agriculture—to reduce overdependence on oil money. But diversification is not easy. Low levels of agricultural technology, lack of skilled workforce, high illiteracy rates—as near as one can judge—even a tiny market are some constraints on progress in the non-oil sector. These pending challenges need to be surmounted in an environment where regional instability, terrorism, conflict legacy, and political unpredictability are reigning in Iraq. The agriculture sector in Kurdistan is highly viable to diversify, as seen by its past prosperity pre-2003. If the means of livelihood shift from the monocultural oil dominant industry to the agricultural sector, then the government can end budget deficits and decrease the dependence of the populace on the government for financing. This causes a more sustainable and resilient economy for the Kurdistan region (Eklund et al. 2016).

Eklund et al. (2016) further commented that several challenges are faced by the agricultural industry in Kurdistan, of which one major issue is that service sectors are overshadowing it.

Such negligence toward agriculture may negatively impact the economic development of the region, especially in terms of self-sufficiency. This should arouse serious concern about extension, education, training, and research since their proper execution will increase productivity and efficiency in the agricultural sector. Furthermore, the impact of the energy sector has meant that urbanization and changes in the structure of the rural population have undermined rural policy, fostered Dutch disease within the region, and created a plethora of problems within its agricultural sector. These problems prevent growth and any potential economic contribution to Kurdistan. The sector primarily consists of family-run farms that lack organization. In 2008, a development plan was proposed to promote a partnership between the government and farmers to diversify the economy. The plan aimed to invest \$10 billion over ten years, but it encountered numerous obstacles.

The budget of \$50 million was deemed insufficient, raising concerns about transparency and accountability. The plan lacked clarity on how to create a conducive environment, and implementing it required costly border control measures. Migration to urban areas and the economic interests of major parties, particularly the KDP and PUK, hampered the plan. External influences, particularly from Turkey and Iran, further complicate matters. Furthermore, the elimination of import taxes that protected local producers resulted in the collapse of local production. Turkey and Iran's geopolitical considerations contributed to political dependency. Despite recent efforts, the agriculture sector's contribution to GDP has declined from 20 percent in the 1970s to 4 percent (Abdullah and Gray 2022).

7.5 Summary

The KRI's economic development is substantially impeded by political instability, which restricts employment creation, capital formation, and foreign investment. This decline in FDI has a broad impact, including losing access to the necessary capital, technology, and expertise for long-term development. Due to the interdependence of these concerns, it is critical to resolve the underlying factors contributing to political instability in the KRI. A stable and predictable environment offers the surest way to encourage business expansion, attract increased investment, and stimulate the creation of jobs.

This presages the challenges the KRI faces in achieving sustainable development, particularly considering that starting from 2013, political instability has marked a decline in bilateral commerce. Other areas that political instability affects are human capital and social development, which result in a brain outflow, increased destitution, and a less professional workforce. Such politically unstable regions usually pitch economic development to the periphery, exacerbating the extant problems of poverty and inequality. For this reason, stability must be put at the apex to handle the complex political and economic challenges that face KRI; this entails collaborative effort and addressing infrastructure development, resource allocation, and governance matters.

Severe challenges of corruption exist in the KRI due to the post-conflict situation. The actions and policies of the ruling parties can be said to have exacerbated this problem. Their power-sharing agreement tends to promote corruption, leading to the favoring of party members by public institutions. Unfortunately, media coverage has proved to be in the hands of the ruling elite and is hence not independent and responsible. This brings forth the situation wherein no proper system of checks and balances exists due to which resources are misallocated, funding irregularities, and commercial monopolies exist. The hegemony of the ruling parties threatens to impair economic growth in the regional grassroots. Long-term efforts to strengthen institutions and comprehensive governance reforms, with a serious commitment to transparency, are urgently required to deal with corruption effectively. Otherwise, this would sustain and harm the public and economic progress in the KRI. It is further observed that the constraints on political opposition, because of the ruling parties' strong influence over important institutions, raise concerns about necessary checks and balances for long-term growth.

However, corruption of that nature could be reduced by comprehensive reforms in governance, institutional strengthening, and regulatory frameworks regarding transparency and accountability. Otherwise, the region risks getting trapped into a cycle of corruption—one that does not help economic development and undermines the general well-being of its people. Over time, numerous challenges have emerged to diversification efforts aimed at building resilience and sustainability in the KRI economy. Such high dependence on only oil and gas is not only undermining the development of other industries but also making the region more susceptible to unpredictable global oil price fluctuations.

Despite the revisit to diversify its economy, over 80 percent of the KRI's revenue still accrues from petroleum. A dilemma where political leaders in the KRI face a problem is whether they should embrace economic diversification with its accruing benefits or maintain control and power by retaining a tight grip over natural resource sectors. This brings along the control strategy that restricts the magnitude of diversification so as not to alter current and political benefits. The resource curse conflicts with the central government, and inner political tensions complicate the process of economic diversification. The literature discusses that Kurdistan Region must solve these issues to reduce the vulnerability of oil price fluctuations and to promote sustainable growth.

One area for diversification is the agriculture sector. Still, some political factors, like a lack of technology, shortage of skilled labor, and market constraints, hindered it from contributing to the growth of the economy of the region. Significantly, political instability in the KRI alienates FDI attraction and international commerce. Instability also characterizes human capital and social development, leading to a brain drain and entrenching poverty and inequality. This further challenging corruption in the region is based on what is termed a power-sharing agreement between the ruling parties and touches on the institutions, media, and economic growth.

Governance, effective reforms, and greater openness are now critical in breaking the cycle of corruption. By equal measure, the entrenchment of ruling parties—in whichever form—weakens political opposition: the check on and balance that can help assure long-term growth. Achieving economic diversification is essential, yet political elites face a dilemma between economic benefits and potential loss of political power. The resource curse, conflicts, and internal tensions complicate diversification efforts. Addressing these challenges, especially in the agriculture sector, is imperative for the region to reduce vulnerability, promote sustainable growth, and overcome economic hurdles.

References

Abdullah FH (2018) The political system in Iraqi Kurdistan: party rivalries and future perspectives. Asian Affairs 49(4):606–624

Abdullah S, Gray T (2022) White collar crimes and corruption at border crossings in the Kurdistan region in Iraq: causes, effects and challenges for reform. J Kurdistani Strat Stud. https://doi.org/10.54809/jkss.vi2.76. Last Access on 6 July 2021

Acemoglu D, Johnson S, Robinson JA (2005) Institutions as a fundamental cause of long-run growth. In: Aghion P, Durlauf S (eds) Handbook of economic growth. North-Holland, Amsterdam. https://doi.org/10.1016/S1574-0684(05)01006-3. Last Access on 6 July 2021

Aga AAK, Hussein JS (2023) The impact of financial globalization on economic growth in the Kurdistan region of Iraq: an empirical investigation. Manag Account Rev 22(3)

Ala'Aldeen D (2016) State-building in a fragmented Kurdistan region of Iraq. Middle East Res Inst 3(13):1–3

Anaid A (2018) The nature of political economy challenges of the Kurdistan region of Iraq. In: Iraqi Kurdistan's statehood aspirations: a political economy approach. Springer, Cham, pp 9–26

Asadi A (2013) The territorial conflict between the central Iraqi government and the Kurdistan regional government. In: Wahlers G (ed) Elections and transitions in the Islamic world. Konrad Adenauer Stiftung, pp 50–80. http://www.jstor.org/stable/resrep10105.6. Last Access on April 8th 2022
Bali A (2016) The political development of Iraqi Kurdistan. Int J Polit Sci Dev 4(6):208–215
Bali A (2018) Communication tools to fight bureaucratic corruption in Iraqi Kurdistan: a case study. SAGE Open 8(4):2158244018811185
Dixit P, Rzgar R (2018) Diversification of economy—an insight into economic development with special reference to Kurdistan's oil economy and agriculture economy. J Public Admin Financ Law 14:105–117
Eklund L, Persson A, Pilesjö P (2016) Cropland changes in times of conflict, reconstruction, and economic development in Iraqi Kurdistan. Ambio 45(1):78–88
Faris J (2023) Media capture: the political reality of media undergoing a transitional democracy: the case of the Kurdistan Region in Iraq after 2003 (Doctoral dissertation, University of Antwerp)
Fidan C (2016) Turkish business in the Kurdistan region of Iraq. Turkish Policy Quart 14(4):117–126
Gelb A (2014) Should Canada worry about a resource curse? 7(2):1–23. Retrieved 8 September 2021, from https://www.policyschool.ca/wp-content/uploads/2016/03/resource-curse-gelb.pdf
Gharib AH (2016) Political communication and the media in Kurdistan. Sheffield Hallam University (United Kingdom)
Gillies A (2020) Corruption trends during Africa's oil boom, 2005 to 2014. Extract Indust Society 7(4):1171–1181
Gunter M (2017) The Kurds; a modern history, 2nd edn. Markus Wiener, Princeton, pp 60–75
Hadfield C (2020) Research economic development of Kurdistan region through the telescope of diversification oil. Tennessee Res Int Social Sci 2(2):16–26
Hafez Z (2009) The culture of rent, factionalism, and corruption: a political economy of rent in the Arab world. Contemp Arab Affairs 2(3):458–480
Hama HH, Ali O (2020) De-politicization of the partisan forces in the Kurdistan region of Iraq. National Ident 22(2):111–131
Heshmati A (2010) The economy of southern Kurdistan. Nova Science, Hauppauge, NY
Irwani M (2015) Clientelism and implementing social security programmes in post-conflict Iraqi Kurdistan region. Cambridge Scholars Publishing
Ismaeli A (2015) The role of the media in developing democracy In Kurdistan: a study of Rudaw journalists perspectives, notions and attitudes
Jameel HN (2017) A case study of political corruption in conflict-affected societies (The Kurdistan Region of Iraq 2003–13). The University of Leicester. Thesis. https://hdl.handle.net/2381/39926. pp 13–54. Last Access on April 6th 2022
Joseph J, Sümer F (2019) Public sector reforms in the Kurdistan Region of Iraq: tackling the socially constructed barriers to change. Iraqi Kurdistan's statehood aspirations: a political economy approach, pp 125–153
Matallah S (2020) Economic diversification in MENA oil exporters: understanding the role of governance. Resourc Policy 66:101602
Mills R (2023) Kurdistan gas and diversification. MEI.edu. https://www.mei.edu/publications/kurdistan-gas-and-diversification. Last Access on April 7th 2023
Mustafa SD (2021) Iraqi Kurdistan independence referendum: political parties, opportunity and timing. Br J Middle Eastern Stud 48(5):890–907
Nazeer AM, Masih M (2017) Impact of political instability on foreign direct investment and economic growth: evidence from Malaysia
Noori NN, Sidiq KA (2021) Poverty as a consequence of structural imbalances and state-led growth failure in Iraq and the Kurdistan region (1970–2020). J Kurdistani Strat Stud 9
Nuri ZM, Karakır İ (2022) The impact of 'rentier state' on economic development: the case of Kurdish regional government (KRG) of Iraq. Türkiye Politik Çalışmalar Dergisi 2(1):1–17
Paasche E (2016) The role of corruption in reintegration: experiences of Iraqi Kurds upon return from Europe. J Ethn Migr Stud 42(7):1076–1093

Paasche TF, Sidaway JD (2015) Transecting security and space in Kurdistan, Iraq. Environ Plan A 47(10):2113–2133

Ross M (2001) Does oil hinder democracy? World Polit 53(3):325–361. Retrieved August 24, 2021, from http://www.jstor.org/stable/25054153. Last Access on April, 29th 2022

Sabir RS, Hassan SM (2020) The economical outcomes of the political Party in the Kurdistan Region of Iraq. Qalaai Zanist J 5(3):79–110

Sachs DJ Warner AM (1997) Natural resource abundance and economic growth. Research paper, Centre for international development and Harvard Institute for international development, Cambridge, MA

Savasta L (2019) The human Capital of the Kurdish Region of Iraq. Kurdish returnee (s) as a possible agent for a state-building process solution. Revista Transilvania 3

Shareef S, Kiani A (2020) Role of corruption and its impact under various regimes: cross country analysis. Int J Manag Res Emerg Sci 10(3)

Sherwani KH, Ahmad W (2023) An exploratory study of economic factors that hinder economic development of Kurdistan region. Int J Social Sci Educ Stud 10(1):82

Chapter 8
Conclusion

The earlier chapters examined the interplay between politics, economics, and development. The analysis in Chap. 4 yielded a favorable result regarding this relationship. That chapter examined the impact of multiple variables on natural resource revenue and the rate of economic development. Additionally, it explained the outcomes and the primary discoveries, contributions, arguments on the constraints, and the consequences for future investigations. The conclusion chapter provides a summary of findings throughout this research.

Moreover, it contributes several policy implications based on the findings. Also, specific suggestions are provided for decision-makers after considering the analysis of the results. Finally, contributions to literature and implications for future research are added to pave the way for related future studies.

8.1 Summary of the Findings

After reviewing the previous literature, collecting data, and analyzing them, this chapter will summarize the results of this research as follows:

The study investigated a range of political barriers that have impacted the developmental progress of the KRI. It specifically focused on issues such as the lack of a well-defined constitutional framework, resistance to reform, corruption, limited transparency, and the imbalance between the public and private sectors. Furthermore, ongoing conflicts with the federal government of Baghdad, declining oil prices, and the aftermath of the global campaign against ISIS present additional challenges. The research delved into the effects of political characteristics on economic development, the post-2003 political environment, and the influence of geopolitical factors and international attention. The literature review emphasized the necessity for empirical data, economic diversification, and the enhancement of institutions.

R. C. Biro, *Political Challenges of Economic Development in Rentier States*, Perspectives on Development in the Middle East and North Africa (MENA) Region, https://doi.org/10.1007/978-981-96-0563-7_8

The summary of findings highlights the intricate correlation between politics and economics in Kurdistan. It identifies challenges within the political system, such as ideological divisions, a lack of trust, and the dominance of major parties such as the KDP and PUK. Economic issues encompass reliance on the oil industry, a predominant public sector, a high dependency on imports, cash transactions, and weak financial institutions. Perturbed relations with the central government in Baghdad, disputes regarding natural resources, and unresolved territorial matters further compound these challenges. The study recommends that these obstacles need to be overcome to ensure regional progress.

Weak governance, poor infrastructure, low political stability, and low investment in non-resource sectors are typical characteristic features of countries rich in natural resources. The unique character of the interplay between politics, economy, and development in resource-rich rentier states could be explained by specific features thrown up by such countries. The rentier state relies primarily upon external rents, typically collected from the export of natural resources, such as oil or gas licensing, rather than the productive sectors of the national economy. The high degree of dependence on rental revenues has profound effects on the interrelations among politics, economy, and development in the following ways:

- Authoritarian Regimes: The political architecture of rentier states is frequently that of authoritarian regimes, where power is concentrated on a ruling elite or a few persons. Authorities of this nature hold overwhelming control over the political scene by simply manipulating the revenues generated from rents. Consolidation could mark limited democratic competition, institutional erosion, and few mechanisms for accountability.
- Economic Dependency: The marked dependence on a single resource or sector, such as oil or gas, which defines rentier states and characterizes their economies, would seem to create an interdependence that can lead to a phenomenon generally described as the "resource curse." Too abundant natural resources hinder the diversification of economies and retard the growth of other industries. Due to their dependence on global commodity prices and fluctuations in the exchange rate of trading currencies, one would expect financial instability in rentier states.
- Rent Distribution: One of the most critical factors in rentier states is how these rental revenues are distributed. The ruling elite utilizes rents primarily to maintain power and dispense political patronage; a good deal also helps in the balancing of society. Such phenomena, however, also give way to patronage networks, corruption, rising income inequality, and a lack of equable redistribution of the state's resources.
- Development Problems: This immense potential revenue, however, is what makes states dependent on rent frustrated in their development. Overdependence on the revenues accruing from rent can undermine investments in sectors other than natural resources, retard the development of activities that are innovative and entrepreneurial, and slow down the creation of an adequate labor force. This is often accompanied by excessive dependence on rental income, which leads to

a greater need for more economic diversification and subjects these countries to economic disruptions that hinder long-term growth.
- Geopolitical Matters: Most rentier states play a crucial geopolitical role due to the high number of natural resources they possess. This tendency may affect the political alliance, diplomacy with other countries, and a nation's economic policy. The geopolitical interests of the rentier states can be dictated or regulated by foreign powers, which can have huge impacts on the political and economic systems of such nations.

The underlying relationship between politics, economy, and development in rentier states is complex and characterized by centralized political authority, economic dependence, dynamics of rent distribution, obstacles to action, and geopolitical factors. Therefore, diversification of the economy is necessary to fight back against the challenges, institutional strengthening is needed, openness and accountability must be encouraged, and investments in human capital and sustainable development beyond resource extraction are a must to deal with the resource curse.

Literature on rentier states has helped gain an understanding of the challenges that such rentier state governments face in their pursuit of economic growth. Several hypotheses have been presented in explaining political impediments to economic growth. Most of the literature reviewed simply addresses some factors that could, a priori, hamper economic development under rentier regimes; it does not provide any in-depth analysis of either the political or the financial dimension.

Much like other rentier states, the political backdrop of Iraqi Kurdistan is a centralized one, sculpted with reliance on its lifeblood: resource rents to provide fuel toward economic growth. Still, development dominates the economic and political terrains of Iraqi Kurdistan. Essentially, such regimes are defined by the ability of the state to generate revenue through natural resources and, at the same time, distribute them so that they fund government activities and services. It simply has its advantages and disadvantages, such as the fact that corrupt practices can be straightforward, and perhaps there will be overdependence on just one industry. This approach to governance makes it hard for rentier states ever to diversify their economies away from natural resources. So, it's essential to understand the differences and similarities between Iraqi Kurdistan and other resource-dependent states to address political and economic problems. This book discussed the impact of natural resources on the process of economic development with a focus mainly on the theory of the "natural resource curse." Some of the factors identified were causes or causative agents: high costs of extraction procedures, high volatility in petroleum prices, and concentration of rent inputs, among others. Institutions are assessed by governance indicators, coupled with analysis about how they directly affect GDP per capita, hence proving its adverse effects as resulting from governmental efficiency and political stability.

The Kurdistan Region of Iraq functions through an independent political entity, with its governance framework and institutions such as the Kurdistan Regional Government, the Presidency, the Kurdistan Parliament, and the judiciary.

These are the leading role players in determining current structures and future directions in the region, considering the Kurdish people's aspirations. The KRG has a democratic electoral system with different roles, such as the President, Prime Minister, ministers, and other governmental roles. This presidency in the Kurdistan Region is the highest administrative role and also combines legislative, operational, and political duties. He is the President and is expected to typically play a significant role in domestic and international matters, acting as an ambassador for the Kurdish people. Legislation goes into practice under his watch. Establishing the Kurdistan Parliament in 1992 was one of the significant steps toward democratic governance in the region. The Parliament plays a very significant role in legislation and regulation, especially in major sectors such as education, health, security, and agricultural matters.

Legislation was passed by the Kurdistan National Assembly for an independent judiciary, providing it with legal authority over all inhabitants. Progress, though limited, has been observed while pending issues are to be resolved, among them further revisions for judicial independence and reduction of reliance on the KRG itself about external financial aid. This book extensively covered the political system in the KRI, which needs help to achieve cohesion and stability. The major political institutions in the region include the Kurdistan Democratic Party and the Patriotic Union of Kurdistan, along with some other minor political parties, which make the entire political scenario further complicated.

After the recognition of the Kurdish state, KDP and PUK have agreed to the power-sharing agreement, but there are reservations regarding how much power the President will possess. Sulaymaniyah and Erbil contain ideological differences, because of which there is a dire need for more trust and closer working; however, the political scene seems to be mainly controlled by KDP and PUK. It investigates the consistency of economic and political structures within the Kurdistan Region of Iraq, enumerating issues such as a shrunk public sector, rent-seeking activity, and the lack of constitutional standards. It then proposes reforms in public sector restructuring, financial strengthening, and improvement of the legal framework for a free market economy. The KRI economy is characterized by dependence on the oil sector, domination of the public sector, high dependence upon imports, strong preference for cash, and weak financial institutions. The oil industry generated substantial revenue for the region. Still, its heavy reliance on oil created difficulties during low oil prices or when the industry faced internal or external disruptions. The public sector substantially impacts the economy, as government spending surpasses 50 percent of the GDP and is a significant source of public employment. The instability in public spending and the dominance of the public sector significantly hinders the expansion of the private sector. The research acknowledges the economic challenges faced by the KRI, including a reliance on cash-based transactions, political biases, centralization, dependence on energy exports, and transparency issues. Weak judicial systems, bureaucratic inefficiencies, and corruption hinder economic freedom. Recommendations entail legal reforms, enhanced protection of property rights, and the establishment of political stability.

Various forms of tensions exist between Baghdad's central government and Erbil's regional government, primarily concerning controlling natural resources. Divergent interpretations of constitutional articles have resulted in conflicts and a breakdown of collaborative efforts. In addition, there is another strain from the issue of disputed territories. The involvement of foreign players in the dynamics further complicates having a win–win situation and improving relations. At the same time, getting an idea about the constituents of KRI is necessary to understand its political scenario and the problems of the Kurdish community. This research goes on to prove this point.

The effectiveness of natural resources on economic development will be traced comprehensively over time in the research. While the presence of resources can contribute to higher income levels and increase in per capita GDP, it must also be noted that it may affect the opposite by rendering lower growth rates. The "natural resource curse" is based on the proposition that an abundance of mineral wealth can potentially have some very detrimental rather than beneficial effects on specific nations. A more interesting underlying issue is the different levels of socioeconomic development in countries richly endowed with natural resources, each as a case study—for instance, Chile and Botswana—while others remain incapable of ensuring robust economic growth despite having vast reserves of natural resources. This project has concluded that the processes involved in extracting natural resources are costly, and such costs can be applied to other industries or services. Furthermore, uncertainty over global petroleum prices poses a significant threat to the economic stability of the rentier economies comprised of large fractions of low and middle-income groups. Moreover, the consolidation of rent inputs facilitates the ability of non-inclusive governing bodies to extract rent rather than promote economic growth, as their structures perpetuate political control. Furthermore, this research has demonstrated that substandard political institutions substantially impede economic progress within rentier states. In contemporary society, institutions play a pivotal role in various aspects of public life, encompassing social, educational, commercial, and bureaucratic realms. Furthermore, empirical evidence supports that developed nations possess more robust institutions, whereas underdeveloped countries typically exhibit weaker institutional frameworks and structures. The inverse correlation between economic growth and the presence of weak institutions found here is consistent with prior research findings.

This study examines the institutional quality of 51 rentier states through data. Specifically, it focuses on six governance indicators identified by Kaufmann et al. (2010). These indicators include voice and accountability, political stability, government effectiveness, regulatory quality, the role of law, and corruption control. Furthermore, the positive influence of institutions is contingent upon various factors, such as the nature of the institutions themselves, prevailing social norms, and the engagement of citizens. Organizations with similar attributes sometimes yield disparate outcomes across diverse groups and geographical areas.

This research uses various political and economic factors to explore how GDP growth relates to institutional quality. The study details the econometric model and estimation procedures in a broad and conventional manner. The research analyzed panel data to examine the presence of endogeneity and interdependence among certain explanatory variables. Nations that generate similar rents often exhibit varying degrees of dependency on resource revenue. This book accounts for various national factors and incorporates all the variations in the data instead of relying primarily on fixed effects specific to each sample country. Based on the empirical findings, it can be observed that voice and accountability substantially influence the growth of the GDP. Additionally, the results indicate that government consumption has a detrimental impact on GDP growth.

The findings indicate that certain nations' institutions cannot ensure economic stability due to various factors. One possible factor contributing to this issue is the inadequate quality of their political systems, which fosters a conducive environment for unscrupulous politicians and public officials to participate in rent-seeking behaviors. This phenomenon leads to a decline in institutional efficiency and poses a potential risk to economic growth. Hence, countries with robust governmental frameworks experience significantly higher GDP growth rates than those with inadequate institutional structures.

Political and economic institutions are essential for the economy to expand steadily and sustainably. These organizations support sustainability, draw capital, ease commerce, and foster competition. With solid political and economic frameworks, lasting economic progress can be attained. This research has tested the coherence of KRI economic and political institutions in democratic government and financial systems that support free markets for economic betterment.

There are some deep-rooted challenges to the KRI at every level of democratic governance, the rule of law, provision of basic services, and maintenance of law and order for property rights to ensure trade. Because of institutional flaws, the weakened public sector, political manipulation, and rent-seeking tactics have grown entrenched. The research argues that stronger constitutional norms and commitment to the rule of law must address these inadequacies. However, the region also faces issues like rent-seeking by special interest groups, self-serving politicians, rent-hiking, and an inefficient bureaucracy that is only becoming bigger. The endemic laws that now prevent the KRI from having a prosperous economic environment may be altered by revising the constitution and enacting new laws. It is decided that clear lines must be drawn between the different government departments, and the power vested in each department should be used to create checks and balances. Better political norms must be made and constitutional limitations on the reach of general government authority have to be imposed.

This has long posed a significant challenge to the economic governance of the KRI, which is divided into multiple ministries, including the Ministries of Planning, Natural Resources, and Finance and Economy. Similarly, a balance sheet only undermines the KRI's ability to formulate and pursue fresh economic policies accordingly. Finally, the several budgeting processes used by the KRI's provinces significantly interrupt how the economy is governed.

The results pointed out that the KRG needs comprehensive restructuring that could help it fight corruption, promote growth in the private sector, diversify its economy from reliance on oil, and bring efficiency to its public sector. Transforming the financial sector from a cash-based system to improve transparency and public accountability is crucial to fostering private sector expansion in the KRI. To maintain a market-based economy, the legislative framework regulating businesses must be reinforced to support and protect domestic SMEs and foreign direct investment.

The public sector's accountability and transparency must be improved to encourage such initiatives. Additionally required are the integration of financial accounts for the public sector and enhanced economic data collection and evidence-based policymaking. Corrupt officials must be identified and brought to justice to cease the industry's pointless activities. More administrative action is anticipated to protect property rights, preserve the rule of law generally, and enforce agreements in the national interest. Without such adjustments, the KRG's economy would continue to suffer as rent-seekers and politicians use the public sector for their political show.

Most of the political and financial institutions of the KRI are still developing after three decades. Additionally, the economic, political, and security policies left behind by the previous Iraqi administrations and the continuation of traditional societal norms and beliefs opposed to a market economy, efficient government, and democracy have left these institutions with shaky foundations. Most of the reform efforts and measures for the region are currently merely on paper. Due to a cash-based economy, political biases, excessive centralization in managing financial and economic resources, high reliance on oil exports, and transparency difficulties, the area must overcome considerable challenges to its economic independence and development. Additionally, the region's economic development is vulnerable due to a shaky and weak legal system, a convoluted bureaucracy, and insufficient and inaccurate data for most sectors.

Even though Iraqi and KRI laws safeguard property rights, the present legal system cannot support substantial private investment. Additionally, there needs to be more solid legal protection for intellectual property; addressing this issue would encourage innovation and entrepreneurship. Adequate protection of property rights and contract enforcement require effective governmental institutions that can assure security and the rule of law.

Political instability is recognized as a significant challenge for development in the KRI. Instability has reduced foreign direct investment and bilateral commerce with other nations because it has facilitated brain drain and challenges in social development. Some of the reasons contributing to it are corruption, power-sharing agreements, and limitations on opposition. The project emphasizes the need to effectively address corruption through comprehensive reforms, strengthen institutions, and promote transparency. Economic diversification is deemed vital to mitigate susceptibilities to fluctuations in oil prices. Challenges within the agricultural sector are identified, with the resolution of these issues crucial for achieving sustainable growth.

The KRI structure must go forward with structural reform to guarantee the long-term viability of its various economic and political institutions and advance openness, accountability, and productivity in its government sector. Open organizations supported by more robust legislative frameworks will ensure fair business opportunities and create a growth-friendly atmosphere. The Kurdistan Region of Iraq will be able to establish the circumstances for more substantial social and economic growth by improving the delivery of crucial public services, including healthcare, education, and infrastructure.

8.2 Policy Implications

The conclusions drawn from this study should be of broad relevance to countries abundant in natural resources, with relevance to the KRI. Accordingly, these countries can overcome the political obstacles in their economic development in several ways; for example, by improving their political and economic institutions. This research suggests policy implications for rentier states, specifically for Iraqi Kurdistan. These consequences desire to tackle problems related to governance weaknesses, economic reliance on natural resources, rent distribution, development barriers, and geopolitical considerations. By adopting these policy implications, rentier states can strive for sustainable economic growth, diminish reliance on natural resources, and enhance the welfare of their individuals. Following are some of the policy-related consequences that warrant considerations in policymaking.

Therefore, the economy's diversification is vital for rentier states in creating non-resource-based revenue sources and deserves priority. This may be accomplished by encouraging investments outside of the natural resource sector, providing an enabling atmosphere for innovation and enterprise, and training a skilled workforce through its tendency to reduce exposure to commodity price fluctuation in the world markets and to stimulate long-term growth, diversification seminar.

The rentier states should work on the economic and political development of their structure. This relates to strengthening the governance system, enhancing openness, accountability, transparency, and reducing corruption. Special attention is required to establish robust frameworks to guarantee investments against any potential threats by protecting financial security and preparing a base for sustainable development. In addition, rentier states need to develop policies about the fair sharing of revenues generated in terms of rentals to reduce income inequalities and prevent the concentration of power among ruling elites. Transparent and reliable sharing system of rents might foster social cohesion, reduce corruption, and help boost economic growth. Countries rich in natural resources need to manage geopolitical risks through diplomacy by creating multidimensional relations with other countries, enlarge the base of economic cooperation, and not be overly dependent on any one country.

The strategic decision-making process must also consider the long-term interests of the state and those of its citizens. In recent times, problems have occurred in the KRI's economy because of deteriorating country relationships with Iraq and its neighbors and with the current governance structures. The prevailing conditions require the strengthening of ties between the KRI and the neighboring countries and improvement in relations between it and Baghdad to achieve speedy economic growth, just like before the September 2017 independence referendum. It is an environment of predictable stability, one that the KRI must have if it intends to gain private investment from across and beyond the state and one that deals effectively with complex subjects such as autonomy. Rentier states can develop further democratization through the political challenges associated with the promotion of democratic competition, consolidation of institutional frameworks, and enhancement of methods of keeping people and institutions responsible. Such establishments mean equal opportunities for political participation, freedom of speech, protection of human rights, and nurturing good governance. It is also posited that rentier states should improve the level of financial and economic governance through the establishment of proper financial institutions and improvement in public accounting methods, as well as a shift from cash-based frameworks toward open and accountable ones for handling finances.

Practical economic growth requires a sound monetary policy well incentivized through efficient fiscal management.

Furthermore, rentier states should continue to foster the rule of law, protect property rights, and ensure contract performance. In addition, there is a further need for better legal frameworks with less corruption and an appropriate regime for protecting intellectual property, which can attract investment, stimulate creativity, and build business-friendly environments. Increased data collection and analysis of economic data in rentier states accommodate informed decision-making for a more effective assessment of progress toward growth objectives. Some of the main issues challenging economic development within the Kurdistan Region of Iraq are political instability, corruption, oil dependency, and problems with economic diversification. Most notably, political instability in the region has caused brain drain, poverty, and an inexperienced labor force because of its effect on human capital and social development. What further worsened these issues was the unpopular decline in bilateral commerce since 2013, hence every need for a stable and predictable environment. Against this background, sustainable development in KRI juxtaposes stability at the top of the agenda, tending to focus efforts on infrastructure development and resource allocation at different levels of government in a collaborative way. In general, corruption is one of the significant challenges to KRI, finding its roots in the post-conflict situation, further perpetuated by actions and policies from the ruling parties. The power-sharing agreement between KDP–PUK has, therefore obviously boosted corruption in the institutions, media independence, and accountability. Ending corruption and breaking these cycles that have been so adverse to general and economic progress will thus call for strengthened institutions and broad governance reforms, accompanied by a dedication to transparency.

The constraints placed on political opposition have instituted fears for the necessary checks and balances needed to sustain a growth prospect in the long run. Regarding that, tackling corruption requires comprehensive reforms in governance structures, institutions, and regulatory frameworks, along with an established commitment toward transparency and accountability practices. Without such actions taken to effect change, corruption was likely to perpetuate the dire situation against economic development and citizen well-being.

Indeed, one of the significant challenges heaped on to achieve long-lasting resilience and sustainable growth would be the diversification of the economy. Reliance solely on oil and gas resources discourages other sectors' self-development, as these countries become quite vulnerable regarding any minute changes in global oil prices. Despite a specific drive toward economic diversification, regional income remains dominated by more than 80 percent derived from oil.

In this regard, three complex problems that bedevil many oil-rich countries as a result of the resource curse, disagreements with the central government, and fiduciary frictions complicate economic diversification because of an over-reliance on natural wealth. This means that the Kurdistan Region must continue dealing with these vulnerabilities stemming from the oil price changes and work toward economics with self-sustaining growth. Agriculture can indeed be touted as one viable option for diversification. Be that as it may, challenges such as suboptimal technology, qualified labor shortages, and market limitations constrained its contribution to economic growth in the region.

In summary, a host of challenges to economic development in the Kurdistan Region of Iraq demands comprehensive reforms, joint effort, and strategic planning. Political instability, corruption, and political opposition will have to be curbed for real diversification for the economy to be stable and lay the foundations for resilient long-term growth.

8.3 Contribution to the Literature

The book elaborates on the complex intermingling of politics and economics within KRI, outlining the challenges that haunt the said region, entailing political fragmentations, economic dependency, and overwhelming controls by powerful political parties. The research adds to the existing literature on economic growth, resource management, and political hurdles in the Kurdistan Region of Iraq. It provides enormous insights into researchers, policymakers, and practitioners who are interested in learning the dynamics of this area. This research makes some critical contributions to the available literature on rentier states, however. It situates the detailed examination of political, economic, and developmental challenges that most rentier states face within the context of Iraqi Kurdistan.

Literature syntheses, data collection, and analysis, therefore, underpin the achievement of in-depth awareness about the complex interplay that exists among politics, economy, institutions, and development in rentier states. It distinguishes between the key challenges most rentier states face, such as governance, institutions, economic dependence on natural resources, wealth distribution, bounds to development, and geopolitical aspects. This will help add literature to research about the specific patterns and challenges the Kurdistan Region of Iraq has gone through, especially in Iraqi Kurdistan. The study has considered and reviewed the challenges posed in the political structure of Kurdistan: most especially political instability, issues of trust, and overlordship of some political groups. It contributes to an immense understanding of the fact that political unity and stability are required for sustainable economic growth.

The book analyzed how political and economic institutions influence the ability to attain economic growth among rentier states. Although scholarship on these issues needs institutional solid frameworks to aid economic development and reduce the adverse effects of rentier or the resource curse, it is essential to create demands for transparency and accountability, and respect for the rule of law. The empirical analysis is used largely by examination of the governance variables about panel data, offering empirical evidence to confirm the findings. In enhancing the credibility and trustworthiness of the conclusions to be administered, econometric models and statistical analyses are carried out. As such, the research findings present policy implications that may guide the policymakers and stakeholders in rentier states, particularly in Iraqi Kurdistan, toward effectively addressing the identified issues.

The epidemiology in this research is relevant in identifying the bidirectional influence of political instability and its impacts, which negatively affect employment, capital formation, and foreign investment. Secondly, it gives detailed inputs on how intricate political dealings interface with economic progress in the Kurdistan Region of Iraq. Accordingly, it provides insights into aspects of the effects resulting from political instability in such a setting. Moreover, the research has pointed out the complexity of corruption: its birth in post-conflict societies and further reinforcement by governing parties. This nuanced perspective adds value to the literature by reflecting how corruption thwarts new institutional development and economic growth in KRI. The study also examines challenges in economic diversification, particularly those created by political elites.

This exemplifies the problems of economic diversification and the reduction of dependence on oil to develop an overview of the general economy within resource-dependent states. Overall, this work adds nuance through context-based and integrated perspectives on the economic challenges that characterize the KRI. It provides practical guidance to policymakers, adds to the academic discourse, and lays a foundation for further research and exploration of context-specific policy solutions in the region and other resource-dependent economies. Moreover, through its exhaustive evaluation, empirical evidence, and bouts of policy implications, this work provides significant additions to the present body of literature on rentier states.

This literature contribution deepens our understanding of the complex relationships between politics, economy, and development in rentier states. It also helps to create valuable knowledge for guiding policymakers on coping with the challenges arising from rentierism.

8.4 Limitations and Implications for Future Research

Although the study has been able to shed more light on the challenges that face rentier nations and how they affect Iraqi Kurdistan, some limitations ought to be recognized, while suggestions for further research are vital. Given that the research has focused on the situation in Iraqi Kurdistan, its conclusions can only be applied to some rentier nations. Comparison among various rentier nations has to be further researched to understand what commonalities or differences may exist among the challenges and behaviors these nations face. The negative implications of no data availability are well understood, more so in this large sample, since many participants come from relatively poor countries. Several critical macroeconomic variables, like literacy rate, human capital development rate, and democracy index, could not find a place in the projections simply because their data was unavailable.

The study is very articulate in its discussion of the problems developed by rentier nations, but perhaps future studies can further explore specific issues and consequences. For example, further research may wish to research how political stability could be influenced by rent distribution or else investigate impediments against economic diversification within chosen rentier governments. The work focuses on the current issues and consequences of rentierism. Future studies should examine the durability and long-term effects of different policy initiatives, such as institutional changes or economic diversification policies, and deeper comprehend their success rate and possible negative aspects in the long term.

The political, institutional, and economic factors of rentier states are prominent topic of discussion in this study. The research might aim to develop further an argument for social and/or environmental grounds—for example, how a rentier economy shapes social inequality, indicators of human capital and its development, or even environmental sustainability. This would provide further elucidation of issues and implications for rentier nations at large.

The study briefly covers the effect of outside forces and geopolitical variables on rentier nations. The patterns of external factors, such as the impact of foreign players, global marketplaces, and regional factors, on politics, economics, and evolution of rentier states might be further explored in future studies.

Scholars can improve their comprehension of rentier states by considering limitations and exploring new research areas. This can result in more advanced understanding and recommendations for addressing the challenges faced by these states.

8.5 Policy Recommendations for Rentier States on Economic Diversification Through Sustainable Energy Transition

Energy from renewable sources is the foundation of environmentally friendly energy growth and energy transition, which is becoming increasingly necessary due to the expanding need for power as well as increasing greenhouse gases and pollution in the environment. The rewards of a shift for sustainable development also call for a more comprehensive viewpoint that takes into account how consumers act, energy effectiveness, stability, and sufficiency of energy supplies.

Working toward developing non-hydrocarbon sector is the first step of economic diversification in resource-rich states. The alternative sector for these countries could be different based on their political systems, geographical situation, and their capabilities. For example, it is more suitable for the Gulf countries to focus on the tourism and free trade zones, whereas some states like Iran could develop agriculture and manufacturing industries. Apart from these sectors, renewable energy could be the best alternative for the economic diversification to distance relying on the oil industry.

Environmental sustainability, diversification of the economy, and the affordability of renewable energy sources are the main forces behind the energy transition in the current age. Using initiatives for alternative energies, the removal of energy subsidies, and energy efficiency improvements are the key points of transition from oil to green energy. The energy transition could be accomplished via large-scale initiatives integrating nuclear and renewable energy sources, as well as planned communities that integrate energy efficiency into the built environment. Additionally, they represent modernity and primacy, giving the ruling class credibility and giving them an advantage in sustainability competition. Renewable energy sources like solar energy have the potential to economically replace nuclear power, which is now included in Saudi Arabia's and the UAE's energy mix regulations.

The advancement of clean energy sources requires essential modifications to national institutions and business structures across economies where petroleum industry is crucial to both political equilibrium and economic prosperity. These changes could clash with the interests of political and economic decision-makers who seek to maintain the current reliance on the extraction of oil and gas. The major modifications occur in the form of privatization of government-owned businesses to improve the competitiveness of renewable energy technologies, liberalization of the electricity market, transformation of electricity tariffs to ensure that costs represent the expense of output, and improvements of incentives for using fewer fossil fuels. A domestic instability scenario might arise from such fundamental shifts, which could also put the present social compact of rentier actors in danger.

A systematic transition to renewable energy must also be made possible by the combined efforts of many players, including the governmental, business, social, and scientific fields, in order to guarantee an efficient and equitable renewable energy transition. Involving stakeholders from numerous industries in decision-making decreases the likelihood of conflicting interests, fragmented policies, and waste of effort while promoting effective integration of activities. Yet, without strong political intent at the top, the implementation of these plans and engagement of the beforementioned parties are impossible.

Since there are regional variations in the relationship between energy usage and economic growth, rentier players should design energy strategies that meet their unique demands. Countries such as Qatar and the United Arab Emirates should prioritize the transition to greener energy sources since renewable energy may supplant fossil fuels stock without negatively impacting their economies. Additionally, governments may promote renewable energy through tax cuts, subsidies, and financial assistance. Reducing the use of fossil fuels may coexist with environmental measures in rentier nations without impeding their economic development. If the economy isn't yet being boosted by renewable energy, improving energy-efficient technologies could be possibly of help. Furthermore, investing on innovations and supplies for renewable energy generates new employment, which would prove beneficial for the overall economy.

Reference

Kaufmann D, Kraay A, Mastruzzi M (2010) The worldwide governance indicators: methodology and analytical issues. Hague J Rule Law 3(02):220–246. https://doi.org/10.1017/s1876404511200046

Appendices

Appendix A.1 Sample of selected rentier states

No.	Country	Indicators	Average between 2003 and 2020
1.	Albania	"Total natural resources rents (% of GDP)"	1.7653
		"Ores and metals exports (% of merchandise exports)"	11.5534
		"Fuel exports (% of merchandise exports)"	10.5034
		"Personal remittances, received (% of GDP)"	12.4834
2.	Algeria	"Total natural resources rents (% of GDP)"	23.9004
		"Ores and metals exports (% of merchandise exports)"	0.3659
		"Fuel exports (% of merchandise exports)"	97.6921
		"Personal remittances, received (% of GDP)"	0.8025
3.	Angola	"Total natural resources rents (% of GDP)"	32.1787
		"Ores and metals exports (% of merchandise exports)"	2.7651
		"Fuel exports (% of merchandise exports)"	96.2217
		"Personal remittances, received (% of GDP)"	0.0152

(continued)

R. C. Biro, *Political Challenges of Economic Development in Rentier States*, Perspectives on Development in the Middle East and North Africa (MENA) Region, https://doi.org/10.1007/978-981-96-0563-7

Appendix A.1 (continued)

No.	Country	Indicators	Average between 2003 and 2020
4.	Azerbaijan	"Total natural resources rents (% of GDP)"	27.6392
		"Ores and metals exports (% of merchandise exports)"	1.3579
		"Fuel exports (% of merchandise exports)"	89.4305
		"Personal remittances, received (% of GDP)"	2.8511
5.	Bahrain	"Total natural resources rents (% of GDP)"	18.9276
		"Ores and metals exports (% of merchandise exports)"	19.5803
		"Fuel exports (% of merchandise exports)"	62.9054
		"Personal remittances, received (% of GDP)"	—
6.	Bolivia	"Total natural resources rents (% of GDP)"	8.6354
		"Ores and metals exports (% of merchandise exports)"	25.9877
		"Fuel exports (% of merchandise exports)"	41.9166
		"Personal remittances, received (% of GDP)"	4.2083
7.	Botswana	"Total natural resources rents (% of GDP)"	2.2678
		"Ores and metals exports (% of merchandise exports)"	9.6641
		"Fuel exports (% of merchandise exports)"	0.3415
		"Personal remittances, received (% of GDP)"	0.4115
8.	Brunei Darussalam	"Total natural resources rents (% of GDP)"	25.2334
		"Ores and metals exports (% of merchandise exports)"	0.1287
		"Fuel exports (% of merchandise exports)"	93.3023
		"Personal remittances, received (% of GDP)"	0.0072

(continued)

Appendix A.1 (continued)

No.	Country	Indicators	Average between 2003 and 2020
9.	Cameroon	"Total natural resources rents (% of GDP)"	6.7545
		"Ores and metals exports (% of merchandise exports)"	5.2841
		"Fuel exports (% of merchandise exports)"	39.9703
		"Personal remittances, received (% of GDP)"	0.6831
10.	Chad	"Total natural resources rents (% of GDP)"	23.0659
		"Ores and metals exports (% of merchandise exports)"	—
		"Fuel exports (% of merchandise exports)"	—
		"Personal remittances, received (% of GDP)"	0.0000
11.	Chile	"Total natural resources rents (% of GDP)"	8.6492
		"Ores and metals exports (% of merchandise exports)"	55.7385
		"Fuel exports (% of merchandise exports)"	1.5580
		"Personal remittances, received (% of GDP)"	0.0188
12.	Congo, Dem. Rep.	"Total natural resources rents (% of GDP)"	23.8169
		"Ores and metals exports (% of merchandise exports)"	63.8308
		"Fuel exports (% of merchandise exports)"	0.6600
		"Personal remittances, received (% of GDP)"	1.9203
13.	Congo, rep.	"Total natural resources rents (% of GDP)"	38.0716
		"Ores and metals exports (% of merchandise exports)"	0.4145
		"Fuel exports (% of merchandise exports)"	66.0372
		"Personal remittances, received (% of GDP)"	0.2254

(continued)

Appendix A.1 (continued)

No.	Country	Indicators	Average between 2003 and 2020
14.	Cote d'Ivoire	"Total natural resources rents (% of GDP)"	3.8906
		"Ores and metals exports (% of merchandise exports)"	0.4785
		"Fuel exports (% of merchandise exports)"	21.7448
		"Personal remittances, received (% of GDP)"	0.7426
15.	Ecuador	"Total natural resources rents (% of GDP)"	11.0144
		"Ores and metals exports (% of merchandise exports)"	0.9639
		"Fuel exports (% of merchandise exports)"	48.9145
		"Personal remittances, received (% of GDP)"	3.8936
16.	Equatorial Guinea	"Total natural resources rents (% of GDP)"	33.3646
		"Ores and metals exports (% of merchandise exports)"	—
		"Fuel exports (% of merchandise exports)"	—
		"Personal remittances, received (% of GDP)"	0.0000
17.	Gabon	"Total natural resources rents (% of GDP)"	28.0009
		"Ores and metals exports (% of merchandise exports)"	3.1644
		"Fuel exports (% of merchandise exports)"	84.2755
		"Personal remittances, received (% of GDP)"	0.1118
18.	Guinea	"Total natural resources rents (% of GDP)"	14.9277
		"Ores and metals exports (% of merchandise exports)"	50.0974
		"Fuel exports (% of merchandise exports)"	0.4140
		"Personal remittances, received (% of GDP)"	0.9703

(continued)

Appendix A.1 (continued)

No.	Country	Indicators	Average between 2003 and 2020
19.	Guyana	"Total natural resources rents (% of GDP)"	13.1852
		"Ores and metals exports (% of merchandise exports)"	9.7906
		"Fuel exports (% of merchandise exports)"	2.4195
		"Personal remittances, received (% of GDP)"	10.2891
20.	Indonesia	"Total natural resources rents (% of GDP)"	6.3237
		"Ores and metals exports (% of merchandise exports)"	7.1553
		"Fuel exports (% of merchandise exports)"	26.1357
		"Personal remittances, received (% of GDP)"	1.0616
21.	Iran, Islamic rep.	"Total natural resources rents (% of GDP)"	25.2323
		"Ores and metals exports (% of merchandise exports)"	2.4468
		"Fuel exports (% of merchandise exports)"	72.5612
		"Personal remittances, received (% of GDP)"	0.6551
22.	Iraq	"Total natural resources rents (% of GDP)"	47.5933
		"Ores and metals exports (% of merchandise exports)"	0.0274
		"Fuel exports (% of merchandise exports)"	99.1993
		"Personal remittances, received (% of GDP)"	0.3776
23.	Kazakhstan	"Total natural resources rents (% of GDP)"	21.2946
		"Ores and metals exports (% of merchandise exports)"	13.6685
		"Fuel exports (% of merchandise exports)"	67.8059
		"Personal remittances, received (% of GDP)"	0.1783

(continued)

Appendix A.1 (continued)

No.	Country	Indicators	Average between 2003 and 2020
24.	Lao PDR	"Total natural resources rents (% of GDP)"	8.7193
		"Ores and metals exports (% of merchandise exports)"	39.9664
		"Fuel exports (% of merchandise exports)"	8.8986
		"Personal remittances, received (% of GDP)"	0.8927
25.	Liberia	"Total natural resources rents (% of GDP)"	21.4793
		"Ores and metals exports (% of merchandise exports)"	—
		"Fuel exports (% of merchandise exports)"	—
		"Personal remittances, received (% of GDP)"	11.4965
26.	Libya	"Total natural resources rents (% of GDP)"	42.6743
		"Ores and metals exports (% of merchandise exports)"	0.4869
		"Fuel exports (% of merchandise exports)"	94.6102
		"Personal remittances, received (% of GDP)"	0.0066
27.	Mali	"Total natural resources rents (% of GDP)"	7.5862
		"Ores and metals exports (% of merchandise exports)"	0.2537
		"Fuel exports (% of merchandise exports)"	0.4746
		"Personal remittances, received (% of GDP)"	5.0334
28.	Mauritania	"Total natural resources rents (% of GDP)"	16.4763
		"Ores and metals exports (% of merchandise exports)"	45.1377
		"Fuel exports (% of merchandise exports)"	10.2801
		"Personal remittances, received (% of GDP)"	0.2968

(continued)

Appendix A.1 (continued)

No.	Country	Indicators	Average between 2003 and 2020
29.	Mexico	"Total natural resources rents (% of GDP)"	4.3403
		"Ores and metals exports (% of merchandise exports)"	2.4736
		"Fuel exports (% of merchandise exports)"	11.0600
		"Personal remittances, received (% of GDP)"	2.4897
30.	Mongolia	"Total natural resources rents (% of GDP)"	20.3884
		"Ores and metals exports (% of merchandise exports)"	45.9072
		"Fuel exports (% of merchandise exports)"	22.9994
		"Personal remittances, received (% of GDP)"	3.9156
31.	Niger	"Total natural resources rents (% of GDP)"	8.2873
		"Ores and metals exports (% of merchandise exports)"	37.1853
		"Fuel exports (% of merchandise exports)"	10.7901
		"Personal remittances, received (% of GDP)"	1.8084
32.	Nigeria	"Total natural resources rents (% of GDP)"	12.2017
		"Ores and metals exports (% of merchandise exports)"	0.3331
		"Fuel exports (% of merchandise exports)"	91.3075
		"Personal remittances, received (% of GDP)"	4.9221
33.	Norway	"Total natural resources rents (% of GDP)"	8.0578
		"Ores and metals exports (% of merchandise exports)"	6.2875
		"Fuel exports (% of merchandise exports)"	62.5693
		"Personal remittances, received (% of GDP)"	0.1563

(continued)

Appendix A.1 (continued)

No.	Country	Indicators	Average between 2003 and 2020
34.	Oman	"Total natural resources rents (% of GDP)"	33.6693
		"Ores and metals exports (% of merchandise exports)"	3.2284
		"Fuel exports (% of merchandise exports)"	80.1393
		"Personal remittances, received (% of GDP)"	0.0741
35.	Papua New Guinea	"Total natural resources rents (% of GDP)"	19.9682
		"Ores and metals exports (% of merchandise exports)"	44.6144
		"Fuel exports (% of merchandise exports)"	11.7498
		"Personal remittances, received (% of GDP)"	0.0712
36.	Peru	"Total natural resources rents (% of GDP)"	7.7554
		"Ores and metals exports (% of merchandise exports)"	41.6276
		"Fuel exports (% of merchandise exports)"	8.5215
		"Personal remittances, received (% of GDP)"	1.6316
37.	Qatar	"Total natural resources rents (% of GDP)"	30.4406
		"Ores and metals exports (% of merchandise exports)"	1.0364
		"Fuel exports (% of merchandise exports)"	87.5821
		"Personal remittances, received (% of GDP)"	0.2043
38.	Russian Federation	"Total natural resources rents (% of GDP)"	13.8580
		"Ores and metals exports (% of merchandise exports)"	6.1527
		"Fuel exports (% of merchandise exports)"	59.6698
		"Personal remittances, received (% of GDP)"	0.4200

(continued)

Appendix A.1 (continued)

No.	Country	Indicators	Average between 2003 and 2020
39.	Saudi Arabia	"Total natural resources rents (% of GDP)"	38.2320
		"Ores and metals exports (% of merchandise exports)"	0.6401
		"Fuel exports (% of merchandise exports)"	85.1481
		"Personal remittances, received (% of GDP)"	0.0384
40.	Sudan	"Total natural resources rents (% of GDP)"	9.0902
		"Ores and metals exports (% of merchandise exports)"	0.3894
		"Fuel exports (% of merchandise exports)"	87.2478
		"Personal remittances, received (% of GDP)"	1.7833
41.	Suriname	"Total natural resources rents (% of GDP)"	14.6219
		"Ores and metals exports (% of merchandise exports)"	0.2711
		"Fuel exports (% of merchandise exports)"	4.9400
		"Personal remittances, received (% of GDP)"	0.8728
42.	Syrian Arab Republic	"Total natural resources rents (% of GDP)"	6.3693
		"Ores and metals exports (% of merchandise exports)"	1.8095
		"Fuel exports (% of merchandise exports)"	51.8172
		"Personal remittances, received (% of GDP)"	0.2911
43.	Timor-Leste	"Total natural resources rents (% of GDP)"	44.4907
		"Ores and metals exports (% of merchandise exports)"	0.0751
		"Fuel exports (% of merchandise exports)"	0.6698
		"Personal remittances, received (% of GDP)"	6.1232

(continued)

Appendix A.1 (continued)

No.	Country	Indicators	Average between 2003 and 2020
44.	Trinidad and Tobago	"Total natural resources rents (% of GDP)"	13.1780
		"Ores and metals exports (% of merchandise exports)"	1.2855
		"Fuel exports (% of merchandise exports)"	59.1088
		"Personal remittances, received (% of GDP)"	0.5739
45.	Turkmenistan	"Total natural resources rents (% of GDP)"	30.8458
		"Ores and metals exports (% of merchandise exports)"	—
		"Fuel exports (% of merchandise exports)"	—
		"Personal remittances, received (% of GDP)"	0.0467
46.	United Arab Emirates	"Total natural resources rents (% of GDP)"	21.4829
		"Ores and metals exports (% of merchandise exports)"	2.5066
		"Fuel exports (% of merchandise exports)"	54.0153
		"Personal remittances, received (% of GDP)"	—
47.	Uzbekistan	"Total natural resources rents (% of GDP)"	16.3098
		"Ores and metals exports (% of merchandise exports)"	8.1388
		"Fuel exports (% of merchandise exports)"	15.9116
		"Personal remittances, received (% of GDP)"	9.2060
48.	Venezuela, RB	"Total natural resources rents (% of GDP)"	20.4765
		"Ores and metals exports (% of merchandise exports)"	1.8543
		"Fuel exports (% of merchandise exports)"	89.2725
		"Personal remittances, received (% of GDP)"	0.0739

(continued)

Appendix A.1 (continued)

No.	Country	Indicators	Average between 2003 and 2020
49.	Vietnam	"Total natural resources rents (% of GDP)"	7.1719
		"Ores and metals exports (% of merchandise exports)"	0.8204
		"Fuel exports (% of merchandise exports)"	11.5096
		"Personal remittances, received (% of GDP)"	5.5290
50.	Yemen, rep.	"Total natural resources rents (% of GDP)"	21.3900
		"Ores and metals exports (% of merchandise exports)"	0.3968
		"Fuel exports (% of merchandise exports)"	77.6189
		"Personal remittances, received (% of GDP)"	6.5640
51.	Zambia	"Total natural resources rents (% of GDP)"	14.3797
		"Ores and metals exports (% of merchandise exports)"	73.4580
		"Fuel exports (% of merchandise exports)"	1.1440
		"Personal remittances, received (% of GDP)"	0.3957

Appendix A.2 Classification of rentier states based on their foreign rents and income group

Countries	Type of natural resources	Income group (World Bank)
Congo, Dem. Rep.	Minerals & oil	"Low income (LICs) and lower-middle income countries (LMICs)"
Liberia	Gold/diamond/iron ore	"Low income (LICs) and lower-middle income countries (LMICs)"
Niger	Uranium	"Low income (LICs) and lower-middle income countries (LMICs)"
Guinea	Mining products	"Low income (LICs) and lower-middle income countries (LMICs)"
Mali	Gold	"Low income (LICs) and lower-middle income countries (LMICs)"
Chad	Oil	"Low income (LICs) and lower-middle income countries (LMICs)"
Mauritania	Iron ore	"Low income (LICs) and lower-middle income countries (LMICs)"
Lao PDR	Copper & gold	"Low income (LICs) and lower-middle income countries (LMICs)"

(continued)

Appendix A.2 (continued)

Countries	Type of natural resources	Income group (World Bank)
Zambia	Copper	"Low income (LICs) and lower-middle income countries (LMICs)"
Vietnam	Oil	"Low income (LICs) and lower-middle income countries (LMICs)"
Yemen	Oil	"Low income (LICs) and lower-middle income countries (LMICs)"
Nigeria	Oil	"Low income (LICs) and lower-middle income countries (LMICs)"
Cameroon	Oil	"Low income (LICs) and lower-middle income countries (LMICs)"
Papua New Guinea	Oil/copper/gold	"Low income (LICs) and lower-middle income countries (LMICs)"
Sudan	Oil	"Low income (LICs) and lower-middle income countries (LMICs)"
Uzbekistan	Gold/gas	"Low income (LICs) and lower-middle income countries (LMICs)"
Côte d'Ivoire	Oil/gas	"Low income (LICs) and lower-middle income countries (LMICs)"
Bolivia	Gas	"Low income (LICs) and lower-middle income countries (LMICs)"
Mongolia	Copper	"Low income (LICs) and lower-middle income countries (LMICs)"
Congo, rep. of	Oil	"Low income (LICs) and lower-middle income countries (LMICs)"
Iraq	Oil	"Low income (LICs) and lower-middle income countries (LMICs)"
Indonesia	Oil	"Low income (LICs) and lower-middle income countries (LMICs)"
Timor-Leste	Oil	"Low income (LICs) and lower-middle income countries (LMICs)"
Syrian Arab Republic	Oil	"Low income (LICs) and lower-middle income countries (LMICs)"
Guyana	Gold & bauxite	"Low income (LICs) and lower-middle income countries (LMICs)"
Turkmenistan	Oil	"Low income (LICs) and lower-middle income countries (LMICs)"
Angola	Oil	"Low income (LICs) and lower-middle income countries (LMICs)"
Gabon	Oil	"Low income (LICs) and lower-middle income countries (LMICs)"
Equatorial Guinea	Oil	"Low income (LICs) and lower-middle income countries (LMICs)"
Ecuador	Oil	"Upper-middle income countries (UMICs) that are rich in natural resources"

(continued)

Appendix A.2 (continued)

Countries	Type of natural resources	Income group (World Bank)
Albania	Oil/gas/ores/metals	"Upper-middle income countries (UMICs) that are rich in natural resources"
Algeria	Oil	"Upper-middle income countries (UMICs) that are rich in natural resources"
Iran	Oil	"Upper-middle income countries (UMICs) that are rich in natural resources"
Peru	Minerals	"Upper-middle income countries (UMICs) that are rich in natural resources"
Azerbaijan	Oil	"Upper-middle income countries (UMICs) that are rich in natural resources"
Botswana	Diamonds	"Upper-middle income countries (UMICs) that are rich in natural resources"
Kazakhstan	Oil	"Upper-middle income countries (UMICs) that are rich in natural resources"
Suriname	Minerals	"Upper-middle income countries (UMICs) that are rich in natural resources"
Mexico	Oil	"Upper-middle income countries (UMICs) that are rich in natural resources"
Russia	Oil	"Upper-middle income countries (UMICs) that are rich in natural resources"
Chile	Copper	"Upper-middle income countries (UMICs) that are rich in natural resources"
Venezuela	Oil	"Upper-middle income countries (UMICs) that are rich in natural resources"
Libya	Oil	"Upper-middle income countries (UMICs) that are rich in natural resources"
Bahrain	Oil	"High income countries (HICs) that are rich in natural resources"
Brunei Darussalam	Gas	"High income countries (HICs) that are rich in natural resources"
Trinidad and Tobago	Gas	"High income countries (HICs) that are rich in natural resources"
Saudi Arabia	Oil	"High income countries (HICs) that are rich in natural resources"
Oman	Oil	"High income countries (HICs) that are rich in natural resources"
United Arab Emirates	Oil	"High income countries (HICs) that are rich in natural resources"
Qatar	Gas	"High income countries (HICs) that are rich in natural resources"
Norway	Oil	"High income countries (HICs) that are rich in natural resources"

MIX
Papier aus verantwortungsvollen Quellen
Paper from responsible sources
FSC® C105338

If you have any concerns about our products,
you can contact us on
ProductSafety@springernature.com

In case Publisher is established outside the EU,
the EU authorized representative is:
Springer Nature Customer Service Center GmbH
Europaplatz 3, 69115 Heidelberg, Germany

Printed by Libri Plureos GmbH
in Hamburg, Germany